"In this historically well-informed, theologically careful, and pastorally sensitive volume, Dr. Marcus Johnson seeks to remedy what he rightly calls 'the glaring omission of the theme of union with Christ in the soteriological understanding of the contemporary evangelical church.' He convincingly demonstrates that the recovery of this central biblical theme helps us as Christians to understand better and more deeply the relation of Christ's person and work, the church as the body of Christ, and the glorious unity of our salvation in Christ. I am happy to recommend this book as an important addition to the growing body of literature on this significant topic."

William B. Evans, Eunice Witherspoon Bell Younts and Willie Camp Younts Professor of Bible, Erskine College

"Johnson is a master mystery writer. Chapter by chapter, he unfolds the mystery of our new life in Christ. He does not solve the mystery, but rather draws us into its wonders."

Bruce K. Modahl, Senior Pastor, Grace Lutheran Church, River Forest, Illinois

"Seeking the core of biblical Christianity, Marcus Johnson probes the understanding of salvation, focusing on restoring to keen awareness the reality of believers' union in Christ as 'the essence and foundation of salvation.' Among the factors he points to as contributing to the sad neglect of this essential doctrine is a too-timid fear of mystery and a too-bold confidence in reason. And, in describing his own pilgrimage, Johnson considers persuasively that our union with Christ suffers from overemphasis on the work of Christ to the detriment of his person. Likewise, strong emphasis on the legal and forensic dimensions of justification has led to weak recognition of personal and participatory categories. He pays special care to the salutary nature of the church. This book, written from the heart, speaks to the heart."

Charles Partee, P. C. Rossin Professor of Church History, Pittsburgh Theological Seminary, Pittsburgh, Pennsylvania

"The tendency in much contemporary evangelical thought is to view salvation as if it were the reception of an abstract and objectified commodity given on account of Christ yet apart from him, as if Christ were the agent and condition of our salvation, but not that salvation itself. Marcus Johnson demonstrates that this is neither the witness of the apostles nor the confession of the Protestant Reformers, who proclaimed salvation to be a life-giving, life-transforming participation in our incarnate substitute. Immensely important and timely, this volume provides a richly textured theology of salvation couched in the only context that allows soteriology to be truly intelligible, pastoral, and doxological—the context constituted by the church and her sacraments."

John C. Clark, Assistant Professor of Theology, Moody Bible Institute

ONE WITH CHRIST

ONE

WITH

CHRIST

AN EVANGELICAL THEOLOGY
OF SALVATION

MARCUS PETER JOHNSON

CROSSWAY

WHEATON, ILLINOIS

Published by Crossway
             1300 Crescent Street
             Wheaton, Illinois 60187

Cover design: Josh Dennis

Cover image: Lucas Cranach the Elder, *The Crucifixion*, 1538, oil on panel

First printing 2013

Printed in the United States of America

Trade paperback ISBN: 978-1-4335-3149-1
Mobipocket ISBN: 978-1-4335-3151-4
PDF ISBN: 978-1-4335-3150-7
ePub ISBN: 978-1-4335-3152-1

Library of Congress Cataloging-in-Publication Data

Johnson, Marcus Peter, 1971–
    One with Christ : an evangelical theology of salvation / Marcus Peter Johnson.
       pages cm
    Includes bibliographical references and index.
    ISBN 978-1-4335-3149-1 (tp)
    1. Salvation—Christianity. 2. Evangelicalism. 3. Reformed Chuch—Doctrines. I. Title.
BT751.3.J64   2013
234—dc23   2013011769

Crossway is a publishing ministry of Good News Publishers.

VP		23	22	21	20	19	18	17	16	15	14	13
15	14	13	12	11	10	9	8	7	6	5	4	3	2	1

To my son, Peter.
You are a joy to me, a living image of the gospel.
May you come to share in the endless joy of the
heavenly Father, in his Son, the Lord Jesus Christ

CONTENTS

PREFACE

This book is the result of a shocking encounter I had, and continue to have, with John Calvin.

When I decided during my graduate studies to pursue the thought of the great pastor-theologian of sixteenth-century Geneva, I expected a number of things. I expected that I would find in Calvin an enormously helpful resource for understanding the depth and significance of evangelical Protestant theology. I expected that I would find in his theological understanding an important historical grounding for the Protestant and evangelical faith that I confess. I expected that I would find rich accounts of doctrines that were central to my understanding of the gospel: for instance, the doctrines of the atonement, of justification, and of salvation by faith alone. And Calvin did not disappoint. My expectations were met and exceeded, not only because his theology is rich and profound, but also because it is consistently pastoral and emotionally penetrating (the caricature that Calvin was an arid intellectual who wrote theology for its own sake is just that, as anyone who actually reads Calvin's works knows).

The fact that Calvin's theology exceeded my expectations was delightful and enriching, but that was not what was shocking. What *was* shocking to me was the way in which Calvin spoke of salvation. His manner was both familiar and foreign to me at the same time. I expected and found familiar concepts, terms, and phrases given sublime expression—faith, grace, atonement, justification, sanctification, election, and others. However, I was constantly disrupted by Calvin's consistent and ubiquitous refrain about being joined to Jesus Christ. At first, I simply absorbed this element of his theology into my pre-existent understandings, assuming that Calvin's language about union with

Christ was simply another, perhaps sentimental, method of expressing that believers are saved by the work of Christ on the cross. But then I realized, in a way that was initially disconcerting, that when Calvin wrote of being united to Christ, he meant that believers are personally joined to the living, incarnate, crucified, resurrected Jesus. Moreover, I realized that this union with Christ, which Calvin described in strikingly graphic and intimate terms, constituted for him the very essence of salvation. To be saved *by Christ*, Calvin kept insisting, means to be included *in the person of Christ*. That is what salvation *is*.

Due either to my theological naïveté or to my theological upbringing (or both), I did not have the categories to grasp what Calvin was saying. It was only when I began to realize that what he was saying was not only thoroughly biblical, but also in concert with many of the theological luminaries of the Christian tradition, that I began to be amazed rather than disconcerted. What at first had seemed foreign to me was nothing other than Calvin's articulation of something basic to the Christian confession, a gospel truth that is fundamental to the biblical Author (and authors) and a living reality that was assumed by Calvin's predecessors and contemporaries in the faith. As it turned out, *I* was the theological foreigner.

Once I began to see that Calvin's language was in line with the language and thought forms embedded in the Bible and in the historic stream of Christian orthodoxy, new vistas of biblical, theological, and historical understanding began to open up to me. Salvation, in particular, took on a meaning that I had never imagined. Calvin had not contradicted anything I had believed, but his understanding of being united to Christ enriched my understanding in ways from which I have yet to recover (and hope I never do). My shocking encounter with Calvin revealed to me the beauty, wonder, and mystery of salvation in Christ, and along with it, the beauty, wonder, and mystery of the church. This surprising encounter is the impetus for this book.

It is customary for an author to express thanks to all those who make the writing and publishing of a book possible, and I am more than glad to do so. This book would not have been possible without the wisdom, generosity, and insights of many willing and capable brothers and sisters in Christ.

Although it is not customary to thank dead theologians (who have never been so alive as they now are in Christ), I cannot help but note my deep indebtedness to Calvin, Martin Luther, and Thomas F. Torrance. Their glorious insights into, and faithful maintenance of, the gospel have forever changed me.

I am very grateful to my friends at Crossway Books, who decided to publish this first-time author. Their reputation for publishing excellence precedes them, and I hope that I have not done any disservice to it. To say that I am honored by their willingness is an understatement.

I also want to thank the hundreds of students at Moody Bible Institute who have attended my classes in theology and have heard me lecture on the substance of this book over several years. I count it among my highest privileges to teach these precious children of God, whose attentiveness, insightful questions, and patient learning have moved me deeply. They have contributed in no small measure to this work. Some of these students were willing to offer helpful observations and critiques of initial drafts—among them, Fred Morelli, Nathan Beck, and Amy Gilbaugh.

Special gratitude goes to John Clark, a colleague, beloved friend, and astute theologian and mentor, whose loving and critical reading of the manuscript proved especially valuable. Whatever defects remain, however, are assignable to me. *Doktorvater* Victor Shepherd also deserves mention, for he engendered and nourished in me an appreciation for the theology of the Reformation, and helped awaken me to the reality of union with Christ that is so essential to that theology.

In a most significant way, I wish to thank my wife, Stacie Jo, who not only offered beneficial corrections to the manuscript but is herself a living picture to me of what it means to be personally joined to Jesus Christ: "'Therefore a man shall leave his father and mother and hold fast to his wife, and the two shall become one flesh.' This mystery is profound, and I am saying that it refers to Christ and the church" (Eph. 5:31–32).

INTRODUCTION: UNION WITH CHRIST AND SALVATION

Christ in you, the hope of glory.

COLOSSIANS 1:27

This book is concerned with repairing an ever-widening fissure in evangelical theology that threatens to put asunder what God has joined together. In far too many evangelical expressions of the gospel, the saving work of Christ has been so distanced from his person that the notion of a saving *personal* union with the incarnate, crucified, resurrected, *living* Jesus strikes us as rather outlandish. We are content, more often than not, to refer to the "atoning work of Christ" or the "work of Christ on the cross" as the basis for our salvation. Yet, as important as such expressions are for a robust evangelical soteriology (the study of salvation), we are in dire need of the reminder that Christ's saving work is of no benefit to us unless we are joined to the living Savior whose work it is. When we entertain the notion—consciously or not, intentionally or not—that we can be saved by the work of Christ apart from being joined to him personally, we are deepening a fissure that, left unrepaired, will continue to move us away from our biblically faithful theological heritage.

The sixteenth-century Protestant Reformer John Calvin insisted that we must never separate the work of Christ from his person if we wish to understand the nature of salvation. However much we may rightly extol and magnify the saving work of Christ on our behalf, however highly we may esteem what he accomplished in his life, death, resurrection, and ascension, we will have missed what is utterly essential to this good news if we fail to understand that our salvation has to do with his very person. The saving work of Christ is not to be thought of as abstracted from the living person of Christ.

Calvin's way of expressing this is striking and emphatic:

> First, we must understand that as long as Christ remains outside of us, and we are separated from him, all that he has suffered and done for the salvation of the human race remains useless and of no value to us. Therefore, to share in what he has received from the Father, he had to become ours and to dwell within us . . . for, as I have said, all that he possesses is nothing to us until we grow into one body with him.[1]

If Calvin's insistence on the intensely relational aspect of salvation—the personal indwelling of Christ—seems somewhat foreign to us, it may be because contemporary evangelical soteriology[2] has largely lost sight of a profound mystery that lies at the heart of the gospel, a mystery that the apostle Paul describes as "Christ in you, the hope of glory" (Col. 1:27). The mysterious reality of our union with Jesus Christ, by which he dwells in us and we in him, is so utterly essential to the gospel that to obscure it inevitably leads to an obscuring of the gospel itself. For a number of reasons, several of which I will explore below, contemporary evangelical theology has routinely failed to incorporate this mystery into the heart of its soteriological understanding. This has led to the danger of what we might call "the objectification of salvation," the creation of a dichotomy between the work and person of Christ or, in Calvin's words, the peril of seeking "in Christ something else than Christ himself."[3] This soteriological oversight needs to be addressed for the purpose of maintaining gospel vitality and the richness of the church's life and confession. To this

---

[1] John Calvin, *Institutes of the Christian Religion*, ed. John T. McNeil, trans. Ford Lewis Battles, Library of Christian Classics, Vols. 20–21 (Philadelphia: Westminster, 1960), Book 3, chapter 1, paragraph 1 (hereafter, 3.1.1).

[2] There is a (growing) challenge in trying to define exactly what is meant by "evangelical." Douglas Sweeney writes succinctly, "Evangelicals comprise a movement that is rooted in classical Christian orthodoxy, shaped by a largely Protestant understanding of the gospel, and distinguished from other such movements by an eighteenth-century twist [the renewal movements of the Great Awakening]" (*The American Evangelical Story: A History of the Movement* [Grand Rapids: Baker, 2005], 24). This book attempts to retrieve a Protestant understanding of the gospel that is rooted in classical Christian orthodoxy and which is, therefore, evangelical.

[3] This memorable comment is from John Calvin, *Calvin's Commentaries* (Edinburgh: Calvin Translation Society, 1844–56; reprinted in 22 vols., Grand Rapids: Baker, 2003), John 6:26.

end, we do well to take a step back and recover the richness that is already present in our tradition, then bring it to bear on the church's life and confession. This book attempts to address this oversight by articulating an evangelical soteriology from within the mystery and reality of the church's union with its Savior.

Evangelicalism has been rightly characterized as a movement devoted to upholding the authority of Scripture, the centrality of the cross in Christ's saving work, and the proclamation of the gospel of Jesus Christ; in other words, the evangelical movement is bibliocentric, crucicentric, and gospel-centric. These emphases constitute an admirable legacy for which we should be thankful. At times, however, in gratitude for one's heritage, and in the interest of continuing its biblical, historical, and theological faithfulness, there is a need for renewed reflection and constructive criticism. Despite its relative clear-sightedness on many essential gospel issues, evangelicalism has largely lost its sense of a profound, essential saving reality that is deeply rooted in both the biblical portrayal of salvation and the appropriation of that portrayal in the historic confession of the Christian church. The apostolic writers, with the church fathers and Reformers following suit, described this reality with a host of stunning and arresting images. This reality, which was central to their understanding of the gospel, was the mystery of the believer's union with Jesus Christ.

There is much more in the pages that follow about what it means to say that salvation consists in, or is rooted in, the believer's becoming one with the Savior—the One who, for us and for our salvation, was crucified, buried, and resurrected, and who then ascended to the right hand of the Father. But before I attend to these crucial matters, a word about a present danger that threatens evangelical theology is in order.

As I mentioned above, evangelical theology generally, and evangelical soteriology more specifically, has been overtaken by a subtle dichotomization of the person and work of Christ. This is reflected in the tendency to discuss salvation in rather abstract, extrinsic, and impersonal terms. In textbooks, sermons, and classrooms, salvation is often conceived of as the reception of some*thing* Christ has acquired for us rather than as the reception of the living Christ. In other words, salvation is described as a gift to be apprehended rather than the apprehension of the Giver himself. To put it yet another way, the gospel is portrayed as the offer of a depersonalized benefit (e.g., grace, justification, or eternal life) rather than the offer of the very person of Christ (who is himself the grace of God, our justification, and our eternal life).[4]

These conceptions, expressions, and portrayals, though certainly not ill-intentioned, fail to fully capture not only the beauty, wonder, and mystery of our salvation, but, more importantly, the personal reality that is its essence. Because they tend to refer to salvation in terms of benefits or gifts that are abstracted from Jesus Christ, these ways of speaking about salvation run the risk of one-sidedly objectifying the saving work of Christ so that his living person—as well as the necessity of our union with him—begins to fade into obscurity. Contemporary evangelical theology has rightly stressed the saving work of Christ, but it has simultaneously overlooked the reality through which we benefit from this saving work. We have emphasized the work of Christ, but too often to the exclusion of the saving person of Christ. The impression we give too often is that salvation is reducible to the work (or gifts) of Christ in isolation from the fullness of his saving person, as though he were a divine Santa Claus, showering us with gifts but not including us in his very person and life. This view subtly succumbs to a dangerous soteriological reductionism in which we begin to speak of receiving the benefits of Christ apart from receiving the Giver himself—Christ *for* us without Christ *in* us. We ought, rather, to insist that the atonement (the saving work of Christ) is indivisible from the One who atones (the saving person of Christ).[5]

This book is an exploration of soteriology expressed within the conviction that *Christ* is our salvation and that we are the recipients of his saving work precisely and only because we are recipients of the living Christ. Our *union* with the living Christ is, in other words, what it means to be saved.

---

[4] Even the familiar phrases "saved by grace" or "saved by the cross" can dissolve into abstractions. Grace saves us only because we enter it by being joined to Jesus Christ, who is the grace of God to us. The cross saves us only because, in our union with the crucified Christ, we experience the benefits of his death. Jesus Christ is, in other words, the content of both grace and cross: we are saved *in Christ*.

[5] As Thomas F. Torrance put it, Christ does not merely perform an action called the atonement, "Christ Jesus IS the atonement" (cited in *Atonement: The Person and Work of Christ*, ed. Robert T. Walker [Downers Grove, IL: IVP Academic, 2009], 94, emphasis in original).

Union with Christ in Scripture and Church Tradition

I have made the claim that the mystery of our union with Christ is deeply rooted in the biblical portrayal of salvation, as well as in the faith confession of the church fathers and sixteenth-century Reformers. A brief substantiation of this claim will help not only to provide biblical and historical context for the substance of this book, but also to demonstrate preliminarily that the doctrine of union with Christ looms large in the sources to which evangelicalism has always been indebted.

"Union with Christ," as I use it in this book, is a collective phrase that is meant to encompass the astonishing number of terms, expressions, and images in the New Testament—in the Pauline and Johannine writings in particular—that refer to the oneness of the believer with Christ. The most common of these expressions is the characteristically Pauline phrase "in Christ," which occurs, in combination with "in Christ Jesus," "in the Lord," and "in him," approximately 164 times in Paul's letters.[6] To cite a few examples, believers individually and the church corporately are said to be possessors of eternal life in Christ (Rom. 6:23); justified in Christ (8:1); glorified in Christ (Rom. 8:30; 2 Cor. 3:18); sanctified in Christ (1 Cor. 1:2); called in Christ (v. 9); made alive in Christ (15:22; Eph. 2:5); created anew in Christ (2 Cor. 5:17); adopted as children of God in Christ (Gal. 3:26); elected in Christ (Eph. 1:4); and raised with Christ (Col. 3:1).

This notion is so embedded in Paul's thought that he refers to Christians (a term he does not use) with regularity as those who are "in Christ" or "in the Lord," as if this phrase is simply what it means to *be* a Christian (cf. Rom. 16:1–13; Phil. 4:21; Col. 1:2).[7] His language extends much further, however. His letters include references to believers being created in Christ (Eph. 2:10), crucified with him (Gal. 2:20), buried with him (Col. 2:12), baptized into Christ and his death (Rom. 6:3), united with him in his resurrection (Rom. 6:5), and seated with

---

[6] J. K. S. Reid, *Our Life in Christ* (Philadelphia: Westminster Press, 1963), 12. Reid refers to the important work of Adolf Deismann, *Die Neutestamntliche Formel 'in Christo Jesu,'* who counts at least 164 occurrences of such language in the writings of Paul alone.

[7] We often hear, in contemporary Christianity, the phrase "in Christ" used as a synonym for "Christian." In one sense, this is accurate. In another sense, however, the phrase and the term are not strictly synonyms, because one can be a "Christian" only *as a result of* being joined to Christ; the constitutive reality of being joined to Christ allows the designation "Christian" to have meaning.

him in the heavenly places (Eph. 2:6); Christ being formed in believers (Gal. 4:19) and dwelling in our hearts (Eph. 3:17); the church as members—limbs and organs—of Christ's body (1 Cor. 6:15; 12:27); Christ in us (2 Cor. 13:5) and us in him (1 Cor. 1:30); the church as one flesh with Christ (Eph. 5:31–32); and believers gaining Christ/being found in him (Phil. 3:8–9). As Bruce Demarest has estimated, the number of occurrences of "union with Christ" terminology in Paul's letters alone exceeds two hundred![8] It is no wonder, then, that the renowned Scottish preacher James Stewart once wrote: "The heart of Paul's religion is union with Christ. This, more than any other conception, . . . is the key which unlocks the secrets of his soul."[9]

"Union with Christ" terminology and imagery are just as ubiquitous and regnant in the Johannine corpus. In John's soteriology, Jesus is the living water (John 4, 7), the bread of life (John 6:33, 48), and the one whose flesh and blood are to be consumed for eternal life (John 6:53–57); we have eternal life only if we have the Son (1 John 5:11–12), we are in the Son—who is true God and eternal life (1 John 5:20)—and we live through him (1 John 4:9). Jesus abides in us and we in him (John 6:56; 15:4–7), and God abides in us and we in him through Jesus and the Spirit (1 John 3:24; 4:12–16). We are one with Christ and the Father (John 14:20; 17:21–23). Jesus is the true vine in whom we abide and apart from whom we can do nothing (John 15:1–5), and he is the resurrection and life in himself (John 11:25; cf. John 1:4). John's assertions about the nature of salvation (often quoting Jesus) are of a vital, organic, and personal nature. We find throughout the Johannine corpus the insistence that Jesus is more than a provider *of* blessings such as eternal life, truth, living bread, living water, or resurrection life; He *is in himself* the blessings he provides. There is an emphatic personalization of salvation in John's writings, as if John were intent on demonstrating that while the benefits of salvation happen because of Christ and through Christ, they are not available to us except *by our participation in Christ's life.*

---

[8] Bruce Demarest, *The Cross and Salvation* (Wheaton, IL: Crossway, 1997), 313, counts 216 such occurrences in Paul. J. D. G. Dunn, *The Theology of Paul the Apostle* (Grand Rapids: Eerdmans, 2006), 396, details Paul's "participation in Christ" language and notes that the phrase *"en Christo"* alone occurs eighty-three times in the Pauline corpus. See also Reid, *Our Life in Christ*, 12.

[9] James Stewart, *Man in Christ* (1935; repr., Vancouver: Regent College, 2002), 147.

The staggering ubiquity of the theme of union with Christ in Paul's and John's writings surely warrants the conclusion that they share the basic soteriological conviction that salvation, in all of its life-altering aspects, consists at root in being united with Christ the Savior.

This centrality of union with Jesus Christ in salvation in the apostolic witness was not overlooked by the early church fathers and Reformers. Donald Fairbairn, in his book *Life in the Trinity*, produced a compelling compilation of the thought of four particularly influential early church theologians: Irenaeus of Lyons (140–200), Athanasius of Alexandria (296–373), Augustine of Hippo (354–430), and Cyril of Alexandria (375–444).[10] Fairbairn asserts that the general consensus among these early framers of Christian doctrine was that salvation is, in its most basic sense, a participation in the Son's relationship to the Father through the power of the Holy Spirit. In our union with Christ through the Spirit, believers share in the personal relation and love between the Father and the Son, and in the manifold blessings that result. Accordingly, for these early churchmen, salvation was understood in characteristically personal terms, an understanding they found first in Paul and John:

> The central reality of the Christian life is that believers are united to Christ, and the reason this is so central is because it links us to the central relationship that there is, Christ's relationship to his Father. . . . The early church recognized this, and so they wrote of salvation by writing of the God in whom we participate when we are saved. They did not normally parcel out different aspects of salvation, discussing them individually as if one could possess one or another of them in isolation. Instead, whenever they wrote of salvation, the context for the discussion was a treatment of God, of Christ, of the Holy Spirit. And whenever they did write of different aspects of salvation, they made clear that these aspects hinged on and revolved around participation in Christ.[11]

The Reformers of the sixteenth century—for whom Holy Scripture was the primary authority in matters of church doctrine, and

---

[10] Donald Fairbairn, *Life in the Trinity: An Introduction to Theology with the Help of the Church Fathers* (Downers Grove, IL: IVP, 2009).
[11] Ibid., 202.

who therefore regarded the faithful interpretation of the Scriptures by the church fathers as immensely important—also emphasized union with Christ in their understanding of salvation. For instance, Martin Luther, usually distinguished by his teaching on justification by faith alone, was clear that justification and faith occur in a broader context of union with the Savior, who alone possesses righteousness. An often-overlooked aspect of Luther's soteriology is his stress on the Christ-intimacy that results from faith:

> But faith must be taught correctly, namely that by it you are so cemented to Christ that He and you are as one person, which cannot be separated but remains attached to Him forever and declares: "I am as Christ." And Christ, in turn, says: "I am as the sinner who is attached to me and I to him. For by faith we are joined together into one flesh and bone." Thus Eph. 5:30 says: "We are members of the body of Christ, of his flesh and bones," in such a way that faith couples Christ and me more intimately than a husband is coupled to his wife.[12]

Justification by faith does not, for Luther, occur in a vacuum. Faith justifies only insofar as it brings us into a personal, intimate union with Christ: "Therefore faith justifies *because* it takes hold of Christ and possesses this treasure, *the present Christ*. . . . Therefore the Christ who is grasped by faith and who lives in the heart is the true Christian righteousness, *on account of which* God counts us as righteous and grants us eternal life."[13] While contemporary evangelical theology has often looked to Luther to articulate its position on salvation/justification by grace alone through faith alone, we have often neglected the *soli Christi* ("in Christ alone") that makes all the other *solas* possible: "It is impossible for one to be a Christian unless he possesses Christ. If he possesses Christ, he possesses all the benefits of Christ."[14]

Luther's emphasis on union with Christ was echoed resoundingly in Calvin's theology. The opening to Book 3 of his justly famous work *The Institutes of the Christian Religion* provides ample support for the contention that Calvin viewed union with Christ as the center of the ap-

---

[12] Martin Luther, "Lectures on Galatians," in *Luther's Works*, 55 vols., gen. ed. Jaroslav Pelikan (St. Louis: Concordia Publishing House; Philadelphia: Fortress Press, 1955–1975), Vol. 26, 168.

[13] Luther, *Works*, Vol. 26, 130 (emphasis added).

[14] Ibid., Vol. 31, 189–190. This excerpt is from Luther's "Explanation of the Ninety-Five Theses (1518)."

plication of salvation. His words, which I have previously quoted, are worth pondering again:

> First, we must understand that as long as Christ remains outside of us, and we are separated from him, all that he has suffered and done for the salvation of the human race remains useless and of no value to us. Therefore, to share in what he has received from the Father, he had to become ours and to dwell within us . . . for, as I have said, all that he possesses is nothing to us until we grow into one body with him.[15]

There is a remarkable soterio-logic in this passage: Calvin claims that all of the blessings the Son has received from the Father, that is, all of what Christ has accomplished on our behalf as Savior, every one of the glorious benefits of his person and work—his assumption of our flesh; his sinless life; his propitiatory, self-sacrificial, sin-expiating crucifixion; his life-giving, justifying resurrection; his prophetic, priestly and royal provision—are *useless* to us unless he "dwell[s] within us . . . until we grow into one body with him." A more emphatic assertion about the saving relevance of union with Christ would be difficult to find.

Not surprisingly, we find the biblical theme of union with Christ running like a thread through Calvin's writings,[16] exemplified perhaps by his easy identification of participation in Christ with the gospel: "For this is the design of the gospel, that Christ may become ours, and that we may be ingrafted into his body."[17] With his understanding of the gospel significance of the believer's union with Christ, Calvin proved himself an attentive student of the Scriptures, of the early church fathers, and of his predecessor in the Reformation movement, Luther.[18]

This chorus of ecclesiastical voices from the classical, orthodox Christian tradition does not exhaust the number of those who have

---

[15] Calvin, *Institutes*, 3.1.1.

[16] Torrance has written, "All Calvin's teaching and preaching have to do with salvation through union with Christ in his death and resurrection" (*Conflict and Agreement in the Church* [London: Lutterworth Press, 1959], 91). This quotation is cited in Charles Partee's excellent work in which he demonstrates the "foundational role of [union with Christ] across the total sweep of [Calvin's] theology" (*The Theology of John Calvin* [Louisville: Westminster John Knox Press, 2008], xvi).

[17] Calvin, *Commentaries*, 1 Cor. 1:9.

[18] Cf. Marcus Johnson, "Luther and Calvin on Union with Christ," in *Fides et Historia* 39, no. 2 (Summer 2007), 59–77.

borne witness to the significance of being united to Christ; it merely represents a sampling of the some of the most influential. Among their number we might also cite other luminaries of the Reformation, such as Martin Bucer, Peter Martyr Vermigli, and Theodore Beza, and many of the catechisms and confessions of their time; leading Puritan thinkers such as Thomas Boston, John Cotton, and Jonathan Edwards; the underappreciated Reformed theologian John Williamson Nevin; and the late Thomas F. Torrance of Edinburgh. All of these church-men shared a profound awareness of the vital, personal, and intimate mystery of which Paul spoke, "Christ in you, the hope of glory." As we pursue a deeper appreciation of this saving mystery, the voices of many of these figures will reappear throughout the book, particularly those of the Reformers and their heirs, who constitute the fountainhead of the evangelical Protestant movement. After all, evangelical theology is its most robust and vibrant when, having listened to the living voice of Jesus Christ in his Word, it finds its bearings in the rich tradition of faithful interpreters in whom Christ has resounded.

Whatever Happened to Union with Christ?

If what I have briefly described is true—that union with Christ is a pervasive theme throughout the New Testament, and is deeply embed-ded in the soteriology of key figures in the Christian tradition—then why, for instance, are almost all of the students in my systematic the-ology courses each semester puzzled at having never heard of union with Christ in any theologically significant way? After all, they come from a wide range of evangelical, or evangelically minded, churches—whether Baptist, Evangelical Free, Lutheran, Presbyterian, Methodist, or non-denominational. Once they are brought to an awareness of "the riches of the glory of this mystery" (Col. 1:27) and the far-reaching significance of this saving union, these students lament this apparent oversight in their theological education. They are not alone, for I, too, have wondered how such a crucial aspect of the biblical portrayal of salvation, woven so deeply into the historic evangelical tradition, for so long escaped my notice. How could it be that these students (and I), most of whom had been raised in gospel-rich, Jesus-exalting, evangeli-cal churches, and had heard hundreds of sermons, attended countless

Bible studies, and read a number of biblical/theological books, could claim not to have heard of union with Christ?

The answer to this question, it seems to me, is complex. But there are important and compelling reasons to try to give an answer. It is complex because, in one sense, my students and I are wrong. We *had* heard of union with Christ before, we just did not know it. We could not have failed to hear of it, because, as we have seen, it saturates the writings of Paul and John (Protestant favorites, to be sure). In so many of the sermons we heard, the Bible studies we attended, and even our private study of Scripture, we encountered the language: "in Christ," "crucified with Christ," "members of Christ," "alive in Christ," "Christ as living bread and water," "his flesh and blood as eternal life," "the vine and branches," and on and on. The concept was all around us, and yet it strangely failed to take hold. All of this language and imagery failed to penetrate into the core of our understanding of salvation. Perhaps we were not sure what to do with the language. Perhaps we were not taught what to do with this concept, and so we let it exist at the outer edges of our thought, content to sentimentalize it or leave it to the "mystics." We lacked the conceptual categories to make sense of it. So, the more precise question is: What accounts for the lack of conceptual clarity that leads to the glaring omission of the theme of union with Christ *in the soteriological understanding of the contemporary evangelical church?*

Allow me to humbly suggest four reasons why contemporary evangelical theology has not, on the whole, incorporated union with Christ into the heart of its soteriological understanding. All of these reasons admit of exceptions, to be sure, but in the main I believe they are pertinent and instructive.

First, many of the texts that the evangelical church turns to for instruction in theology, or more specifically soteriology, whether more popularly written or for more academic purposes, do not include adequate treatments of the doctrine. These texts fall into three broad classes: those that do not mention union with Christ at all; those that mention union with Christ in a non-substantive way, either subsuming it under another category (e.g., sanctification or the Christian life) or sentimentalizing it; and those that recognize the importance of the doctrine, ostensibly at least, but ultimately fall short of demonstrating why it is central to understanding salvation as a whole.[19]

A second reason, related to the first, is that personal, organic, participational categories have been assigned at best a secondary place in evangelical soteriological understanding. The dominant motif in evangelical Protestant salvation has been the legal/forensic type. This is manifest in the emphasis that has been placed on the doctrine of justification, and is easily demonstrated by a perusal of theology textbooks and the library shelves they inhabit. Indeed, the *raison d'être* of this book is the difficulty of even finding a text that treats union with Christ on its own merits.[20] This is not at all to say that the evangelical Protestant emphasis on justification is without warrant or is not extremely important—far from it. Neither is it to say that justification and union with Christ are somehow incongruent; in fact, Luther and Calvin believed that justification *depends on union with Christ* for its cogency, and it is from them that we draw our typically forensic emphases. I will argue later that union with Christ is the reality from which to articulate a particularly rich, classically Protestant understanding of justification.

Third, the contemporary evangelical church has failed to pay sufficient attention to the theological tradition from which it springs. That is to say, evangelicalism has often neglected the study of church history and the theologians and pastors who have guided the church in its doctrinal confession and preserved the truths of the gospel for centuries. While Douglas Sweeney's definition of evangelicalism includes the phrase "rooted in classical Christian orthodoxy, shaped by a largely Protestant understanding of the gospel,"[21] he is expressing what is optimal in the tradition, not necessarily what is characteristic. In too many instances, evangelicalism is in danger of historical amnesia, in which case it runs the risk of losing not only its theological

---

[19] This does not mean that these texts are not helpful or important in what they affirm. The reader is especially encouraged to read chapter 8 in Demarest, *The Cross*, and John Murray, *Redemption Accomplished and Applied* (Grand Rapids: Eerdmans, 1955), 161–173.

[20] This deficiency has begun to be addressed by Robert Letham, *Union with Christ: In Scripture, History and Theology* (Phillipsburg, NJ: P&R, 2011); Todd Billings, *Union with Christ: Reframing Theology and Ministry for the Church* (Grand Rapids: Baker, 2011); Constantine Campbell, *Paul and Union with Christ: An Exegetical and Theological Study* (Grand Rapids: Zondervan, 2012). For an excellent, more scholarly treatment, see William B. Evans, *Imputation and Impartation: Union with Christ in American Reformed Theology*, Studies in Christian History and Thought (Eugene, OR: Wipf & Stock, 2009).

[21] Sweeney, *The American Evangelical Story*, 24.

depth, but also its identity. Union with Christ is among those doctrines that, while historically well attested, have escaped the notice of our churches.

Finally, and more conjecturally, the relative absence of a robust understanding of our participation in Christ may be explained by a particularly modern reticence to embrace mystery at the heart of our faith confession. This hesitation is evidence of Protestant theology's dangerous liaison with rationalism. To many evangelical ears, "union with Christ" terminology and imagery sound "mystical," and we prefer to cede mystical concepts and categories to Roman Catholic and Eastern Orthodox theologies. This is a failure, however, to distinguish between *mysticism* and *mystery* in theology.

Mysticism is a vague, speculative, unmediated, and direct experience of God, or absorption into God. By contrast, nearly all of the central biblical doctrines we embrace are rooted in mystery (e.g., the creation of the world *ex nihilo*, the virgin birth, the incarnation, the hypostatic union, the resurrection, the Trinity, the inspiration of Scripture, and others). This is why theology requires a healthy dose of modesty. "The modesty that theology needs," writes Hans Boersma, "is the recognition that we cannot rationally comprehend God. Theology is based on mystery and enters into mystery."[22] Despite the obvious truth of this assertion, modern evangelicals often seem more prepared to embrace doctrines apparently amenable to logical, rational systematization than to embrace the mysteries of our faith in a state of wonder and confession. This may explain our tendency to spend an inordinate amount of time *explaining* the mysteries of our faith rather than adoring and savoring them.[23] Mystery speaks of a reality that can be apprehended, pointed to, and described, but *never* explained, let alone explained away. This may also explain the disappearance of a sacramental understanding of the gospel, the church, and her sacraments, topics we shall explore at greater length. Our union with Christ

---

[22] Hans Boersma, *Heavenly Participation: The Weaving of a Sacramental Tapestry* (Grand Rapids: Eerdmans, 2011), 26–27. Boersma goes on to note, provocatively, "Modern theology's problem is its rational confidence—and thus, ultimately, its pride" (27).

[23] Theology certainly attempts to explain God's relationship to the world, but it simultaneously accepts and exults in God's ultimate transcendence. K. Scott Oliphint phrases this notion rather well: "It is certainly not the case that the relationship of God to the world is absolutely inexplicable; rather, in whatever ways it is explicable, it will always remain for us incomprehensible as well" (*God with Us: Divine Condescension and the Attributes of God* [Wheaton, IL: Crossway, 2012], 225).

is indeed one of the great mysteries that lies at the heart of Christian confession, and it is thoroughly evangelical.[24]

So, reasons for the general absence of union with Christ in evangelical soteriology are manifold, and the true cause is very difficult to identify. But no matter which of these reasons (or combination of reasons) best explains this deficiency, Augustus Strong's words still ring true nearly a century after he wrote them: "[T]he majority of Christians much more frequently think of Christ as a Savior outside of them, than as a Savior who dwells within."[25] The consequence of this oversight in the church is that salvation has often been thought of as dislocated from the living person Jesus Christ, as a blessing or set of blessings that exist and are given independently from our being joined to the incarnate, crucified, resurrected, ascended, glorified Lord himself.

Furthermore, the rich, compelling imagery in Scripture that testifies to the church's living, organic relationship to Jesus Christ tends to recede into mere metaphors and sentiments, and so on to a reductionistic ecclesiology that cannot but fail to take the church seriously as the mystery of Christ's body. Correspondingly, baptism and the Lord's Supper, the identity markers of that body, which show forth and seal the good news that we truly share in Christ's death, burial, and resurrection, fade into obscurity in a regrettable bifurcation of soteriology and ecclesiology. The church as the body of Christ becomes barely relevant to the gospel of salvation "in Christ Jesus." A retrieval of the central significance of union with Christ will provide a way for the evangelical church to see once again why the work of Christ cannot be separated from his person; why the gloriously good news about salvation rests in the church being joined to the One who *is* salvation himself; and why Jesus Christ *is* the essence of the church, or else the church is no more than a voluntaristic religious club of like-minded folk.

---

[24] Vernon Grounds's remarkable essay on the importance of mystery and paradox in the Christian confession deserves a wide reading among Christians: "The Postulate of Paradox," in *Bulletin of the Evangelical Theological Society* 7, no. 1 (Winter 1964), 3–21. Grounds reminds us that Christians *confess the mysteries* of our faith; our faith confession is grounded in truths that are impossible to fully comprehend. In this sense, Christians are not so unlike the White Queen in Lewis Carroll's *Through the Looking Glass*, who "believed as many as six impossible things before breakfast." This is a feeling I often have during breakfast after Sunday church services.

[25] Augustus Strong, *Systematic Theology* (1907; repr., Valley Forge, PA; Judson Press, 1976), 795.

Overview

The premise of this book is that the primary, central, and fundamental reality of salvation is our union with Jesus Christ, because of which union all the benefits of the Savior flow to us, and through which union all these benefits are to be understood. This book comprises an introduction to evangelical soteriology (or applied soteriology) oriented around the most basic of all saving truths, the union God the Father forges between the believer and his Son, Jesus Christ, through the power of the Holy Spirit. To put it plainly, *to be saved is to be united to the Savior*. I develop this premise along the following chapter outline.

Chapter 1 provides an orientation to the nature and character of our union with Christ, a biblical theme so rich and complex, and so sweeping in scope, that we must begin by defining terms and parameters. The most important questions this chapter addresses are these: What *kind* of union is the Bible referring to? What does it mean to say that I am truly joined to Christ? How does this union come about? This chapter is crucial in that the nature and character of this union go very far in determining how we conceive of its effects. In other words, how we understand the essence of salvation profoundly affects how we conceive of the benefits that follow.

Chapter 2 is also an orienting chapter. It takes a soteriological step backward, so to speak, in order to describe the human predicament that makes union with Christ necessary. That predicament is the tragic and deserved fall of humankind into condemnation and depravity as described in Genesis 3 and Romans 5. The good news about our union with the last Adam, Jesus Christ, is predicated on the bad news about our prior union with the first Adam. Though both of these unions defy precise, logical description (they are mysteries), this chapter seeks to show how our sinful condition "in Adam" is perfectly rectified "in Christ." Further, the saving significance of the incarnation is explored. The incarnate humanity of Jesus Christ, in which we find the perfect union of God and man, is the basis for the church's union with Christ.

Chapters 3, 4, and 5 describe, in turn, the benefits most commonly associated with salvation: justification, sanctification, and adoption. Although these sublime benefits are certainly distinguishable, and so warrant their own chapters, they are also inseparable as benefits that

issue forth from Christ, the One who is our justification, our sanctification, and the true Son of the Father. We see the depth and wonder
of these blessings of Christ when we consider them as results of our
participation in him. Justification (chap. 3) is that saving blessing by
which sinners are declared righteous in God's sight through the forgiveness of our sins and the imputation of Christ's righteousness. This
comes about precisely as we are brought to share in the righteous
life, the sin-bearing death, and the triumphant resurrection of Jesus.
Sanctification (chap. 4) is that saving blessing wherein believers, by
virtue of being joined to the Holy One, share in the holiness of Christ,
bear the title of saints, and progressively realize the holiness that is
already theirs. It is therefore that act of salvation in which God richly
blesses us by bringing us into increasing conformity to his perfect
image, Jesus. Adoption (chap. 5) is that saving blessing wherein believers, by virtue of their communion with the true Son of God, share in
his sonship by grace, are given the right to be called and received as
beloved children of the Father, and inherit the immeasurable rights
and privileges secured by the only begotten Son, Jesus.

Chapter 6 explores two additional benefits of our saving union
with Christ: preservation and glorification. While these saving graces
are perhaps lesser-known and sometimes relegated to the periphery
of our soteriology, they are, in fact, integral to God's salvation for us
in Christ. When God includes us in Christ, he promises that he will
never lose us and will faithfully preserve us in his love and holy care.
Furthermore, as God preserves us in Christ, he also glorifies us in him.
Glorification is the full and final realization of our union with Christ,
in which the saints will be transformed so as to bear perfectly the
image of Jesus Christ for eternity.

Chapters 7 and 8 are an attempt to demonstrate the relationship
between salvation and the church, that is, the relationship between
soteriology and ecclesiology. When evangelicalism fails to incorporate
union with Christ into the heart of its theology—opting instead for a
dangerous soteriological abstractionism, reductionism, and individualism—it fails to see how the church and her sacraments relate to God's
promise to redeem us only as we are included in Jesus Christ as his
body. If we begin our understanding of salvation with the staggering

reality that we are joined to Jesus Christ, we may begin to see why being joined to him is simultaneously our salvation *and the constitution of the church*. Salvation is a communal reality whereby sinners are joined to Christ *and to one another*, entering the saving reality of Christ's body. Those who are saved into the body of Christ commemorate, celebrate, and continue to participate in their union with Christ in his life, death, and resurrection through the preaching of God's Word (the audible gospel) and the sacraments of baptism and the Lord's Supper (the visible gospel). The church, in other words, is brought into being through her union with the Lord, and continues to grow and be sustained in that union through the presence of Christ in Word and sacrament. Any understanding of salvation that loses sight of the centrality of union with Christ is bound to lose sight of the saving relevance of the church and her sacraments.

This book is not meant to be a comprehensive soteriology. Each of the chapters describe wonders of salvation that cannot be exhausted in a single chapter, that are, in fact, worthy of books of their own. But although this book is not comprehensive, it is cohesive. It seeks to describe how the manifold blessings of salvation find their significance and foundations in the union believers have with Christ. I hope that the reader will come away with a deeper sense of the significance of the person of Christ and his work, why they should not and cannot be separated, and why our union with Christ's person is the fount of all of his blessings. So, I do hope this book is foundational, always orienting us to the living Lord and Savior Jesus, and our participation in him, as the grounding of salvation. Like any evangelical theology true to its name, this book looks to the written Word of God as the primary and authoritative source for its arguments and conclusions, and enlists the help of theologians past and present for interpretive guidance and depth.

1

THE NATURE OF
UNION WITH CHRIST

Whoever feeds on my flesh and drinks
my blood abides in me, and I in him.

JOHN 6:56

Trying to explain mysteries is counterintuitive. If we succeed in the task, we risk losing the mystery; if we retain the mystery, we risk losing the explanation. We fail in succeeding and succeed only in failing.

However, we must at least *attempt* to describe mystery, for, after all, so much of the mysterious, enigmatic language in the New Testament is wrapped up with the theme of the believer's union with Christ. We read of feeding on flesh and drinking blood; of body parts and flesh-unions; of vines, branches, and living water; of dying in another's death and living in another's life; and of the indwelling Spirit and God becoming flesh. Perhaps it is because this language and these images mystify and puzzle us that we fail to reckon properly with them. We feel a bit like many of Jesus's contemporaries, confused and even troubled by what he says. But we must reckon with these words, because embedded in them are the most astounding of promises—eternal life, the hope of glory, forgiveness, holiness, redemption, resurrection, bodily transformation, and, most astonishing of all, the Son of God dwelling in us. This is the language of salvation and the logic of the gospel, and so we must attempt to understand and articulate the mystery of our union with Christ if we are to understand and articulate our salvation.

As I discussed in the book's introduction, "union with Christ" language pervades the writings of the New Testament, particularly the letters of Paul and the writings of John. The sheer number of instances in which such language occurs is instructive in its own right, for the repetition gives us an indication of the importance of this theme. But these instances occur in an array of contexts that address different aspects of this union and shed light on the manifold ways in which we may conceive of it.

In order to bring some clarity to such an expansive theme, this chapter will (1) explore the immense scope of union with Christ as it is presented in the Bible and offer some defining parameters; (2) define the nature or character of the union positively, so as to describe what our union with the Savior consists of and how it comes about; and (3) define the nature or character of the union negatively, so as to describe erroneous or inadequate notions. In one respect, this chapter is the most important of all, because our conception of the nature of our saving union with Christ inevitably (consciously or subconsciously) determines how we conceive of the nature of salvation more generally.

The Scope of Union with Christ

John Murray, longtime professor of systematic theology at Westminster Theological Seminary, was keenly aware of the massive redemptive scope of union with Christ in the Scriptures:

> Nothing is more central or basic than union and communion with Christ. Union with Christ is really the *central truth of the whole doctrine of salvation* not only in its application but also in its once-for-all accomplishment in the finished work of Christ. Indeed the whole process of salvation has its origin in one phase of union with Christ and salvation has in view the realization of other phases of union with Christ.[1]

Murray's words succinctly summarize the breadth involved when one undertakes to explain the centrality of union with Christ in the

---

[1]John Murray, *Redemption Accomplished and Applied* (Grand Rapids: Eerdmans, 1955), 161 (emphasis added).

accomplishment and application of salvation in Christ. He was referring to the fact that the biblical account of salvation "in Christ" has an
enormous reach. God elects people "in Christ" before the foundation of
the world, Jesus assumes our human flesh in the incarnation, believers
are savingly united to Christ, and, finally, that union is consummated
in the resurrection and glorification of the saints "in Christ." To offer
some conceptual clarity and dimension to the matter, let us consider
these four phases of union with Christ.[2]

I. UNION WITH CHRIST IN ELECTION

God's redemptive plan for humanity began long before the incarnation,
crucifixion, resurrection, and ascension of his Son. Astonishingly, as
Paul informs us, God "chose us *in [Christ]* before the foundation of the
world" (Eph. 1:4). In some inscrutable sense, the saints can be comprehended as *in Christ* before the temporal accomplishment and application of salvation through Christ in space and time. We gladly accept
the pronouncement that God the Father blesses us "in Christ with
every spiritual blessing in the heavenly places" (v. 3). But as we read on,
we find to our amazement that these blessings occur in the sphere of
God's *predestinating* will and grace, so that the Father's eternal purpose
and love for us are ours only and ever as we are included in Christ.
In fact, Paul indicates that God's calling of us to salvation through the
gospel is the magnificent outworking of what God has *already* given us
"*in Christ Jesus* before the ages began" (2 Tim. 1:9). Whereas Paul's use of
"in Christ" is usually reserved for the temporal inclusion of believers
in Christ (and constitutes the focus of this book), in the case of election
we can speak of a kind of pre-temporal union with Christ—a union
that somehow existed before and above time—that is the source of the
time-and-space application of that union to the people of God. As Murray writes, "And that means that those who will be saved were not even
contemplated by the Father in the ultimate counsel of his predestinating love apart from union with Christ—they were chosen in Christ."[3]

---

[2] Scholars have various ways of classifying these phases of union with Christ. For example, Richard B.
Gaffin Jr. refers to predestinarian, redemptive historical, and existential or applicatory phases in "Union
with Christ: Some Biblical and Theological Reflections," in *Always Reforming: Explorations in Systematic
Theology*, ed. A. T. B. McGowan (Downers Grove, IL: IVP, 2006), 275. See also Sinclair Ferguson, *The Holy
Spirit* (Downers Grove, IL: IVP, 1996), 103–11.
[3] Murray, *Redemption*, 162.

The fact that our union with Christ in election predates the realization of that union in time helps us to see how Paul can make the apparently audacious claims that Christians have been crucified, buried, and raised with Christ (Rom. 6:3–6; Gal. 2:20; Col. 2:12–13; 3:1). In some ineffable way,[4] those whom God has chosen as his own have always been "in Christ," and so they come to enjoy the realization of that union in their earthly lives. Although the doctrine of election has been subject to unbiblical distortion—sometimes used as the occasion for speculating about whether someone is saved or not, apart from God's definitive self-disclosure and self-giving in Jesus Christ—it functions in Scripture in a very different way. It speaks to the church of the unconditioned love of God in Christ, insisting that the initiative of our salvation always rests with God—he loved us in Christ before we were born and will always love us so!

If we wish to know whether this eternal love is ours, John Calvin wrote, we are to look to Jesus Christ:

> But if we have been chosen in him, we shall not find assurance of our election in ourselves; and not even God the Father, if we conceive of him as severed from his Son. Christ, then, is the mirror wherein we must, and without self-deception may, contemplate our own election. For since it is into his body the Father has destined those to be engrafted whom he has willed from eternity to be his own . . . we have sufficiently clear and firm testimony that we have been inscribed in the book of life if we are in communion with Christ.[5]

2. UNION WITH CHRIST IN THE INCARNATION

I will say more regarding the incarnation in chapter 2, but it is important to notice even here the theo-logic of the incarnation and hypostatic union, in which God the Son took on flesh and wrought in himself a perfect union of the divine and the human in one person. Why was it that the "Word became flesh and dwelt among us" (John 1:14)? Was it not so that in this union of our humanity with his divin-

---

[4] I am sensitive here that I may be in violation of G. C. Berkouwer's warning, "He who attempts to define this more clearly will easily employ more words than Paul needed for his song of praise to God's election in Christ" (Berkouwer, *Studies in Dogmatics: Divine Election* [Grand Rapids: Eerdmans, 1960], 148).
[5] John Calvin, *Institutes of the Christian Religion*, ed. John T. McNeill, trans. Ford Lewis Battles, Library of Christian Classics, Vols. 20–21 (Philadelphia: Westminster, 1960), 3.24.5.

ity we might be restored to fellowship with God? Was not his taking on human flesh the taking on or assumption of *our* human flesh and humanity? According to the famous dictum of Gregory of Nazianzus, salvation depends upon the incarnate Christ assuming the fullness of our humanity: "For that which He has not assumed He has not healed; but that which is united to His Godhead is also saved."[6] If Gregory is right, then we are surely justified in claiming that we have been united to Christ in his incarnation.

The great mystery of the incarnation is that God, without ceasing to be God, became what he created in order to join us to himself. Thus, the Son of God entered into human existence to dwell among and *in us*, assuming our humanity into union with himself. Jesus's humanity was no phantasm, having only the appearance of genuine flesh and blood (Heb. 2:14). He entered into the ontological depths of our humanity, sinlessly assuming our sinful nature (Rom. 8:3; 6:6; 2 Cor. 5:21), in order that he might sanctify and justify our flesh in his birth, life, death, and resurrection, bringing us into his filial relation with the Father. All that Christ did in union with our flesh, in other words, was done vicariously for us. This is among the reasons why Paul, for instance, can speak of our participation in Christ's death, resurrection, and ascension in the *past tense* (Romans 6; Colossians 2–3; Ephesians 2). Herein we see the awesome logic of the incarnation—God has joined himself to us through Jesus Christ in order to save us.

Listen to the words of the church fathers Athanasius and Irenaeus:

> You must understand why it is that the Word of the Father, so great and so high, has been manifest in bodily form. He has not assumed a body as proper to His own nature, far from it, for as the Word He is without body. *He has been manifested in a human body for this reason only, out of the love and goodness of His Father, for the salvation of us men.*[7]

> But how could we be joined to incorruptibility and immortality, unless, first, incorruptibility and immortality had become that which we also are, so that the corruptible might be swallowed up by incor-

---

[6] Gregory of Nazianzus, "Against Apollinarius" (Epistle 101), in *Nicene and Post-Nicene Fathers*, Second Series, Vol. 7, ed. Philip Schaff and Henry Wace (Grand Rapids: Eerdmans, n.d.), 440.

[7] Athanasius, *On the Incarnation* (Crestwood, NY: St. Valdimir's Seminary Press, 1977), 26 (emphasis added).

ruptibility, and the mortal by immortality, that we might receive the adoption of sons?[8]

So at the very apex of God's redemptive action in history we see the joining of the eternal Son of God and humanity. The incarnation forms the basis on which our estranged humanity—flesh and bones, mind and spirit—may be united to our Maker once again. The incarnation tells us that God intends to save the whole of our humanity in Christ and that he is doing so through the flesh-and-blood existence of his Son. Indeed, the flesh of Jesus Christ is life-giving to us, a point Calvin thought crucial to emphasize: "For no one will ever come to Christ as God, who despises him as man; and, therefore, if you wish to have any interest in Christ, you must take care, above all things, that you do not disdain his flesh."[9] The flesh-and-blood union of our humanity with the Son of God—in all that he did to achieve our salvation through his birth, life, death, resurrection, and ascension—is the objective basis for salvation, which is then realized in us as we are joined to him through faith.

3. UNION WITH CHRIST IN ACTUAL EXPERIENCE

The most common referent to union with Christ in Scripture is the union that follows both our election in Christ and the union of God and humanity in the incarnation. It is the union that occurs when these prior unions come to fruition and are subjectively realized and experienced by those who are savingly united to Christ through faith by the power of the Spirit. This union is what Paul has in mind, for instance, when he writes that we have been called by God "into the fellowship of his Son, Jesus Christ our Lord" (1 Cor. 1:9).

This fellowship (*koinonia*: "sharing, participation") is expressed in numerous ways in Scripture. To experience fellowship with the Son

---

[8] Irenaeus, *Against Heresies*, 3.19.1, in *Ante-Nicene Fathers*, Vol. 1, ed. Alexander Roberts and James Donaldson (1885; repr., Peabody, MA: Hendrickson, 1994).

[9] John Calvin, *Calvin's Commentaries* (Edinburgh: Calvin Translation Society, 1844–56; reprinted in 22 vols., Grand Rapids: Baker, 2003), John 6:56. For Calvin, our only access to God is through the incarnate humanity of Christ: "And though righteousness flows from God alone, still we shall not attain the full manifestation of it any where else than in the flesh of Christ.; for in it was accomplished the redemption of man, in it a sacrifice was offered to atone for sins, and an obedience yielded to God, to reconcile him to us; it was also filled with the sanctification of the Spirit, and at length, having vanquished death, it was received into the heavenly glory. It follows, therefore, that all the parts of life have been placed in it, that no man may have reason to complain that he is deprived of life, as if it were placed in concealment, or at a distance" (*Commentaries*, John 6:51). This is why Calvin insisted that the work of Christ is useless to us unless we are joined to the incarnate humanity of Christ.

is to be made alive in Christ, justified in Christ, sanctified in Christ, seated in the heavenly realms in Christ, built up into Christ, and given fullness in Christ. Those joined to Christ are "members of Christ," "crucified with Christ," "included in Christ," "baptized into Christ," and the "body of Christ." They eat and drink Christ; they are one with Christ; Christ dwells in them and they dwell in him; and they can do *nothing* apart from him. Salvation is realized and appropriated in the lives of fallen humans only as they apprehend Jesus Christ, who gives himself and all of his blessings to us in our Spirit-empowered faith response to his gospel. Through this gospel, God the Father incorporates us into Jesus Christ, who is the sum of all blessings: "And because of [God] you are *in Christ Jesus*, who became to us wisdom from God, righteousness and sanctification and redemption" (1 Cor. 1:30).

Because this book specifically deals with the subject of applied soteriology (the application of Christ's saving work and person), the normal referent of the phrase "union with Christ" in this book is to this subjectively realized experiential union—that which occurs through faith in the gospel of Jesus Christ by the power of the Spirit. It is because of this union that Christians are so named, and this union is the reason why Christians receive all the blessings of salvation. Anthony Hoekema views union with Christ as "having its roots in divine election, its basis in the redemptive work of Christ, and its actual establishment with God's people in time."[10] It is this third aspect with which we are primarily concerned in applied soteriology, and therefore this aspect shall constitute the focus of the chapters that follow.

4. UNION WITH CHRIST IN CONSUMMATION

Even though believers have truly been united to Christ and have shared in all of his blessings, there is still a hope for which we wait—the final, full manifestation of that union in the *eschaton*. Thus, at one and the same time, we are included in Christ and yet we pray *maranatha!*— "Our Lord, come!" (1 Cor. 16:22). We are "found in [Christ]," and yet

---

[10] Anthony Hoekema, *Saved by Grace* (Grand Rapids: Eerdmans, 1989), 55. In organizing the scriptural treatment of union with Christ in this way, Hoekema improved on Louis Berkhof, but he did not give sufficient expression to the reality of Christ's *assumption carnis*, his assumption of our flesh into his person in the incarnation. In other words, the *basis* of our union with Christ involves more than merely his redemptive work. It involves *our humanity joined to his person* in his work.

await his glorious return (cf. Phil. 3:9, 20–21). Jesus Christ returned to his Father, and yet he says, "You in me, and I in you" (cf. John 14:12, 20). The church does not await the return of Christ so that we *may* be united to him; rather, the church *is* united to Christ, and so eagerly awaits the consummation of this union.

The consummation of union with Christ is nearly synonymous with resurrection and glorification, when the blessings of our union with him will well up into their completed fullness. For instance, we read that "Our citizenship is in heaven. And we eagerly await a Savior from there . . . who . . . will transform our lowly bodies so that they will be like his glorious body" (Phil. 3:20–21, NIV1984). Similarly, "As we have borne the image of the man of dust, we shall also bear the image of the man of heaven" (1 Cor. 15:49). These are phenomenal pictures of the coming glory we will share with Christ. We think also of the marriage supper of the Lamb, where the Bridegroom and his bride-church will feast forevermore.

Chapter 6 will unfold in more detail the eschatological blessings of this consummated union—the glorification of those who have been preserved by God's grace. For now, we simply note, along with Hoekema, that "future glory . . . will be nothing other than the continued unfolding of the riches of our union with Christ. Much of what the future holds in store for us is left undescribed in the Bible. But of one thing we can be sure: we shall be eternally in Christ and with Christ, sharing his glory."[11]

The Nature of Union with Christ

I began this book with the observation that a profound mystery lies at the heart of the gospel of our salvation. The mystery is that Jesus Christ, the eternal Son of God in the flesh, is "in" us (Col. 1:27); or, as Paul puts it elsewhere, we, the church, have become "one flesh" with Christ (Eph. 5:31–32). Jesus's words in the Gospel of John are equally mysterious and arresting: "Unless you eat the flesh of the Son of Man and drink his blood, you have no life in you" (6:53). I suspect most of us, when confronted with these kinds of passages, react with equal joy and bewilderment. After all, we certainly desire to be one with Christ

---

[11] Ibid., 64.

and to have the eternal life of which he speaks. But what can it possibly mean to say that we are united to the One whom we confess as God himself? What are we to make of the assertion that eternal life comes only through partaking of his flesh and blood? We know that we are to believe and confess it, but how do we understand and embrace it?

The words of the great fourth-century theologian Hilary of Poitiers seem especially appropriate at times like these:

> We are compelled to attempt what is unattainable, to climb where we cannot reach, to speak what we cannot utter. Instead of the bare adoration of faith, we are under an obligation to entrust the deepest matters of faith to human language.[12]

The "bare adoration of faith," the normal and felicitous posture of the Christian who confesses the mysteries of the faith, sometimes calls for clarification (the heavy burden and privilege of theology). And with respect to the mystery of our union with Christ, we have a plethora of biblical representations to guide our expression. This union is likened to that of a building and its cornerstone (Eph. 2:20–22), a vine and its branches (John 15:1–8), the members of a human body and its head (Eph. 1:22–23; 1 Cor. 12:12), and the union between husband and wife (Eph. 5:31–32; 2 Cor. 11:2).

It is true that these representations, and others, are shadowy approximations of a reality that transcends our comprehension. This should not keep us, however, from saying what we can and must, even if "our descriptions must therefore be inadequate."[13] To say nothing would be to run the risk of losing the significance of the mystery and to push what is central to the periphery. This is true of other saving mysteries of our faith, such as the Trinity and the incarnation, and it is true of our union with Christ.[14] I offer the descriptions that follow

---

[12] This is a common paraphrase of Hilary's words from *De Trinitate*, 2.2 (in *Nicene and Post-Nicene Fathers*, Second Series, Vol. 9). Although Hilary was struggling to put into human language the mystery of the Trinity, our attempt to grasp what it means that we are united to Christ is also an obligation that we must entrust to human language.

[13] Augustus Strong, *Systematic Theology* (1907; repr., Valley Forge, PA: Judson Press, 1976), 798.

[14] The evidence that this risk is real and dangerous can be demonstrated by the tendency in evangelical Protestant theology to treat the doctrines of the Trinity and the incarnation as removed from soteriology. Often, these doctrines are treated as conundrums to be solved or defended (apologetics) rather than as revelations about salvation. See Fred Sanders, *The Deep Things of God: How the Trinity Changes Everything* (Wheaton, IL: Crossway, 2011).

with the conviction that when we express the nature of our union with Christ, we are simultaneously expressing the very nature of our salvation.

OUR UNION WITH CHRIST IS TRINITARIAN

To say that our union with Christ is Trinitarian means that by virtue of being incorporated into the life of Jesus Christ, we participate in the life, love, and fellowship of the Trinity. Because the Son is one with the Father, our being joined to the Son means we are joined to the Father. And because the Spirit exists as the bond of communion between the Father and Son, he brings us into that communion by uniting us to Christ. This staggering biblical revelation forms the personal foundation for all the benefits that constitute our salvation.[15]

Augustine opens his *Confessions* with one of the best-known passages in Christian literature: "For you [God] have made us for yourself, and our heart is restless until it rests in you."[16] Calvin likewise affirms that the perfection of human happiness "is to be united with God."[17] Both were expressing a basic scriptural truth—the greatest need and desire (whether conscious or not) of human beings, fallen and estranged from God, is to be restored to the One who created us and loves us, and apart from whom we perish. This is precisely what our union with the God-man Jesus Christ accomplishes. The apostle John records various ways in which Jesus spoke of this reality: "I am the way, and the truth, and the life. No one comes to the Father except through me" (John 14:6); "Believe me that I am in the Father and the Father is in me" (v. 11). Jesus speaks of including believers in the intimacy he has with his Father: "The glory that you have given me I have given to them, that they may be one even as we are one, I in them and you in me" (17:22–23); "I made known to them your name, and I will continue to make it known, that the love with which you have loved me may be in them, and I in them" (v. 26).

As staggering and incomprehensible as it may seem, our union

---

[15] In the words of Jonathan Edwards: "There was, [as] it were, an eternal society or family in the Godhead, in the Trinity of persons. It seems to be God's design to admit the church into the divine family as his son's wife" (cited in Brad Harper and Paul Louis Metzger, *Exploring Ecclesiology: An Evangelical and Ecumenical Introduction* [Grand Rapids: Brazos Press, 2009], 37).

[16] Augustine, *Confessions*, trans. Henry Chadwick (Oxford: Oxford University Press, 1998), 1.1.

[17] Calvin, *Institutes*, 1.15.6.

with Christ is a union with the triune God, for Christ incorporates us into his relationship with his Father. And because Christ is identical in nature (*homoousion*) with the Father, to be united to the person of Christ (through his incarnate humanity) is to be united to the whole Christ, the One who is fully human and fully God in one person. As it turns out, the doctrine of the hypostatic union is more than mere christological ontology—it tells us that the One who took on our flesh unites that flesh indivisibly to his deity so that we experience fellowship with our Maker again. This is good news indeed!

> For the Word of God is a divine nature even when in the flesh, and although he is by nature God, we are his kindred because of his taking the same flesh as ours. Therefore the manner of the fellowship is similar. For just as he is closely related to the Father and through their identity of nature the Father is closely related to him, *so also are we [closely related] to him and he to us, in so far as he was made man. And through him as through a mediator we are joined to the Father.*[18]

I will say a word below about why being joined to God the Father through Christ does not mean that Christians become God or gods (deification). We are affirming here that the union of our humanity with the humanity of Christ necessarily involves our sharing in the whole person of Christ as divine and human. To be united to Christ is therefore to share in his oneness with the Father. We are united to God the Father through God the incarnate Son.[19]

Furthermore, we are united to Christ by the Holy Spirit. Theologians have often expressed this truth by referring to the union as "spiritual." We must take care when we express ourselves this way, however. Speaking of a "spiritual" union—as opposed to speaking, as we should, of a union with Christ that occurs by way of the third person of the Trinity—might conjure up some conceptions that are problematic and unbiblical. One potential problem is that referring to our union with Christ as "spiritual" risks obscuring the specific,

---

[18] Cyril of Alexandria, *Commentary on John* (cited in Donald Fairbairn, *Life in the Trinity: An Introduction to Theology with the Help of the Church Fathers* [Downers Grove, IL: IVP, 2009], 138, emphasis added).

[19] It is important to stress that our union with God is mediated by the incarnate humanity of Christ, not only because this is the theo-logic of the incarnation, but also so that we avoid speaking in an unqualified sense of a union with God in his very essence or substance.

essential reality of the union (Christ himself) in ambiguous religious sentiment.[20] Another is that the term *spiritual* may imply that the union is merely between Christ's Spirit and our spirits, as if the union consisted in our shared convictions or dispositions. Finally, and perhaps most dangerous of all, references to a "spiritual" union may be taken to imply that the union occurs between believers and the Holy Spirit *in abstraction from Jesus Christ*. According to this view, the indwelling Holy Spirit functions as a replacement for the absent Christ, and it has been my experience that many Christians think of the Spirit in this way.[21] These views need to be corrected.

To say that our union with Christ occurs by the power of the Spirit means that the Holy Spirit is himself the bond who unites us to the living Christ. Christ sent the Spirit not so that we might have a roughly suitable replacement in his absence, but that we might enjoy the *actual presence of Christ* (through the Spirit). The Spirit is the personal manner or mode of Christ's dwelling in us. Thus, in the Scriptures we see that the presence of the Spirit is closely associated with the presence of Christ, and the Spirit is even called the "Spirit of Christ" (Rom. 8:9–11; cf. Gal. 4:6; Phil. 1:19). Christ's sending of the Spirit means that, through the indwelling of the Spirit, *Christ* is in us and we are in him (John 14:16–20). Notice his words in this passage: "I will not leave you as orphans; I will come to you." Jesus did not send an alternative but his very presence through the Spirit. The Spirit did not come to mediate his own presence, to glorify his own name, to teach us about himself, or to form the body of the Spirit. The Spirit was not incarnated, crucified, or resurrected for our salvation. The Spirit came to make Christ known, to glorify Christ's name, to teach us about Christ, and to form us together as the body of Christ (John 15:26; 16:14–15; 1 Cor. 2:14–16; 12:13).

The heart of the Spirit's ministry is to join us to the incarnate, cru-

---

[20] Often, the term *spiritual* is used as a synonym for *religious* to describe someone's religious disposition (whether Christian or not). When the apostle Paul uses the term, it is nearly always a reference to the third person of the triune God, necessarily excluding non-Christians.

[21] I suspect this is because of a truncated reading of John 14–17 and Acts 2, where the sending of the Spirit is interpreted as something other than *Christ's* presence through the Spirit. This misreading is often reinforced by notions of Spirit baptism that fail to stress that the Spirit baptizes believers *into Jesus Christ*. Familiar choruses we sing may also reinforce such notions: "Thank you, oh my Father, for giving us your Son, and leaving your Spirit 'til the work on earth is done" (from the song "There Is a Redeemer," written by Melody Green; © Universal Music Publishing Group).

cified, resurrected, ascended, and living Lord Jesus Christ. J. I. Packer writes that "the distinctive, constant, basic ministry of the Holy Spirit in the New Covenant is . . . to mediate Christ's presence to believers."[22] Therefore, describing union with Christ as a "spiritual" union can mean only that it is a union with *Christ* that takes place through the power of the Holy Spirit—it is a *Spirit*ual union. After all, the essential point of the Spirit's coming is not to unite us to the Spirit, but to bring us the Savior:

> Nothing, therefore, is bestowed on us by the Spirit apart from Christ, but he takes it from Christ, that he may communicate it to us . . . for he does not enlighten us to draw us away in the smallest degree from Christ. . . . In a word, the Spirit enriches us with no other than the riches of Christ, that he may display his glory in all things.[23]

Thus, our union with Christ is fully Trinitarian, a participation in the relations of the triune God. In our union with the Word of God, Jesus Christ, we are beneficiaries of the perfect union of God and man in himself, and we now share in his oneness with the Father. And the same Holy Spirit—in the words of the Nicene Creed, "the Lord, the Giver of life"—who conceived the incarnate Christ also conceives us anew by incorporating us into the One who is life in himself.

OUR UNION WITH CHRIST IS INTENSELY
PERSONAL AND INTIMATE

The personal and *intimate*[24] nature of our union with Jesus is often overlooked or obscured. In part, this may be due to the one-sided emphasis on forensic, substitutionary aspects of salvation that is so prevalent in contemporary evangelical Protestantism. But it may also be due to our reticence to embrace what seems too impossible to be true; we have a hard time believing what God declares to us in his Word. Let us consider three of these hard-to-believe passages.

The first is Ephesians 5:29–32, which reads:

---

[22] J. I. Packer, *Keep in Step with the Spirit* (Grand Rapids: Fleming H. Revell, 1984), 49.
[23] Calvin, *Commentaries*, John 16:14.
[24] By "personal," I mean that our human persons are united to Christ's person. By "intimate," I mean that this union involves our deepest nature. In other words, this union reaches down into the deepest and broadest part of our being, and thus cannot be reduced to mere sentiment.

For no one ever hated his own flesh, but nourishes and cherishes it, just as Christ does the church, because we are members of his body. "Therefore a man shall leave his father and mother and hold fast to his wife, and the two shall become one flesh." This mystery is profound, and I am saying that it refers to Christ and the church.

The last sentence is especially startling. We are conditioned to assume that this passage is principally about the joining together of a man and a woman in marriage. But Paul uses the intimate bond first described in Genesis 2:18 to interpret the intimacy between Christ and the members of his body. The "profound mystery" is that Christ and his bride, the church, have become "one flesh."[25] This mystery is illustrated with the personal intimacy shared by husband and wife, the most intimate of all human unions.[26] We are supposed to understand our union with Christ in a way that approximates, but exceeds, this closeness.

Paul could hardly speak in more personal and intimate terms—unless we take into consideration what he writes in 1 Corinthians 6:15–17:

> Do you not know that your bodies are members of Christ? Shall I then take the members of Christ and make them members of a prostitute? Never! Or do you not know that he who is joinedto a prostitute becomes one body with her? For, as it is written, "The two will become one flesh." But he who is joined to the Lord becomes one spirit with him.

Again, Paul draws a (more explicit) comparison between sexual union and union with Christ, or between bodily participation with a prostitute and bodily participation in Jesus Christ. Paul again refers to Genesis 2, but this time to point out the defilement that occurs in joining oneself sexually to a prostitute. The truly astonishing point for

---

[25] The imagery of the church as the wife or bride of Christ occurs elsewhere in the New Testament (Rom. 7:4; 2 Cor. 11:2; Rev. 19:7; 22:17) and is part and parcel of a larger biblical theme in which God's people are viewed as his wife (even if they are often unfaithful). See Isa. 54:5; Jer. 3:20; the book of Hosea; and the especially stunning imagery in Ezekiel 16.

[26] The Greek word translated "hold fast" means to "glue or cement together." It has reference to more, but not less, than physical, sexual union between husband and wife. See Harold Hoehner, *Ephesians: An Exegetical Commentary* (Grand Rapids: Baker Academic, 2002), 773. I cannot help but wonder whether the rampant sexual distortions in our culture, and in our minds, keep us too embarrassed to embrace the beautiful sexual imagery that is used to describe the unity between Christ and the church.

our purposes is this: Paul thinks that bodily union with a prostitute is shamefully unholy *because believers are already in a union with Jesus Christ that includes their bodies.* The fact that we become "one spirit" with the Lord affirms, rather than contradicts, the notion that through the Spirit our very bodies are involved in this union: "Paul does not intend to suggest that Christ unites only with the human spirit or soul. The Spirit creates the union with Christ and makes the body its temple."[27] So intensely personal is this union that it incorporates our bodies as well.

A final passage, maybe the most astonishing of all, gives us further reason to know that our union with Christ is profoundly personal and intimate. It occurs in the midst of what we have come to refer to as Jesus's High Priestly Prayer, wherein he prays to his Father for the unity of those who believe in him:

> I do not ask for these only, but also for those who will believe in me through their word, that they may all be one, just as you, Father, are in me, and I in you, that they also may be in us, so that the world may believe that you have sent me. The glory that you have given me I have given to them, that they may be one even as we are one, I in them and you in me, that they may become perfectly one, so that the world may know that you sent me and loved them even as you loved me. (John 17:20–23)

I wonder whether we sometimes miss the startling point of Jesus's prayer in this passage. What is truly startling in his prayer—"that they may all be one"—lies in the description of the *nature* of that oneness: "Just as you, Father, are in me, and I in you." Jesus not only compares the unity of believers to the unity shared by the Father and the Son, a thought that is staggering enough, but he goes on to explain that this unity is a result of believers existing "in" the unity of the Father and the Son. "The thought," writes D. A. Carson, "is breathtakingly extravagant."[28] Indeed it is. There can be no union of greater personal intimacy than that which exists between God the Father and God the

---

[27] David Garland, *1 Corinthians*, Baker Exegetical Commentary on the New Testament (Grand Rapids: Baker, 2003), 235. As Calvin put it, "Observe that the spiritual connection which we have with Christ belongs not merely to the soul, but also to the body. . . . Otherwise the hope of a resurrection were weak, if our connection were not of that nature—full and complete" (*Commentaries*, 1 Cor. 6:15).

[28] D. A. Carson, *The Gospel According to John*, Pillar New Testament Commentary (Grand Rapids: Eerdmans, 1991), 569.

Son. But here Jesus tells us that we are incorporated into that relationship as he dwells in us, and the Father in him. Our union with Jesus Christ is a participation in the most personal and intimate union that has ever, and will ever, exist. In fact, it is important that we go further and say that God's triune relationality is the foundation for, the *raison d'être*, of all human relational capacity and existence. And we are brought into this divine, relationship-constituting communion when Jesus Christ joins us to himself. To say, then, that our union with him is personal and intimate may even be selling the truth short.

OUR UNION WITH CHRIST IS VITAL AND ORGANIC

Describing our union with Christ as vital and organic may seem redundant given what I have said above, but it is worth expanding upon, however briefly. The Scriptures reveal that we stand in a vital, "life-giving" relation to Christ that exceeds any relation of mere external or peripheral influence. Christ is the source of our life and activity as a vine is to its branches, so that apart from him, we can do nothing (John 15); he is our sustenance as living bread and water (John 4 and 6); he is our resurrection and life (John 11); and he is our eternal life in his own being (John 5). Paul writes that "it is no longer I who live, but Christ who lives in me" (Gal. 2:20), and further, that our lives are now "hidden with Christ in God. When Christ who is [our] life appears, then [we] also will appear with him in glory" (Col. 3:3–4). Our union with Christ is "vital" because Christ *is* our life.

Furthermore, the union we have with Christ is organic in that we are integral elements of a living wholeness. We are actually joined to one another in Christ. Each believer is described as a part of the body of Christ (1 Cor. 12:27), and believers as a whole are described as "members" (or limbs and organs) of Christ's body (Eph. 5:30). The church exists (in a reciprocal but subordinate fashion) for and through Christ as he exists in and for the church. As such, Christ is the head of the church, "which is his body, the fullness of him who fills all in all" (Eph. 1:23). As members together of one Jesus Christ, believers make up an organic unity in which each member belongs to all the others (Rom. 12:5). We function properly only in reciprocal relationships, so that we may "grow up in every way into him who is the head, into

Christ" (Eph. 4:15). Christ is both the source of our life and the source of our relational dependence.

OUR UNION WITH CHRIST IS A PROFOUND MYSTERY

The depth of this mystery ultimately lies beyond our comprehension; it is finally ineffable. This does not mean for us, nor did it for Paul, that there is nothing we can affirm about it. On the contrary, the language and images of Scripture help us gain important insights into the nature of the union. The profound mystery of the union does mean, however, that in the end we confess in sheer wonder the truth of our union with Jesus rather than attempt to subject it to the limited capacities of our reason. Calvin put it this way:

> For my own part, I am overwhelmed by the depth of this mystery, and am not ashamed to join Paul in acknowledging at once my ignorance and my admiration. How much more satisfactory would this be than to follow my carnal judgment, in undervaluing what Paul declares to be a deep mystery! Reason itself teaches how we ought to act in such matters; for whatever is supernatural is clearly beyond our own comprehension. Let us therefore labor more to feel Christ living in us, than to discover the nature of that intercourse.[29]

We must be cautious, when we refer to this union as a mystery, of imagining that it is somehow less than fully real. God's triune existence is a mystery to us, yet he is the very source of all existence and reality. The union of divine and human natures in Jesus Christ is also a mystery, but this does not mean that the union is less than "real." The same applies to the mystery of our union with Christ. Eighteenth-century Scottish church leader Thomas Boston wrote:

> The Gospel is a doctrine of mysteries. O what mysteries are here! The Head in heaven, the members on earth, yet really united! Christ in the believer, living in him, walking in him: and the believer dwelling in God, putting on the Lord Jesus, eating his flesh and drinking his blood! This makes the saints a mystery to the world, yea, a mystery to themselves.[30]

---

[29] Calvin, *Commentaries*, Eph. 5:32. This passage is one of hundreds in Calvin's corpus that demonstrate that, contrary to popular conceptions, his theology is essentially confessional.
[30] Thomas Boston, *Human Nature in Its Fourfold State* (Carlisle, PA: Banner of Truth Trust, 1964; repr., 1989), 257.

Union with Christ: What It Is *Not*

To this point in the chapter, I have described in positive terms the most important aspects of the nature of our union with Christ. However, because there have been many misconceived, superficial, and reductionistic notions surrounding this topic, I also need to offer some clarifying points. Often, in trying to articulate what something *is*, it is also helpful to articulate what it is *not*.

WE ARE UNITED TO GOD THROUGH CHRIST, BUT WE ARE NOT THEREBY DEIFIED

Affirming, as we have, that believers are truly joined to Jesus Christ in the fullness of his divine-human person—and through him to God the Father, and to both through the powerful, relational operation of the Holy Spirit—is not the same thing as affirming that Christians become God or gods. Classical Christian orthodoxy has always rejected the idea of deification (the transformation of humanity into divinity). Among the reasons for this rejection is a very important theological one: human beings were not created to ever be something other than human. A human being flourishes and is greatly blessed in intimate fellowship with her Creator, but she does not flourish and live blessedly by being something other than human. God did not become incarnate ("enfleshed") to make us other than human, but to heal our sin-disfigured humanity.

The hypostatic union in Jesus Christ is helpful here. As Robert Letham points out, "Strictly speaking, we are united to [Christ's] humanity, but his humanity is inseparable from his deity, due to the hypostatic union." Because our union with him is with his whole person, we are thereby united to the eternal Son, and so united to God. However, "this does not mean any blurring of the Creator-creature distinction, any more than the assumption of humanity by the Son in the incarnation does. His humanity remains humanity (without confusion, without mixture). So, we remain human, creatures."[31]

In our union with the God-man, our humanity is not obliterated, but restored. We do not become fused with Christ in such a way that

---

[31] Robert Letham, *The Holy Trinity: In Scripture, History, Theology, and Worship* (Phillipsburg, NJ: P&R, 2004), 468.

our individual existence disappears into his. Neither do we become mixed with Christ so as to become something neither human nor divine. Rather, in our union with him, we come into *authentic* existence. We are redeemed from the only kind of existence there is apart from Christ: estranged and distorted existence.

So, the idea that we become something other than human in union with Jesus Christ is to be rejected, while the idea that we truly participate in the life of God *in Christ* is to be wholeheartedly affirmed. The crucial distinction can be discerned by differentiating between *deification*, an ontological sharing in the Godhead in which the human literally becomes divine, and *theosis*, a participation in the life of God the Father *through union with Jesus Christ* by the power of the Holy Spirit in which the human becomes truly human.[32] Defined in this way, theosis has a rich history in the tradition of the classical, orthodox (even evangelical Protestant) Christian church.[33]

OUR UNION WITH CHRIST OCCURS THROUGH FAITH, BUT CANNOT BE REDUCED TO THE HUMAN FAITH EXPERIENCE

This point may be best illustrated by our difficulty interpreting Jesus's words in John 6:54: "Whoever feeds on my flesh and drinks my blood has eternal life, and I will raise him up on the last day." The difficulty did not originate with us; Jesus's original disciples struggled to understand this "hard teaching," and many since have struggled, too. Interpretive efforts often fall into one of two extremes. One interprets this passage as a reference to a partaking of the flesh and blood of Jesus in the Lord's Supper. Not surprisingly, this is the tack taken by Roman Catholic commentators.[34] The other, favored by most evangelical Protestants, "spiritualizes" this passage. According to this interpretation, Jesus's words were nothing more than an admonition to believe in

---

[32] Part of the complexity of this issue is exactly the problem of definition, as there is no widespread agreement on how to define our terms. *Theosis* is a Greek word that is usually rendered into the Latin as *deificatio*, and so into English as "deification." One person's deification is another one's theosis. Perhaps the term "Christification" would best suit our purposes in describing our union with God. For a very helpful article on this subject that shows that Calvin certainly had a doctrine of theosis (properly understood), see Myk Habets, "Theosis, Yes; Deification, No," in *The Spirit of Truth: Reading Scripture and Constructing Theology with the Holy Spirit*, ed. Myk Habets (Eugene, OR: Pickwick, 2010).

[33] Fairbairn has a nuanced, introductory discussion of theosis in the early church fathers in *Life in the Trinity*, chapter 1. His book implicitly demonstrates that the Protestant Reformers shared much more with the early church soteriologically than is often understood.

[34] Raymond E. Brown, *The Gospel According to John I–XII* (Garden City, NY: Doubleday, 1966), 284–85.

him for eternal life. In other words, if we were to replace the phrase "whoever *feeds on my flesh and drinks my blood*" with the phrase "whoever *believes*," the meaning would remain the same. This interpretive strategy, the genesis of which can be found in one of the earliest Reformers, Ulrich Zwingli, seems to square nicely with classic Protestant doctrine; after all, we are *saved by faith alone*, not by partaking of Jesus's flesh and blood. So we look to "faith" as a way to exegete Jesus's difficult teaching.

However, there is a third way to interpret this passage that is of genuine Protestant pedigree. Calvin strenuously objected to Zwingli's equation of faith with partaking of Jesus Christ.[35] Calvin sensed the danger that the gospel might be obscured in any attempt to reduce "eating and drinking" terminology to mere allusions or invitations to human faith. If Christ meant nothing more in these words than a veiled reference to faith activity, if he is not truly present in his saving person ("flesh and blood") through faith, then whence salvation? Saving intimacy or union with Christ is not the *same thing* as faith; rather, our saving union with him is the *result of faith*. The insight here, of Johannine and Pauline origin,[36] is that while faith is surely saving, faith is not salvation; *Christ* is salvation. Faith should never be separated from salvation in Christ, but faith surely needs to be distinguished from the Christ whom faith receives. Therefore, Calvin insisted, Christ actually meant what he said: we truly partake of him—we are actually united to him and receive eternal life in the One who took on our flesh and blood. And this union cannot be equated with or reduced to our act of faith.[37] Luther wrote similarly:

> There are still many among us who suppose that Christ is in them when they ponder Christ and His suffering. They do not construe

---

[35] This section is excerpted from my paper "'The Highest Degree of Importance': Union with Christ and Soteriology in Evangelical Calvinism," in *Evangelical Calvinism: Essays Resourcing the Continuing Reformation of the Church*, Princeton Theological Monograph Series, eds. Myk Habets and Robert Grow (Eugene, OR: Pickwick, 2011).

[36] Cf. 2 Cor. 13:5; Gal. 2:20; 3:26–27; Eph. 1:13; Col. 2:12; John 1:12; 6:32ff.; 17:21, 26. Herman Ridderbos, *Paul: An Outline of His Theology* (Grand Rapids: Eerdmans, 1975), 232–33.

[37] Calvin's words are: "Those who infer from this passage that to eat Christ is faith, and nothing else, reason inconclusively. I readily acknowledge that there is no other way in which we eat Christ than by believing; *but the eating is the effect and fruit of faith rather than faith itself*. For faith does not look at Christ only as at a distance, but embraces him, that he may become ours and may dwell in us. It causes us to be incorporated with him, to have life in common with him, and, in short, to become one with him. It is therefore true that by faith alone we eat Christ, provided we also understand in what manner faith unites us to him" (*Commentaries*, John 6:35, emphasis added).

faith in Christ as the true spiritual indwelling of Christ in us and our indwelling in Christ. . . . But by this they actually perverted the suffering of Christ and cast it to the ground. The Lord does not say "Your thoughts of me are in me" or "My thoughts are in you" but rather: "You, you are in me, and I, I am in you."[38]

Evangelical Protestant doctrine has been marked by its allegiance to the *solas* of the Reformation, one of which is *sola fide* (saved "by faith alone"). However, the Reformers never meant that faith is saving *because* one believes, but rather that faith is saving *because of whom faith receives*. We are saved, in other words, not because of some intrinsic merit in our faith, but because we actually become united to the object of our faith, Christ himself. This is a constant refrain from the pens of the Reformers. Luther wrote: "The third incomparable benefit of faith is that it unites the soul with Christ as a bride is united with her bridegroom. By this mystery, as the Apostle teaches, Christ and the soul become one flesh."[39] Notice that Luther saw union with Christ as a *benefit* of faith. Calvin concurred:

> What a remarkable commendation is here bestowed on faith, that, *by means of it*, the Son of God becomes our own, and "makes his abode with us!" By faith we not only acknowledge that Christ suffered and rose from the dead on our account, but, accepting the offers which he makes of himself, we possess and enjoy him as our Saviour.[40]

Strictly speaking, the theo-logic of the Reformation *sola fide* is not that we are saved "*on account of* our faith alone," but that we are saved "*in Christ* through faith alone." If we do not insist on this, we are at great risk of collapsing salvation back into our human experience of faith, which is precisely the danger Calvin saw in Zwingli's interpretation.[41] By all means, let us insist that sinners are saved through faith

---

[38] Martin Luther, *Luther's Works*, 55 vols., gen. ed. Jaroslav Pelikan (St. Louis: Concordia Publishing House; Philadelphia: Fortress Press, 1955–1975), Vol. 23, 144.

[39] Ibid., Vol. 31, 151. Jonathan Edwards echoes Luther: "Now it is by faith that the soul is united unto Christ; faith is this bride's reception of Christ as a bridegroom" (*The Works of Jonathan Edwards* [New Haven, CT: Yale University Press, 1994], Vol. 13, 220).

[40] Calvin, *Commentaries*, Eph. 3:17. On the Reformer's understanding of faith and salvation, see my "Luther and Calvin on Union with Christ," in *Fides et Historia*, 39:2 (Summer 2007), 63–67 (emphasis added).

[41] Calvin also saw the danger here with respect to Zwingli's view of the presence of Christ in the Lord's Supper. See Calvin, *Institutes*, 4.17.5. To put the matter another way, Calvin's question regarding Zwingli's understanding, and that of those who are his theological heirs (most evangelical Protestants), was this:

alone. But let us insist all the more that it is not faith that saves, but Christ who saves (through faith).[42]

UNION WITH CHRIST TRANSCENDS MERE LEGAL AND MORAL NOTIONS, AS WELL AS UNIONS REDUCED TO SHARED SENTIMENT OR PURPOSE

It is not accurate to say that our union with the Savior has no legal and transformative aspects or results. In fact, it has vastly significant legal and transformative aspects, the most blessed of which are our justification and sanctification. It is also true that in this bond we share sentiments with Christ, such as mutual love, and that we share purpose with him, such as the exaltation and proclamation of his name. But by reducing our union with Christ to any of these notions, the comprehensive scope and personal reality of the union become lost to sight. Let me illustrate these briefly in turn.

Legal notions of union with Christ often prevail in evangelical soteriology, in large part because of the emphasis we place on the doctrines of penal substitution and forensic justification, which have become practically synonymous with salvation. These hallmarks of evangelical doctrine, which must always be resolutely affirmed, are often conceived of in rather abstract, extrinsic ways, as if our association with Christ could be reduced to a *mere* legal representation. Unhappily, when we conceive of salvation primarily (or solely) in legal ways, then our primary conception of union with Christ is bound to follow suit. The result is often that we think of a legal union with Christ as the basis for any subsequent (personal, intimate, profoundly real) relation to him.[43] So, the problem is not that evangelicals emphasize forensic aspects of union with Christ, but that we tend to think of union with Christ as *fundamentally* legal in nature. But, as we will see in chapter 3, the legal benefits of union with Christ are just that, *benefits* of a union that is vital, organic, and extremely personal. It is because

---

If Christ is not actually, truly present through faith, then how is anyone ever saved? Are we saved by our faith disposition or by exalted memories of Christ?

[42] The pastoral benefit of this insight from our evangelical forebears is enormous, given that most who struggle with assurance of their salvation tend to go "navel-gazing" (examining the state of their faith) rather than Christ-gazing (examining the utter trustworthiness of Christ).

[43] See chapter 3 for an extended discussion on this point.

we are actually joined to the person of Jesus Christ that we can glory in the legal benefits of that union.

The opposite, and more problematic, reduction is to conceive of union with Christ in mere moral terms. This view, often associated with moral or ethical theories of the atonement, pictures Christ as the moral exemplar of the Christian life.[44] To be in "union" with him means to follow his righteous example, to be joined to him in seeking moral transformation. Although this blatant misconception is usually put forth by liberal theologians and theologies, a more chastened version is not altogether absent from conservative Christian thought. This may take the form of a soteriology in which a sinner is thought of as saved (i.e., "justified") apart from union with Jesus Christ and then, in gratitude for that salvation, pursues a relationship with Christ based on emulating his holiness. Union with Christ is thus relegated to what takes place *after* salvation as the Christian pursues holiness. In other words, union with Christ is reduced to sanctification or the "Christian life." Again, as with justification, it is certainly true that sanctification is a *benefit* of this union, but it does not constitute the union. To reduce union with Christ to sanctification or, worse, moral improvement is to run the very real risk of succumbing to moralism, an ever-present threat in inadequate, impersonal notions of salvation. I will spell this danger out in greater detail in chapter 4.

The final reductions are those that equate our union with Christ with our joint affections or purposes. To be united to Christ is sometimes taken to mean no more than a bond of love that is established by Christ and reciprocated by those he saves. In this sense, the union is not much more than what is established in common human friendships. It also may be taken to mean that because we share with Christ in a common task or purpose—for instance, the advancement of his kingdom—we are therefore bound together. In this sense, the union is not much more than what is established between business associates. There is some truth to be found here—we are indeed united to Christ in sympathetic love and purpose—but these conceptions fail to capture the vital, personal nature of the union.

---

[44] Bruce Demarest, *The Cross and Salvation* (Wheaton, IL: Crossway, 1997), 153–54.

Conclusion

Given the relative lack of formal attention that union with Christ has received in evangelical soteriology, and the corresponding lack of general awareness of the vast significance of this reality among many Christians, this chapter has advanced some rather bold claims. The first is the immense redemptive scope of this doctrine in biblical revelation. All of the various stages of God's redemptive plan for humankind are, in one way or another, comprehended "in Christ." Christians were chosen before the foundation of the world in Jesus Christ. The eternal Word of God, furthermore, joined himself to our estranged humanity in the incarnation, so that by bearing us in him through his life, death, and resurrection, he might restore us to fellowship with God. He then realized this union with him in our actual existence so that we experience through faith the manifold blessings of his person and his benefits. Finally, we live in union with Christ in the anticipation of our resurrection and glorification in him, the eternal consummation of our union.

The second claim is the mysterious, beautiful, and staggering nature of this union as it is portrayed in the Scriptures. In our actual experience, we are joined to the One who is divine and human in his one person. This conjunction, brought about through the power of the Holy Spirit, brings us into the most real of all unions, that between the Son and the Father. We are joined to God himself through union with Christ by the indwelling Spirit. Through faith, we enjoy participation in the life of the Trinity in Christ. The biblical portrayal of our incorporation into Christ is most intimate and personal, so much so that it is pictured by the physical union between husband and wife, and, more than that, by the intimacy shared by the Son and the Father. Because of this, all reductionistic and external notions about the union are inadequate; instead, our understandings must be grounded in the deep, personal reality that is our union with the Savior. Augustus Strong writes:

> Such is the nature of union with Christ,—such, I mean, is the nature of every believer's union with Christ. For, whether he knows it or not, every Christian has entered into just such a partnership as this. It is

this and this only which constitutes him as a Christian, and which makes possible a Christian church. We may, indeed, be thus united to Christ, without being fully conscious of the real nature of our relation to him. We may actually possess the kernel, while as yet we have regard only to the shell; we may seem to ourselves to be united to Christ only by an external bond, while after all it is an inward and spiritual bond that makes us his. God often reveals to the Christian the mystery of the Gospel, which is Christ *in* him the hope of glory, at the very time that he is seeking only some nearer access to a Redeemer outside of him. Trying to find a union of sympathy or cooperation, he is amazed to learn that there is already established a union with Christ more glorious and blessed. . . . Christ and the believer have the same life. They are not separate persons linked together by some temporary bond of friendship—they are united by a tie as close and indissoluble as if the same blood ran in their veins.[45]

"It is this and this only which constitutes him [or her] a Christian." Let us be quite clear before we proceed into the following chapters: the union believers have with Jesus Christ—this breathtaking, nearly unutterably glorious, deeply personal, profoundly real participation in the crucified, resurrected, living Lord and Savior Jesus Christ—is the essence and foundation of salvation. To properly understand the riches of salvation, we must grapple with this mystery. All of the saving benefits of Christ that I will describe in the chapters that follow flow from this central reality and are enriched by an understanding of it. That is why we have started here.

---

[45] Strong, *Systematic Theology*, 802 (emphasis in original).

2

SIN AND THE INCARNATION

For as by the one man's disobedience the
many were made sinners, so by the one man's
obedience the many will be made righteous.

ROMANS 5:19

For as in Adam all die, so also in
Christ shall all be made alive.

1 CORINTHIANS 15:22

For our sake [God] made him to be sin who knew no sin,
so that in him we might become the righteousness of God.

2 CORINTHIANS 5:21

Just as salvation makes sense only in the context of sin, sin can be understood only in the context of salvation. To speak of sin without grace not only makes sin incomprehensible but also belittles the redemptive work of God in the world. "But to speak of grace without sin," writes Cornelius Plantinga, "is surely no better. To do this is to trivialize the cross of Jesus Christ. . . . What had we thought all the ripping and writhing on Golgotha were all about?"[1] A loss of consciousness about

---

[1] Cornelius Plantinga, *Not the Way It's Supposed to Be: A Breviary of Sin* (Grand Rapids: Eerdmans, 1995), 199.

the devastating nature of sin makes the "ripping and writhing" of the Son of God—the blood, sweat, spit, and ridicule—incomprehensible and merely grotesque. A failure to take sin seriously enough also renders the incarnation, faithful life, and resurrection of Jesus superfluous or incidental. "The sober truth is that without full disclosure on sin, the gospel of grace becomes impertinent, unnecessary, and finally uninteresting."[2]

Space will not allow for a full disclosure on sin here, but some context is essential to the chapters that follow. This chapter is about the contexts in which a helpful discussion of soteriology must be couched. The previous chapter described the nature of salvation in terms of our being united to Christ. But we must pause to ask, why do we need to be united to Christ? Why is it pertinent, necessary, or finally interesting? These questions can be answered—and, thus, the chapters that follow can make sense—only if we first have a grasp of the nature of sin and its effects.

As it turns out, sin and salvation have a mutually reciprocating, albeit highly paradoxical, relationship. The darkness of sin is exposed in the light of Jesus Christ, and the effulgence of Jesus Christ is magnified by the darkness of sin: "The light shines in the darkness" (John 1:5a). Along these lines, this chapter will shed light on how our understanding of salvation (soteriology) ought to simultaneously determine and be determined by our understanding of sin (hamartiology); that is, how the nature of salvation reflects the nature of sin. The apostle Paul tells us that humans exist in one of two states: we are either "in Adam" or "in Christ." The former is a depraved, condemned, death-dealing existence. The latter is a sanctified, justified, life-giving existence. We are united either to Adam in death or to Christ in life. We will explore how union with Christ helps us to see what it means to be united to Adam.

The chapter concludes with reflection on the soteriological significance of the incarnation of Jesus Christ, the last Adam. Along with sin, the incarnation provides a necessary context in which salvation must be understood. Evangelical theology has often neglected the incarnation and needs to recover it so that the theo-logic of salvation is not obscured.[3] The "enfleshing" of the eternal Word of God needs to

---

[2] Ibid.

[3] It is regrettable that the incarnation is usually topically divorced from salvation in most theology textbooks and is usually neglected altogether in soteriology texts. I suspect this is because union with

be viewed as much more than a perfunctory step that allowed for the crucifixion. Not only was Jesus's *entire* existence in the flesh a saving existence, but his incarnation demonstrates that God's purpose in salvation is to join us to himself through his Son.

The Problem of Original Sin[4]

The transmission of Adam's sin to his posterity remains a complex and thorny issue in Christian theology. Among Reformed theologians, where conversation on this issue has been most lively, there is still no general consensus on the central question involved: How exactly have Adam's guilt and corruption been transmitted to his descendants? The fact that humanity has sinned in Adam, and that the guilt and corruption of his sin has been transmitted to us, has not historically been in dispute; neither do most deny the mysterious nature of the question. Romans 5:12–19, the crucial text in this discussion, is both the source of the doctrine and the source of the mystery. Paul there affirms the fallen estate of humanity in and through Adam, but he does not specifically explain the nature of the relationship.

The doctrine of the transmission of original sin in the Reformed tradition seeks to describe the results of Adam's sin for his posterity. It typically includes two aspects: original *guilt* and original *pollution*. Original guilt refers to the state of condemnation human beings incur on account of Adam's transgression of God's commandment; it is legal in nature. Original pollution refers to the corruption of human nature that people inherit from Adam, which corruption produces actual sins; this is a moral concept.[5] Given these categories, any view that seeks to explain the transmission of original sin must grapple with at least three interrelated questions: (1) How do we, the descendants of Adam, become guilty of his sin? (2) How do we inherit his polluted nature? (3) What is the relationship between the declaration of our guilt (condemnation) and the corruption of our nature (depravity)?

Christ has largely disappeared from the evangelical theological landscape, which is dominated by legal notions of salvation. In what follows, I hope to make clear that the incarnation provides the basis for robust, realistic accounts of legal solidarity and penal substitution, in both soteriology and hamartiology.
[4] The material in this section draws on my "Participation in Christ and in Adam: A Way Forward on the Question of the Transmission of Original Sin," in *Evangelical Calvinism: Essays Resourcing the Continuing Reformation of the Church*, ed. Myk Habets and Robert Grow (Eugene, OR: Pickwick, 2012).
[5] Cf. Anthony Hoekema, *Created in God's Image* (Grand Rapids: Eerdmans, 1986), 148; Louis Berkhof, *Systematic Theology* (1938; repr., Grand Rapids: Eerdmans, 1996), 245–47.

Heretofore, two viewpoints have dominated Reformed hamartiology: federalism and realism.[6] In the pages that follow, I will briefly expound both views and note their attendant strengths and weaknesses. I will then advance a third position, one I call "christological realism," which, without jettisoning the truths of the other views, develops and seeks to correct them by drawing heavily on the rich and pervasive Pauline theme of union with Christ. This theme is implied in Romans 5 and developed elsewhere in the Pauline corpus. The position draws on the implied parallel in Romans 5 between the condition humanity inherits "in Adam" and that which the redeemed enjoy "in Christ"— but Paul elaborates only on the latter in a substantive way so as to give us true, though limited, insight into what is ultimately a mystery. Christological realism represents a step forward in answering the three interrelated questions involved in the doctrine of original sin.

FEDERALISM

As to the first question regarding the transmission of original sin— How do we become guilty of Adam's sin?—the federalist position holds that Adam was divinely constituted as the federal head of humankind, representing his posterity in his actions. Adam thus stood in the place of humanity when he sinned, and the guilt and condemnation of his transgression is therefore accounted to all his descendants. The relationship between Adam and subsequent humanity is typically framed in forensic terms, such that humanity is declared guilty on account of Adam's sin by virtue of his legal headship.[7] The guilt and condemnation that accrues to humanity from Adam's sin is said to be immediately imputed (or, perhaps better, "directly imputed"[8]) insofar as the declaration of guilt is unmediated by any intervening factor (such as

---

[6] The federalist view is variously known as the "representative" or "immediate imputation" view, the latter of which has specific reference to the imputation of Adam's *guilt*, making this label too conceptually narrow for our purposes. Realism is often referred to as "Augustinian realism," recognizing its debt to its most famous advocate, but this term also is too narrow given the consequent development of realism in Reformed theology. Theologians in the Reformed tradition recognize other views on the transmission of original sin, such as those associated with Pelagius (humanity is born essentially unaffected by Adam's sin) and Placeus (mediate imputation), but rightly find them biblically and therefore theologically untenable. Cf. Hoekema, *Created in God's Image*, 154–57; Berkhof, *Systematic Theology*, 240–43; S. Lewis Johnson, "Romans 5:12—An Exercise in Exegesis and Theology," in *New Dimensions in New Testament Study*, ed. Richard N. Longenecker and Merrill C. Tenney (Grand Rapids: Zondervan, 1974), 306–13.
[7] Cf. Berkhof, *Systematic Theology*, 242–46; Johnson, "Romans 5:12," 312.
[8] Hoekema, *Created in God's Image*, 161.

our ungodliness). Because Adam acted as our federal representative, his transgression of God's commandment serves as the judicial ground for the condemnation of those united to him.

As to the second question—How have we inherited Adam's polluted nature?—federalists maintain that, in addition to directly imputed guilt, humanity also inherits a corrupt nature by reason of its solidarity with Adam. This transmission of a corrupted condition is typically thought to be biological in nature as opposed to legal. In other words, Adam's depraved condition is propagated rather than directly imputed. On this point, many federalists stress that they do not reject in total the realist position, which may account best for the transmission of Adam's corrupt nature.[9] Thus, while the guilt of Adam's sin has relation to his federal headship, the transmission of his corruption is related to his natural or "seminal" headship. It should be said, however, that federalists are not of one accord regarding the transmission of corruption, and some of their conceptions are not altogether clear.

As to the third question—What is the relationship between the declaration of guilt and the transmission of corruption?—again, federalists do not appear to have reached a consensus. Some, such as John Murray, appeal to two kinds of union with Adam to relate the two aspects of original sin: the guilt/condemnation of Adam's primal sin is said to be imputed by virtue of his representative headship, and the corruption of his nature is said to be transmitted by virtue of his natural or seminal headship. Others, curiously, hold that innate corruption is the result of the direct imputation of Adam's guilt. Corruption is viewed as part of the penalty of legal involvement in Adam's guilt.[10] Still other federalists, such as Anthony Hoekema, conflate the two positions. They hold that corruption is linked both to the direct

---

[9] Johnson, "Romans 5:12," 308–9; John Murray writes, "With reference to misrepresentation or at least misconception on the part of opponents, it may not be unnecessary to repeat that the representative view does not deny but rather affirms the natural headship of Adam, the seminal union of Adam and posterity, and that all derive from Adam by natural generation a corrupt nature, and that therefore original sin is passed on by propagation" ("The Imputation of Adam's Sin," in *Westminster Theological Journal* 19, no. 1 [1956], 40).

[10] Berkhof, *Systematic Theology*, 242: "In his righteous judgment God imputes the guilt of the first sin, committed by the head of the covenant, to all those that are federally related to him. And as a result they are born in a depraved and sinful condition as well." See also Robert Reymond, *A New Systematic Theology of the Christian Faith* (Nashville: Thomas Nelson, 1998), 439, 449. Henri Blocher refers to this federalist account as a "rather provocative thesis" in *Original Sin: Illuminating the Riddle* (Downers Grove, IL: IVP, 1997), 73.

imputation of Adam's guilt and to a mediated transmission through propagation.[11]

Despite the valuable contributions of federalism, this brief account reveals some salient weaknesses. The first concerns the problem of *peccatum alienum* ("alien sin") and the justice of God: How is it just that God imputes the sin of Adam to those who did not personally commit his sin? Federalism posits what Oliver Crisp calls a "rather peculiar state of affairs wherein God ordains that one person represents everybody else, and commits a sin that everybody has to suffer for."[12] The difficulty, as even some federalists recognize, lies in the fact that Adam's descendants are accounted guilty of a sin for which they were not personally present and in which they were not volitionally involved—thus, the imputation of an "alien sin."[13] On this view, Adam's posterity are removed, by quite some distance, from actual participation in his sin, except by way of divine, legal fiat. Typically, advocates of federalism appeal to the imputation of Christ's righteousness in justification as a plausible solution: just as Christ acts as the representative head of those "in him" in such a way that his righteousness is imputed to them, even though they are not themselves actually righteous, so Adam's guilt is imputed to those who did not themselves commit his trespass.[14] This solution may not be as convincing as it first appears, perhaps running the danger of justifying one "legal fiction" by appeal to what some regard as another. The question of injustice is not necessarily rectified by an appeal to a merely extrinsic notion of imputation, whether of Adam's guilt or Christ's righteousness, unless of course this imputation is grounded in a logically antecedent and realistic union with the first or last Adam (there is more on this to follow).

The second weakness pertains to the federalist position that the direct imputation of guilt leads to, or has as its consequence, the corruption of our nature.[15] Those who hold this position have not made

---

[11] Hoekema, *Created in God's Image*, 161–62.

[12] Oliver Crisp, "Federalism vs. Realism," *International Journal of Systematic Theology* 8, no. 1 (January 2006), 67.

[13] See G. C. Berkouwer, *Studies in Dogmatics: Sin* (Grand Rapids: Eerdmans, 1971), 449–61. Johnson candidly admits, "We do not for one moment belittle the problem of the *peccatum alienum*, acknowledging that it tends to weaken the case for immediate imputation" ("Romans 5:12," 315).

[14] Murray, "Imputation," 42–44.

[15] Johnson says, "Human sinfulness in the sense of hereditary depravity stands in relation to Adam's first sin as an effect stands to a cause" ("Romans 5:12," 311).

clear, in my view, why a forensic declaration of guilt/condemnation necessarily or theo-logically entails a corruption of nature, unless it is by divine ordination (which is difficult to sustain biblically). Guilt and corruption may both be real consequences of original sin, but it is not obvious that they are related by way of cause and effect. The legal declaration of guilt associated with Adam's sin is a judicial reckoning; therefore, to contend that this legal declaration results in an actual transformation of nature does violence to the forensic metaphor. It is not at all transparent that Adam's depraved nature came about as a consequence of his first sin; does his primal sinning not imply that he was already spiritually compromised?[16] In defense of the view that the imputation of guilt leads to sinful corruption, federalists are prone to appeal again to the parallel with the imputation of Christ's righteousness, which leads to the moral transformation of the sinner. In other words, as justification leads to sanctification "in Christ," so guilt leads to corruption "in Adam."[17] I will challenge this construal below.

REALISM

Realism constitutes the other main Reformed option for addressing the question of the transmission of original sin. With regard to the imputation of Adam's guilt, Augustus H. Strong writes: "(Realism) holds that God imputes the sin of Adam to all his posterity, in virtue of that organic unity of mankind by which the whole race at the time of Adam's transgression existed, not individually, but seminally, in him as its head. The total life of humanity was then in Adam; the race as yet had its being only in him."[18] This view postulates that the descendants of Adam were "realistically" present in him as he sinned. Realists have construed this "real presence" in various ways,[19] but the uniformly integral insight provided here is that the imputation of Adam's sin is predicated upon a real, rather than merely representational, participation in his sin. Whereas in federalism, Adam's sin is imputed and so becomes mine, in realism, the sin is imputed precisely because it *is* mine, as I am in

---

[16] For a nuanced account of Jonathan Edwards on this point, see Oliver Crisp, "The Theological Pedigree of Jonathan Edwards's Doctrine of Imputation," *Scottish Journal of Theology* 56, no. 3 (2003), 308–327, esp. 322.

[17] Reymond, *Systematic Theology*, 438–39.

[18] Augustus Strong, *Systematic Theology* (1907; repr., Valley Forge, PA: Judson Press, 1976), 619.

[19] See esp. Crisp, "Federalism vs. Realism," for nuanced accounts of William G. T. Shedd and Strong.

Adam.[20] Realism thus avoids the charge of injustice, for God is said to declare guilty people who actually are guilty. We may say that the sin that is imputed is at one and the same time *peccatum alienum* and *peccatum proprium*—it is the sin of Adam (*peccatum alienum*) but also my sin (*peccatum proprium*) by virtue of a realistic union with Adam.[21]

By positing a realistic union between Adam and his progeny, realists are able to seamlessly account for the second aspect of the transmission of original sin: pollution. All who are really united to Adam in his first sin, and in the guilt and condemnation that follow, are also participants, by propagation, of his corrupt condition. As we have seen, some federalists have appealed to a "natural" or "seminal" union with Adam as the explanation for the transmission of pollution. Thus, on the question of the relation between the transmission of guilt and pollution, realists differ markedly from federalists. Federalists either posit two headships—a federal headship with respect to the imputation of Adam's guilt/condemnation and a natural headship with respect to the transmission of pollution—or they postulate that innate pollution is a *consequence* of the guilt established through the legal representation of Adam. Realism, on the other hand, accounts for both the imputation of guilt and the transmission of pollution by appealing to a realistic, natural union with Adam. In other words, this one union has both legal and transformative implications. The realist thus avoids the difficulties associated with positing two distinct headships and the apparent incongruity of making innate corruption the consequence of a forensic declaration of guilt.[22]

---

[20] Crisp, "Federalism vs. Realism," 60. The term *impute* is thus used by realists in the sense of "to reckon or to regard Adam's sin as mine." Federalists use the term in a more causal and remote way, as in the sense of "to cause Adam's sin to become mine." Both are legitimate uses of the term *impute*, but they may convey different realities, as in the case of the doctrine of the *imputation* of Christ's righteousness.

[21] Berkouwer writes: "On the one hand, federalism has pointed to a real guilt and to sin as *peccatum proprium*; on the other hand, it speaks of a declaration of guilt on the basis of God's ordinance. Thus we are left with a different doctrine of *imputation* from when man is held responsible for an act which he himself commits. No matter how the federalists try to combine the *peccatum proprium* and *peccatum alienum*, the relativizing that is implicit in the words 'in a certain sense' compels them to understand 'imputation' as a forensic judgment of God. Therefore the federalists have been challenged to show how *such* an imputation is in harmony with Scripture. How can we speak of an "imputation" when we do not mean *an active and personal sinning* in the fullest sense of those words?" (*Sin*, 459).

[22] There is a sense for the realist in which pollution does in fact follow upon guilt/condemnation, specifically in the case of Adam's primal sin. It is safe to say that, in one sense, the corruption of Adam's nature followed upon the breaking of God's commandment. Part of the effect of this transgression of God's commandment was therefore depravity (although it might be equally valid to suggest that Adam must have been spiritually compromised in order to break the command in the first place). See Strong, *Systematic Theology*, 620, for comments to this effect.

However, opponents of realism have pointed to several weaknesses in the position, which have been ably catalogued elsewhere.[23] Two criticisms are of special importance and deserve careful attention. The first, which all federalist stress in varying degrees, is the admittedly difficult task before the realist of attempting to define the *nature* of a realistic union with Adam that is metaphysically/ontologically coherent. What does it mean to say that humanity as a generic whole really existed in Adam? Each version of realism—the *classical Augustinian seminal version*, the *common human nature version* propounded by William G. T. Shedd, and the *unindividualized whole of humanity version* maintained by Strong—is conceptually and/or metaphysically obscure or even implausible.[24] Further, even if realism appears to best account for the question of the justice of God in the imputation of Adam's sin, opponents still wonder whether God's justice is truly vindicated by attributing Adam's sin to those who did not *personally* and *individually* sin.[25] Attempts by realists to be overly precise about the nature of a union that is, at bottom, inscrutable have been basically unsuccessful in clarifying the issue.

Another weakness federalists see in realism is its failure to render congruent the analogy between Adam and Christ that Paul draws in Romans 5. Federalists assert, rightly, that Christ acts as the representative head for the redeemed, and that his righteousness is directly imputed to them rather than something they inherently possess. Similarly, therefore, humanity must be condemned in Adam for an unrighteousness that is not personally their own.[26] The realistic account has shredded the analogy, it is thought, dissolving the parallel between Christ and Adam as representative heads of humanity by positing a "realistic" account of Adamic union that does not exist with respect to Christ and his people. Surely there is no "common human nature" or "unindividualized whole of humanity" that exists in seminal form or otherwise in Christ and through which people are justified. As Murray has noted, the natural union (advanced by realists) that exists between

---

[23] Cf. Johnson, "Romans 5:12," 309–10; Berkhof, *Systematic Theology*, 241; Murray, "Imputation," 35–39.
[24] These helpful delineations are borrowed from Crisp, "Federalism vs. Realism," who nicely brings out the nuances and potential weaknesses in Shedd and Strong.
[25] Cf. Johnson, "Romans 5:12," 309; Blocher, *Original Sin*, 115–16.
[26] Johnson, "Romans 5:12," 310.

Adam and his posterity "provides no analogy to the union that exists between Christ and his people." He goes on to write:

> We conclude, therefore, that more than natural headship is necessary, that natural headship does not carry with it the notion of "specific unity" in Adam, that the *plus* required to explain the imputation of Adam's *first* sin and no other is not shown by Scripture to be the kind of union which realism postulates, and that when we seek to discover the specific character of the union which will ground the imputation of Adam's first sin we find it to be the *same kind of union as is analogous to the union that exists between Christ and his people and on the basis of which his righteousness is theirs unto justification and eternal life.*[27]

Thus, one of the more forceful objections leveled against realism is its incongruity on the Adam-Christ analogy of Romans 5, an analogy that seems so conspicuous in Scripture as to justify an attempt at symmetry. If the relationship that obtains between Christ and his people—particularly with respect to the imputation of righteousness—is that of a representative headship, then this must certainly bear forcibly on one's interpretation of the Adam-progeny relationship—it must also be essentially representative in order to preserve the symmetry.

This symmetry rests, of course, on the assumption that the relationship of Christ to his people in justification is exclusively or primarily a federal-representational headship, an assumption shared by most federalists, who tend to view justification as the primary paradigm of soteriology. But this assumption only seems to beg the (key) question: What if the relationship between Christ and his people is *not* primarily or exclusively federal-representational, and what if Paul had in mind a rather mysterious but certainly "realistic" union with Christ, as we saw in the previous chapter? And, further, what if this "realistic" union Paul envisages allows him to speak both in *forensic* terms regarding the imputation of righteousness and *transformative* terms regarding the transmission of holiness? If what I have already said about the nature of this union is largely correct, then it seems by analogy that we have an instructive Pauline paradigm for understanding the transmission of

---

[27] Murray, "Imputation," 43–44 (emphasis added). It should be noted that Murray does not deny the natural/seminal headship of Adam; he simply finds it unable to account for the imputation of Adam's sin.

original sin, one that is able to encompass the truths of both federalism and realism without succumbing to the inherent weaknesses of either. Admittedly, Paul does not elaborate a sophisticated metaphysical argument. He is content, it seems, with a degree of mystery. Nevertheless, his account of the nature of union with Christ and its implications may prove highly instructive for understanding our union with Adam.[28]

CHRISTOLOGICAL REALISM

Federalism offers a number of important insights into the nature and implications of our dreadful condition "in Adam." Its salutary emphasis on the forensic aspects of our relationship with Adam has proved exceptionally influential, but it is weakened by its undue stress on the representational character of that relationship. Realism is an advance on federalism in this respect, but it is weakened by the obscurity or implausibility of its metaphysical construals, which tax biblical, theological, and philosophical credulity.

In this section, I advance what I am tentatively calling "christological realism,"[29] which may be viewed as a chastened, evangelical Reformed version of classical realism. I call it "chastened" because I do not attempt a technically sophisticated metaphysical construal of the union of which Paul writes, opting instead to affirm the element of mystery in Paul's thought. However, it is still "realistic" or "actual" in the sense that the union between Christ and the believer, which has its analogy in Adam and his posterity, transcends the merely representational or virtual. In an attempt to offer some conceptual clarity, I will describe this union with Christ as vital, organic, and personal.[30] The crux of this proposal rests on the pervasive theme of union with

---

[28] Lewis Smedes writes: "How does life 'in Adam' help us to understand how we are 'in Christ'? Paul looks at everything from his vantage point in Christ; this was true of the law, and it is true of Adam. When he says that we are 'in Christ' as we are 'in Adam,' he brings in the parallel because he first sees man as in Christ" (*Union with Christ: A Biblical View of the New Life in Jesus Christ* [Grand Rapids: Eerdmans, 1983], 82). See also Berkouwer, *Sin*, 509–10.

[29] Every term or phrase is bound to have both strengths and liabilities. For instance, "christological realism" is helpful in that it attempts to convey the extreme intimacy or personalism of Paul's thought on this matter. However, it is not meant to suggest that federalism is somehow less than "real."

[30] Interestingly, these terms are exactly those used by Berkhof in his description of the mystical union with Christ (*Systematic Theology*, 450). Berkhof, a federalist, is willing to speak of union with Christ in these intimate ways because he has essentially reduced this union to sanctification alone, reserving a prior legal union for justification. William B. Evans writes that for Berkhof, "union with Christ has, for all intents and purposes, ceased to function as an umbrella category unifying all of salvation . . . the term 'mystical union' applies only to sanctification, and not at all to justification" (*Imputation and Impartation: Union with Christ in American Reformed Theology* [Eugene, OR: Wipf & Stock, 2009], 236–37).

Christ in Pauline theology.[31] If Paul's notion of union with Christ does indeed qualify as "realistic," even if not in any metaphysically or ontologically sophisticated sense, then it seems appropriate by way of analogy to apply christological realism to our understanding of union with Adam, along with the implications that follow for the transmission of original sin.

Thus far, this book has demonstrated that the theme of union with Christ, or participation in Christ, is ubiquitous in the Pauline corpus, and has consequently occupied a formally prominent place in Reformed soteriology.[32] It is indeed central to Paul's understanding of the redemptive relationship between Christ and his people.[33] His use of various closely related terms and phrases to denote the believer's incorporation into Christ numbers well into the hundreds.[34] Many of these uses indicate that Paul understands union with Christ in "realistic" ways (vital, organic, and personal). While Paul's understanding of union with Christ includes the idea that Christ is our vicarious representative, his understanding extends beyond that idea. It eclipses mere imaginative or sympathetic participation in the actions of another, and it certainly exceeds mere moral exemplarism. Paul gives no indication that he is thinking of multiple unions, as if there were a "federal" kind of union through which we receive legal benefits in Christ and a "mystical" union through which we receive transformative benefits. Indeed, the argument advanced in the pages that follow rests on the assumption that when Paul writes of our salvation "in Christ," he is thinking of no other union than one that is vital, organic, and personal (and also representative). If we receive any benefit from being "in Christ," it is because we have really been united to the person of Christ himself.[35]

We are now in a position to extend Paul's realistic understanding of union with Christ and demonstrate its relevance for understanding the Christ-Adam analogy. Doing so necessitates a return to the three

---

[31] Of course, union with Christ is an extensive theme in the Johannine corpus as well, but our focus will remain on Paul, given that he clearly posits an Adam-Christ analogy.

[32] Evans, *Imputation and Impartation*.

[33] Cf. J. D. G. Dunn, *The Theology of Paul the Apostle* (Grand Rapids: Eerdmans, 2006), 390ff.

[34] See introduction for bibliographic material.

[35] Smedes writes: "There is, it is safe to say, no hint that when Paul says 'Christ lives in me,' he has anyone or anything else in mind than the very person of Jesus Christ. He means Jesus who died and rose again and is coming to establish his kingdom. He means the Jesus who is nothing if not an authentic and concrete person" (*Union with Christ*, 133).

questions with which we began regarding the transmission of original sin, all the while keeping in mind Murray's words regarding the
respective headships of Adam and of Christ:

> All who die die in Adam; all who are made alive are made alive in
> Christ. In view of this comprehensive philosophy of human history
> and destiny and in view of the pivotal and determinative roles of the
> first and last Adam, we must posit constitutive ordination on God's
> part to these unique relationships. And since the analogy instituted
> between Adam and Christ is so conspicuous, *it is surely necessary to
> assume that the kind of relationship which Adam sustains to men is after the
> pattern of the relationship which Christ sustains to men.*[36]

How do we become guilty of Adam's sin?

Drawing on Paul's analogy in Romans 5:18, we may say that we are
condemned in Adam in a way that corresponds to our justification in
Christ. Justification is a declaration by God that we are "in the right,"
that is, not subject to the condemnation we deserve as Adamic sinners. Justification is a crucial redemptive category in Paul; it does not
exhaust union with Christ, but it cannot be properly understood apart
from being "in Christ."[37] D. A. Carson writes, "If we speak of justification or of imputation . . . *apart* from a grasp of this incorporation into
Christ, we will constantly be in danger of contemplating some sort of
transfer *apart* from being included in Christ, *apart* from union with
Christ."[38] A host of passages bears out this observation. For example,
"There is therefore now no condemnation for those who are in Christ
Jesus" (Rom. 8:1). Just as through/in Adam we inherit his trespass, are
declared guilty, and are sentenced to death, so through/in Christ we
inherit his righteousness, are declared not guilty, and receive eternal
life. Through the disobedience of Adam we are "made sinners," and
through the obedience of Christ we are "made righteous" (Rom. 5:19).

At this point, we come face to face with the federalist insistence

---

[36] Murray, "Imputation," 42 (emphasis added).

[37] I will cover this subject in greater depth in chapter 3.

[38] D. A. Carson, "The Vindication of Imputation: On Fields of Discourse and Semantic Fields," in *Justification: What's at Stake in the Current Debates*, ed. Mark Husbands and Daniel J. Treier (Downers Grove, IL:
IVP, 2004), 72. Anthony C. Thiselton writes, "Being in Christ is the horizon of understanding within
which the various problems associated with justification by grace through faith alone become simply questions that receive intelligible answers" (*The Hermeneutics of Doctrine* [Grand Rapids: Eerdmans,
2007], 349).

that in justification Christ's righteousness is directly imputed to us, insofar as he acts as our representative and legal head. The righteousness that is imputed to us is an *aliena iustitia* ("alien righteousness"). We do not realistically participate in Christ's righteousness any more than we realistically participate in Adam's trespass. Recall that this is at the center of the federalist objection to realism with respect to the imputation of Adam's sin. Realism insists that Adam's primal guilt is imputed to us on account of the fact that Adam's sin really is ours. This is an apparent incongruency for the federalist because Christ's relationship with his people—with respect to justification—is construed along merely representational lines. The imputation of Christ's righteousness is a forensic mechanism that is based on a legal solidarity.

If we follow Paul, must we sacrifice his "realism" in order to accommodate his "federalism"? I think not. Paul's understanding of intimate union with Christ *includes* the forensic notion of imputation. It is "in Christ" that we "become the righteousness of God" (2 Cor. 5:21). As he writes elsewhere, "I count [all things] as rubbish, *in order that I may gain Christ and be found in him*, not having a righteousness of my own that comes from the law, but that which comes through faith in Christ, the righteousness from God that depends on faith" (Phil. 3:8–9). In other words, we are reckoned/regarded as righteous because we have been included in Christ. "Because of [God] you are *in Christ Jesus*, who became to us wisdom from God, righteousness and sanctification and redemption" (1 Cor. 1:30). To put it another way, intimate union with Christ includes a forensic aspect: God declares us righteous because *Christ's* righteousness has become ours, and therefore he imputes it to us as such.

Only as we participate in Christ, the Righteous One, do we share in a righteousness not inherently our own, and so become justified. According to this reading, a "real" union with Christ does not preclude the crucial legal aspect, but it is not reduced to mere legal representation either. The ready advantage here is that the charge of legal fiction evaporates: God declares sinners righteous precisely because they *are* righteous, but only "in Christ."

The benefits of this Pauline notion become obvious when applied to Adamic solidarity. If we assume that our union with Adam is analogous to our union with Christ, we are in a position to assert that our participation in Adam's sin is "real" because our participation in Adam is real.

God, therefore, imputes the sin of Adam to us in very much the same way that he imputes the righteousness of Christ to us: he regards it as ours *because we really share in it*. Just as there is a real union with Christ that includes a forensic aspect (justification), so there is a real union with Adam that includes a forensic aspect (condemnation). And just as union with Christ protects justification from the charge of legal fiction, so union with Adam protects the imputation of his guilt from being capricious or unjust. Thus, the federalists are right to insist that the imputation of Adam's primal sin is a forensic affair (and so corresponds with the imputation of Christ's righteousness), but they are mistaken in their insistence that this imputation is best conceived apart from a real union with Adam. The realists, on the other hand, are right to insist on the reality of the Adamic union, but their attempts to articulate the nature of this union metaphysically are less than convincing.

How has the pollution of Adam's nature become ours?

This question is less debated among federalists and realists, but Paul's conception of union with Christ may again lend some conceptual clarity to this ambiguity. For Paul, our intimate union with Christ has both legal and transformative benefits. We are both justified and sanctified "in Christ Jesus" in a way that answers both our guilt and pollution in Adam.[39] Our nature was corrupted in Adam and is being restored in Christ. Just as we are born spiritually dead in Adam, we are reborn spiritually alive in Christ. So the doctrine of justification, which answers the question of our guilt/condemnation, is paralleled by the doctrine of sanctification, which answers the question of our inborn depravity.

Paul writes of this newness of life and holiness in myriad ways, typically grounding his teaching in our participation in Christ. For instance, when we participate in Christ, he is our holiness (1 Cor. 1:30);

---

[39] For the sake of conceptual simplicity, I am using *sanctification* in its broadest sense as inclusive of both its definitive and progressive aspects. In the former sense, sanctification is related to the doctrine of regeneration: newness of life in Christ. On this point, see Anthony Hoekema, *Saved by Grace* (Grand Rapids: Eerdmans, 1989), 107.

we have newness of life (Romans 6) we are new creations (2 Cor. 5:17); we are transformed into his image (2 Cor. 3:18; 1 Cor. 15:49); we are created to do good works (Eph. 2:10); and we have life in our mortal bodies (Rom. 8:10–11). This list could easily be extended, but it suffices to show that in union with Christ we receive more than legal benefits that absolve us of guilt and condemnation. Christ is also the One through whom we are being made new and transformed from our state of spiritual deadness and depravity.[40] In other words, by being "in Christ," we are thoroughly delivered from being "in Adam."

The vast majority of Reformed theologians, be they federalist or realist on the question of original sin, agree that the union by which we receive newness of life in Christ must be described in something more than mere external or representational terms. That is, something more than federal headship is required to account for our status as new creatures who are being transformed into the likeness of Christ. Our union with Christ is, with respect to the transformation of our persons, a vital, intimate, organic, personal union through which believers are empowered by Christ to overcome Adamic depravity.[41] We have noted that some federalists posit two unions with Adam, representative and natural/seminal, in order to account for the dual problem of original sin.[42] But the Adam/Christ analogy seems to suffer on this point unless one is willing to affirm *two* unions with Christ, as Louis Berkhof does—one legal and one vital. The federalist position certainly points in this direction, and yet this hardly seems to do justice to Paul's theology.

The union believers have with Christ appears to be *singular and comprehensive*, encompassing both legal and transformative benefits (1 Cor. 1:30). The problem is that federalists are willing to affirm a vital, organic, personal, and real union with both Adam and Christ, but unwilling—in many cases—to extend the implications of this union to the imputation of either Adam's guilt or Christ's righteousness. To put

---

[40] Sanctification will be spelled out in greater detail in chapter 4.

[41] E.g., Berkhof, *Systematic Theology*, 449–51, refers to this union with Christ as mystical, organic, vital, personal, spiritual, and transforming. However, as we have noted, he distinguishes this "mystical" union from "legal unity" with Christ, which is the basis of justification.

[42] Hoekema writes regarding federalism ("immediate imputation") that Adam's guilt is thought to be directly imputed, while Adam's corruption is thought to be mediately transmitted from parents to children. This implies two kinds of union, one legal and one natural (*Created in God's Image*, 161–2).

it another way, many have been willing to adopt a kind of realism, but they are willing to apply this realism only to the transmission of corruption or of newness of life. And, historically, realism (for federalists and others) has appeared to be a metaphysically implausible solution to Adamic guilt. Is there a way forward in relating the guilt and pollution transmitted from Adam while simultaneously maintaining the analogy between Christ and his people?

What is the relationship between the declaration of our
guilt and the corruption of our nature?

The apostle Paul's conception of the relationship between justification and sanctification "in Christ," and the analogy it provides for the relation between guilt and pollution "in Adam," proves extremely helpful on this question. As we have noted, Paul conceives of our dilemma in Adam as answered by the multiple consequences of our union with Christ: justification and sanctification.[43] To put it clearly: by virtue of a vital, organic, intimate, and personal union with Christ, one receives justification (forgiveness of sins and imputation of righteousness) and sanctification (newness and holiness of life). If this reading of Paul is correct, we may say that he distinguishes these benefits without confusing or separating them. They are concurrent, inseparable benefits that issue forth from our participation in the righteous, holy, life-giving Christ.[44]

Paul does not posit multiple unions to account for the multiple benefits, nor does he make one benefit the cause or consequence of the other. The singular, realistic union with Christ is the ground of all blessings. If we take this understanding of the implications of being in Christ and apply it to the implications of being in Adam, we derive the following assertion: by virtue of our singular, realistic union with Adam, we experience both the guilt and condemnation of his primal trespass, as well as the corrupt condition into which he fell. Guilt and pollution are distinguishable but inseparable dilemmas that issue forth from our union with Adam.

---

[43] We may, of course, speak of union with Christ as the source of many more benefits besides, as the following chapters indicate.

[44] See Richard B. Gaffin Jr., *Resurrection and Redemption: A Study in Paul's Soteriology* (Phillipsburg, NJ: P&R, 1987), esp. 129–143.

As we have noted, some federalists relate guilt and pollution in terms of cause and effect.[45] On this view, the guilt imputed to Adam's descendants by reason of his federal headship is the cause of the corruption of their nature as well. Again, it is not immediately clear why the imputation of Adam's legal guilt should *cause* one to become corrupt. After all, imputation is a forensic notion while corruption is a moral one.[46] Imputation is, by definition, not intended to describe the change in one's corrupt condition; it is the reckoning of one's legal status. The analogy with Christ is especially instructive here. We do not say that in the imputation of Christ's righteousness one's corrupt condition is changed; we say, rather, that one is forensically *declared* to be in the right—he is justified *in Christ*. The change in our corrupt condition is brought about not by justification but by transformation into the likeness of Christ—sanctification *in Christ*. Justification and sanctification address different aspects of the transmission of original sin, and both benefits are ours through union with the last Adam. The fruit of this understanding, when applied to the first Adam, allows us to avoid the problem of relating guilt and pollution in terms of cause and effect, as well as the awkwardness of positing two distinct unions.

Illustratively, we may point to the problems that surface in Murray's treatment of original sin and recall that he proposes both a federal headship to account for the imputation of Adam's guilt and a natural/ seminal headship to account for the transmission of his corruption. Murray then writes, without noticing the ostensible inconsistency, that in our union with Christ there are both legal and transformative effects: justification and renewal.[47] It is not altogether clear whether Murray intends us to think of a federal and natural union with Christ

---

[45] Many Reformed theologians mirror this thinking in their soteriology, referring to justification as the cause or basis of sanctification, or of sanctification as the consequence of justification. See Berkhof, *Systematic Theology*, 418, 536; Reymond, *Systematic Theology*, 438–39; Michael Horton, *Covenant and Salvation: Union with Christ* (Louisville, KY: Westminster John Knox, 2007), chap. 7, esp. 129–30, 139, 143. The realist Shedd put it as bluntly as any federalist: "Sanctification does not justify, but justification sanctifies" (*Dogmatic Theology*, vol. 2 [Nashville: Thomas Nelson, 1980], 559). Lane Tipton has argued that a soteriological paradigm in which justification stands in a causal relationship to sanctification is more typically Lutheran ("Union with Christ and Justification," in *Justified in Christ: God's Plan for Us in Justification*, ed. K. Scott Oliphint [Ross-shire, Scotland: Mentor, 2007], 41–45). For a stimulating historical account, see Peter A. Lillback, "Calvin's Development of the Doctrine of Forensic Justification: Calvin and the Early Lutherans on the Relationship of Justification and Renewal," in *Justified in Christ*, 51–80.
[46] I use the term *moral* here hesitatingly and provisionally. To be specific, our corrupt state is one of *unholiness*, a distortion of the holiness we share in proper relation to the Holy One. I describe this important difference at greater length in chapter 4.
[47] Murray, "Imputation," 19.

(or legal and mystical, as Berkhof puts it) that is consistent with his Adamic construal, or of a single union with Christ with dual implications. If the former, we have the difficulty of finding such an idea in Paul's theology. If the latter, we are suggesting that Murray (et al.) apply in full the Adam/Christ analogy as they have rightly insisted we ought. If there is a single union with Christ with multiple implications, why not say the same of union with Adam?

In an important essay, S. Lewis Johnson voiced the concern of many who sympathize with federalism when he criticized realism on the following point:

> (R)ealism has difficulty in handling the analogy drawn in the passage (Rom. 5) between Adam and Christ. Just as men are justified for a righteousness which is not personally their own, so they were condemned for a sin which was not personally their own. Of course, it must be recognized that this analogy is not a complete one. But it does seem essential to Paul's point to maintain that the *nature of the union* between the principals and their people is parallel.[48]

The "nature of the union" is precisely the point in question. We have attempted to show that Paul understood the relationship between Christ and his people to be more than merely representational/legal. It is, rather, a union that is vital, organic, and personal—it is a union grounded in a personal reality. If we allow the nature of this saving union with Christ to shed light on the nature of the predicament from which we are saved, we arrive at the conclusion that our existence "in Adam" requires the kind of union Paul describes "in Christ."

Sin, Salvation, and the Incarnation

In the foregoing pages, I have attempted to show that our understanding of sin directly affects our understanding of salvation; they are inherently connected revelations. The solution to our sin dilemma tells us a great deal about the nature of that dilemma; in turn, the nature of that dilemma informs the nature of our salvation. Only in the revealing light of Christ do we see clearly enough to understand the depth of our predicament: Christ penetrates our lives in order to expose our darkness.

---

[48]Johnson, "Romans 5:12," 310 (emphasis added).

The advent of Christ demands that we must pursue another crucial avenue that significantly informs the nature of salvation. To this point, my contention has been that the central reality of salvation lies in our being vitally, intimately, and personally united to Jesus Christ (and to the Father through him). I hope this contention has been amply supported biblically. But there is another reason, which lies at the heart of the biblical narrative, to believe strongly that salvation is fundamentally about being joined to Christ: he came to first join himself to us.

THE THEO-LOGIC OF THE INCARNATION

As Athanasius described it, God was presented with a dilemma.[49] Through the fall, his beloved creatures, his "images," had become estranged from him and subject to corruption and death. God had decreed that humankind would surely die if they were to transgress his commandment and suffer alienation from him—and it was unthinkable that he should go back on his word. But to let sin and death have the last word among his beloved images was equally unthinkable. What was God to do?

The solution to this divine dilemma, Athanasius said, lay in the inconceivable notion that God should become very flesh of our flesh, that he should *incarnate* himself. The incorporeal, incorruptible, and immaterial Word of God should become corporeal, corruptible, and material to bring us out of our corruption and death.

This is not the answer many of us might have expected. Is not the answer to this divine dilemma the crucifixion or the resurrection of Christ? Do not these together constitute the fullness of God's answer to the sin dilemma? In one sense, they most certainly do, as Athanasius would have agreed, but even the cross and resurrection are predicated on a prior saving initiative that gives reality and meaning to them: the "enfleshing" of the eternal Word of God. As Thomas F. Torrance puts it:

> Everything in Christianity centers on the incarnation of the Son of God, an invasion of God among men and women in time, bringing and working out a salvation not only understandable by them in their

---

[49] Athanasius, *On the Incarnation* (Crestwood, NY: St. Vladimir's Seminary Press, 1977).

own historical and human life and existence, but historically and concretely accessible to them on earth and in time, in the midst of their frailty, contingency, relativity and sin.[50]

Without the incarnation—that is, without the Son of God truly assuming our flesh-and-blood humanity—the death and resurrection of Jesus would be unreal and merely hypothetical; salvation would remain in the abstract. After all, it is human beings—flesh-and-blood, corrupted human beings—who need salvation. If the Son of God had not joined himself to us in our humanity, what could it possibly mean to say that Jesus is Savior? Unless he bore in himself our true human flesh and blood as he lived faithfully before the Father; as he experienced wrath and alienation from his Father in crucifixion, forsakenness, and death; and as he was raised in victory over death to newness of life—unless he bore our humanity in all that he did—why should we believe that Christ is *our* Savior?

But incarnation is precisely what we find: "And the Word," John writes, "became flesh and dwelt among us . . ." (John 1:14a). Amazingly, John tells us just a few verses earlier that the Word who became flesh *is God himself, who created everything that is*: "In the beginning was the Word, and the Word was with God, and the Word was God. He was in the beginning with God. All things were made through him, and without him was not anything made that was made" (1:1–3). The Word who "became flesh" is God himself, the eternal Son of God who has eternally existed in perfect oneness with the Father as God. This same Word created and sustains the whole universe: "By him all things were created . . . and in him all things hold together" (Col. 1:16–17; cf. Heb. 1:2). The eternally existing, universe-creating Son of God and self-same God joined himself to our humanity, flesh and blood.

It is no wonder, in the face of this awesome gospel mystery, that the early church fathers fought so long and hard to define and protect the church's understanding of the person of Christ. Wrapped up in the mystery of the incarnate Word of God is the very theo-logic of salvation. The incarnation shows us in the clearest possible way that God's intention is to join us to himself through Jesus Christ:

---

[50] Thomas F. Torrance, *Incarnation: The Person and Life of Christ* (Downers Grove, IL: IVP Academic, 2008), 8.

The Trinity created us with a capacity to live *in him*, as creatures in and with our Creator. The incarnation proves it. If it were not so and could not be so, then Jesus Christ—God and man—could not be one person, for the difference between Creator and creature would be so great that incarnation would not be possible. But now our humanity in Jesus Christ is in full and personal union with God, and so in union with Christ we are brought into union with God.[51]

The incarnation of the Word of God, by which he became fully human without ceasing to be fully God, explains what it means for us to be saved. We can participate in the eternal-life-giving relationship between the Father and the Son because the Son has assumed our humanity into his person. We may be joined to God because he has already joined himself to us. In Richard Hooker's exquisite wording, there can be "no union of God with man, without that mean between both which is both."[52]

For those who are concerned that this idea minimizes the centrality of the death and resurrection of Jesus Christ, let me offer this clarification. It was the *incarnate* Son of God who was crucified for our salvation and the *incarnate* Son of God who was resurrected. The incarnation included all that Christ did for us and for our salvation; the crucified, resurrected Son of God is the incarnate Son of God, who assumed our human existence into his own, and crucified and resurrected our human existence in order to give us participation in his life (and through him, life with the Father—eternal life indeed!). In other words, the crucifixion and resurrection of Christ are given their personal reality only in the incarnation. This is why, as we shall see later, Paul can say that we have "died" with Christ and have been "raised with Christ" (Col. 2:20, 3:1; cf. Romans 6; Gal. 2:20). We experience the fullness of Christ's person and work in our salvation (through faith, by the power of the Holy Spirit) precisely because he joined us to himself in the incarnation.

Because the incarnation is basic to our soteriological understanding, we need to pause to spell out a few significant truths that flow

---

[51] Robert Letham, *The Holy Trinity: In Scripture, History, Theology, and Worship* (Phillipsburg, NJ: P&R, 2011), 470.
[52] Richard Hooker, *Laws of Ecclesiastical Polity*, in *The Works of That Learned and Judicious Divine Mr. Richard Hooker* (Oxford: Clarendon Press, 1865), Vol. 50, 3.

from what we have said. First, the incarnation helps us to see that salvation is "in Christ," for it is only in him that humanity has been reconciled to God. Salvation cannot be abstracted from the person of Christ because salvation *is* Christ. It is the joining of our persons to his person, and so salvation cannot be objectified or "thing-ified," as if it were some*thing* Christ could give to us apart from himself. He offers himself to us because that is what it means to be saved.[53]

Second, the incarnation shows us that salvation is a pure act of grace from the side of God. God did what humankind could never do; salvation is truly *sola gratia*:

> Here is an act of pure grace, the stupendous and absolutely free act of God almighty, and it carries with it the irresistible inference that what God has done here for us, we cannot do for ourselves. In fact the incarnation tells us plainly that all our efforts to go from humanity to God are useless and false—all our efforts to join man to God are judged and disqualified, and by this *fait accompli* in Jesus Christ they are completely set aside and revealed to be utterly wrong. God has done the impossible, the incredible thing in Jesus Christ, but it is only now that he has done it that we see how utterly impossible it actually is, impossible for us to accomplish from the side of humanity.[54]

Third, what we have said allows us to see in clearer light the importance of the christological controversies of the fourth and fifth centuries. The Nicene-Constantinopolitan Creed (AD 381) and the Chalcedonian Definition (451) were the result of very serious, sober, and necessary reflection on the person of Christ. They were necessary because how the church thinks of and understands the person of Christ reflects how she thinks of and understands the nature of salvation. This is why, at root, the church fathers fought so diligently to articulate what it means that "the Word became flesh." The church's soteriological life was at stake. When the church confesses, as the

---

[53] See Donald Fairbairn, *Life in the Trinity: An Introduction to Theology with the Help of the Church Fathers* (Downers Grove, IL: IVP, 2009), 136ff., who demonstrates how this insight was articulated in the early church fathers. Torrance writes: "Christ is not only the author and agent of our salvation, but is in himself, even in his human nature, the Source and Substance of it; therefore every one of the saving acts of Christ must carry with it, in our understanding, the whole substance of Christ's human life and nature" (*The School of Faith: The Catechisms of the Reformed Church* [1959; repr., Eugene, OR: Wipf & Stock, 1996], lxxxii).

[54] Torrance, *Incarnation*, 9–10.

Chalcedonian Definition puts it, that the Lord Jesus Christ is "consubstantial with the Father according to the Godhead, and consubstantial with us according to the Manhood," she is confessing nothing other than her saving union with Christ.

Nearly all theological confusion and error is a result of the failure of the church to incorporate the incarnation into the inner logic of its beliefs. Separated from the union of God and humanity in the incarnate Christ, the gospel, the church, and the sacraments are at risk. If history is any indication, when the saving significance of the incarnation is lost to view, the gospel, the church, and the sacraments are loosed from their moorings in the person of Christ and dissolve into sentiments and empty metaphors.

In sum, the incarnation is much more than the means to the end of the crucifixion; it is the constitutive reality of God's redemptive and revelatory action in the world, from which all theological reflection should begin. As John Williamson Nevin exclaimed: "'*The Word become flesh!*' In this simple, but sublime enunciation, we have the whole gospel comprehended in a word. . . . The incarnation is the key that unlocks the sense of all God's revelations."[55]

THE INCARNATION AND PENAL SUBSTITUTION

Soteriological models that focus on the incarnation are often viewed with suspicion by evangelicals. The theological tradition of the Western church, from which American evangelical Protestantism draws most deeply, has typically emphasized juridical/substitutionary models of atonement/salvation. By contrast, the theological tradition of the Eastern church has typically emphasized personal/participatory models of atonement/salvation. Because of the many important theological differences between the Western and Eastern traditions, Western Christians (including evangelicals) have tended to regard personal/participatory soteriological models, such as that found in the Eastern church, with suspicion. The regrettable result is that the incarnation has played a very insubstantial role in evangelical ideas about

---

[55]John Williamson Nevin, *The Mystical Presence: A Vindication of the Reformed or Calvinistic Doctrine of the Holy Eucharist*, American Religious Thought of the 18th and 19th Centuries, Vol. 20 (New York: Garland, 1987), 187 (emphasis in original).

salvation.[56] Evangelicals basically assume that personal/participatory soteriological models, which tend to emphasize the incarnation, are incompatible with judicial/representative models, which tend to emphasize the cross and penal substitution.[57]

For instance, many evangelicals have assumed that the doctrine of the incarnation has no essential connection to the doctrine of penal substitution—the biblical teaching that God gave *himself* in the person of his Son to suffer the death, punishment, and curse due to fallen humanity as the penalty for sin.[58] This is because, in models of salvation that are primarily, or exclusively, juridical or substitutionary, it is not always transparent why our relation to Christ need be anything more than representative and impersonal. After all, could not someone act as my legal representative without the necessity of being personally united to me?

However, the incarnation gives the doctrine of penal substitution its cogency, depth, and reality; indeed, it protects penal substitution from dissolving into a legal fiction. The reason the Son can suffer the death, punishment, and curse due to fallen humanity as the penalty for sin in our place is not that he acts as an unrelated third party, but precisely and only because he is God himself united to our humanity. The doctrine of penal substitution rests upon a real union between God and man in Jesus Christ; apart from it, the condemnation, wrath, and death that Christ experienced on the cross as our substitute becomes a forensic illusion. In what sense would it be just for God to impute our guilt, depravity, and their consequences to his Son unless the Son was truly united to us sinners, unless God "made him to be sin" (2 Cor. 5:21)? This in no way means that Christ himself *committed* sin, but it must mean that he truly identified with us in our sinful flesh in order to be our true substitute.[59]

---

[56] To corroborate this point, one might simply look for books by Protestant evangelicals on the incarnation. The pickings are slim at best. In most contemporary evangelical systematic treatments, the incarnation is treated either apologetically (an enigma to be explained or defended) or mechanistically (Christ's flesh is the instrument God uses to act in our place, to die as our substitute), but almost never as participatory (through the incarnation we are able to participate in the person of Christ). One may, however, consult at least one evangelical who develops a fully participatory, incarnation-based soteriological model: Myk Habets, *Theosis in the Theology of Thomas Torrance* (Burlington, VT: Ashgate, 2009).

[57] I hope that these overly simplistic characterizations have already been seriously challenged in this book. The emphasis the Reformers placed on real union with the person of Christ is alone enough to expose these generalizations as superficial. Regrettably, old habits (and generalizations) die hard.

[58] This excellent definition is found in Steve Jeffrey, Michael Ovey, and Andrew Sach, *Pierced for Our Transgressions: Rediscovering the Glory of Penal Substitution* (Wheaton, IL: Crossway, 2007), 103.

[59] See ibid., 242ff., for an excellent defense of this point.

As it turns out, a great deal rests on how we conceive of the word *substitution*. If we understand this word to mean that Christ acts outside or apart from us in a *merely* representative way, so that our sin and its consequences are somehow mechanically transferred from us to him, then we have a doctrine of penal substitution that flounders in unreality. If, on the other hand, we understand it to mean that our sin and its consequences are transferred from us to him *because he assumed our human nature*, then penal substitution is invested with its full reality and significance. In this case, personal/participatory and judicial/representative models of salvation cohere perfectly: the incarnation provides the personal grounds for the forensic benefits that flow from Christ's substitutionary death.

Torrance has spelled this out in a way worth quoting at length:

> It will not do to think of what Christ has done for us only in terms of representation, for that would imply that Jesus represents, or stands for, *our* response, that he is the leader of humanity in humanity's act of response to God. On the other hand, if Jesus is a substitute in detachment from us, who simply acts in our stead in an external, formal or forensic way, then his response has no ontological bearing upon us but is an empty transaction over our heads. A merely representative or a merely substitutionary concept of vicarious mediation is bereft of any actual saving significance. But if representation and substitution are combined and allowed to interpenetrate each other within the incarnational union of the Son of God with us in which he has actually taken our sin and guilt upon his own being, then we may have a profounder and truer grasp of the vicarious humanity in the mediatorship of Christ, as one in which he acts in our place, in our stead, on our behalf, but out of the ontological depths of our actual human being.[60]

Conclusion

It is no wonder that union with Christ is such a pervasive theme in the New Testament. Because God has joined himself to us through his Son's assumption of our humanity, we can now experience full and final reconciliation with God by being joined to Christ in his crucified and resurrected humanity. The incarnation provides the logic of salva-

---

[60] Thomas F. Torrance, *The Mediation of Christ* (Colorado Springs, CO: Helmer & Howard, 1992), 80–81 (emphasis in original).

tion, for it allows for us to be joined to Christ in all that he is for us and all that he has done on our behalf. In our faith-union with Christ, the benefits of his incarnate life, death, and resurrection become ours. Martin Luther expressed this in terms of the marriage between Christ and his bride, the church:

> And if they are one flesh and there is between them a true marriage . . . it follows that everything they have they hold in common, the good as well as the evil. Accordingly, the believing soul can boast of and glory in whatever Christ has as though it were its own, and whatever the soul has Christ claims as his own. Let us compare these and we shall see inestimable benefits. Christ is full of grace, life, and salvation. The soul is full of sins, death, and damnation. Now let faith come between them and sins, death, and damnation will be Christ's, while grace, life, and salvation will be the soul's; for if Christ is a bridegroom, he must take upon himself all the things which are his bride's and bestow upon her the things that are his. If he gives her his body and very self, how shall he not give her all that is his? And if he takes the body of the bride, how shall he not take all that is hers?[61]

This truly wonderful exchange between Christ and sinners is inexplicable without the context of sin and the incarnation. They tell us why it is that "Christ in you" is indeed the hope of glory. Our corrupting, condemning, death-dealing union with Adam is answered only in our sanctifying, justifying, life-giving union with Christ. And our union with the last Adam, Jesus Christ, is predicated upon the union he has already established with our humanity in the incarnation.

Understanding the nature of sin and the incarnation better situates us to explore the principal subject of this book, what theologians refer to as the application of salvation (often referred to as "applied soteriology," and which might be more appropriately phrased "applied christology": the application of Christ and his benefits). Luther's question nicely captures this point: "If he gives her his body and very self, how shall he not give her all that is his?" The remainder of this book is a description of the various saving benefits we receive when, having been joined to Christ through faith by the power of the Holy Spirit, we receive "all that is his."

---

[61] Martin Luther, "The Freedom of a Christian," in *Luther's Works*, 55 vols., gen. ed. Jaroslav Pelikan (St. Louis: Concordia Publishing House; Philadelphia: Fortress Press, 1955–1975), Vol. 31, 351.

3

JUSTIFICATION
IN CHRIST

... in order that I may gain Christ and be found
in him, not having a righteousness of my own.

PHILIPPIANS 3:8–9

There is therefore now no condemnation
for those who are in Christ Jesus.

ROMANS 8:1

Since the Reformation in the sixteenth century, the doctrine of justification has been the soteriological measuring rod for evangelicals'
orthodoxy, constituting the heart of their understanding of the gospel.
Unfortunately, justification by faith alone has been so thoroughly enshrined in our understanding of salvation that the two have become
synonymous, or nearly so. Justification has almost become theological
shorthand for the gospel.

There are many reasons for the prominent place the doctrine of
justification occupies in evangelical thought: it is thoroughly biblical,
the gospel is incomprehensible without it, and it is deeply comforting
to the Christian troubled by sin. But perhaps the most telling reason is
that it runs in our theological blood. The evangelical Protestant movement was birthed in the midst of Martin Luther's fresh insights into the

nature of God's immense, freely given grace in Christ Jesus. At the very heart of these insights was his articulation of justification, the biblical teaching that God declares us righteous and forgives us completely in Christ through faith, apart from any merit of our own. The doctrine of justification was so important to Luther that he referred to it as:

> Master, prince, lord, leader and judge of all kinds of teachings, which preserves and guides all churchly teaching and establishes our consciences before God. . . . For so you have heard, and it is always preached, that this one article preserves the church of Christ; when it is lost, Christ and the church are lost. . . . This article is the sun, the day, the light of the church and of all believers.[1]

John Calvin followed Luther in his exuberance for, and spirited defense of, justification. He wrote eloquently and forcefully on this doctrine, both doxologically and apologetically, and even referred to it as "the main hinge on which religion turns."[2] The evangelical Protestant movement has ever since been marked by its emphasis on justification, as a perusal of any theological library will demonstrate. The doctrine of justification has generated an immense amount of literature, and it shows no signs of abating. In fact, important controversies, debates, and discussions about justification abound today even *among* evangelicals.

So what is the doctrine of justification exactly? And why is it so important for understanding evangelical theology? Let us begin with a working definition:

> Justification is that benefit of our union with Christ, in his life, death, and resurrection, in which God declares us to be righteous through the forgiveness of our sins and the imputation of Christ's righteousness.

As we noted briefly in chapter 2, justification addresses a key aspect of humanity's twofold sin problem: in Adam, all of humanity is in a state of guilt and condemnation before the Lord, a state in which God de-

---

[1] Martin Luther, cited in Bernhard Lohse, *Martin Luther's Theology: Its Historical and Systematic Development* (Minneapolis: Fortress Press, 1999), 258–59. This last quote is the closest I have seen to approximating the famous Reformation slogan, usually attributed to Luther, that justification is "the article by which the church stands or falls."

[2] John Calvin, *Institutes of the Christian Religion*, ed. John T. McNeill, trans. Ford Lewis Battles, Library of Christian Classics, Vols. 20–21 (Philadelphia: Westminster, 1960), 3.11.1.

clares us unrighteous and we are spiritually dead (Rom. 5:17–19). Thus, one of our greatest needs as sinners is to be "put in the right" with God as regards our guilty and condemned state. To address this enormous problem, we need a Savior through whom we find not only *forgiveness*, in order that we might be found not guilty, but also One in whom we find *righteousness*, in order that we might be freed from condemnation.

This is the thrust of Paul's argument in Romans 3–5. No one can claim to be righteous before the Lord because all are sinners and have sinned—we are guilty of sin, we are condemned and in a state of unrighteousness because of it, and death is our sentence. Paul goes on to tell us that the solution to our horrific dilemma is found in Jesus Christ, through whose life, death, and resurrection we have forgiveness, righteousness, and life. "In Adam" we are unrighteous sinners who are condemned to death. "In Christ" we are declared righteous and freed unto life eternal. We express this glorious truth when we say that we are justified in Christ.

Among the many praiseworthy expressions of the biblical teaching on justification in the history of the church, Calvin's explanation is particularly clear and succinct:

> We explain justification simply as the acceptance with which God receives us into his favour as righteous men. And we say that it consists in the remission of sins and the imputation of Christ's righteousness.[3]

It is easy to see from this classic definition why Protestants have regarded the doctrine of justification as so integral to the gospel. To say that we sinners are justified means that God receives us into his favor as righteous, and this because he remits our sins and imputes Christ's righteousness to us.

The doctrine of justification has traditionally been formulated in judicial, forensic terms in the recognition that Paul's teaching on justification reflects the language of the divine courtroom. Just as our condemnation in Adam is legal in nature, a declaration of our guilt and unrighteousness, so our justification in Christ is legal in nature, a declaration of our forgiveness and righteousness. As we shall see,

---

[3] Ibid., 3.11.2.

the forensic nature of justification is integral to a proper understanding of justification because it protects the truth that God declares us
righteous on behalf of another—Jesus Christ, whose life, death, and
resurrection alone secure God's verdict. Righteousness is not inherent
to us and not obtainable by us; therefore, we cannot be righteous in
God's sight apart from Christ.

The extraordinarily good news about justification requires that we
explore the context in which Christ, in his saving person and work,
accomplishes and secures it for us. After all, we are inclined to wonder:
What does it mean that we are received into God's favor as righteous?
How does it come about that our sins are forgiven? What is meant by
the imputation of Christ's righteousness? And there are many questions besides.

It is not possible in the space we have to articulate the doctrine of
justification comprehensively, so the purpose of this chapter is more
modest. I will attempt to show that justification is best understood
as a benefit of, or a consequence of, the more basic saving reality of
being truly joined to Jesus Christ, who is in himself our justification.
In other words, I will attempt to show that union with Christ provides
the basis for our justification. This point has not always been accorded
the significance it deserves in many treatments of justification, particularly in more contemporary expressions of the doctrine. In an effort
to remedy this oversight, this chapter will (1) investigate the inseparable connection between our union with Christ and our justification;
(2) demonstrate the relationship between Christ's passive obedience and
the forgiveness of our sins; (3) demonstrate the relationship between
Christ's active obedience and the imputation of his righteousness; and
(4) examine some problems that surface when the doctrine of justification is articulated apart from union with Christ. In all, I hope that
the gloriously good news about our union with Christ brings to fuller
expression the gloriously good news about our justification in him.

Union with Christ and Justification

The definition above purposely prioritizes union with Christ to indicate that it is the basis upon which God justifies us. In other words,
just as justification must not be abstracted from Christ's work on our

behalf (which is universally affirmed by Protestants), so it must not be considered apart from our being truly joined to him (which is often obscured or neglected). It is not uncommon to come across soteriological works that define and discuss justification without explicit reference to union with Christ, suggesting that justification can be understood apart from it. Justification is often conceptualized and defined in *merely* judicial and extrinsic categories. For example, in Wayne Grudem's highly popular and influential *Systematic Theology*, he describes the doctrine as follows: "Justification is an instantaneous legal act of God in which he (1) thinks of our sins as forgiven and Christ's righteousness as belonging to us, and (2) declares us to be righteous in his sight."[4] There is, of course, much to be commended in such definitions. They are true as far as they go. But we may be left wondering about the precise nature of the connection between our sins and Christ's death, our unrighteousness and Christ's righteousness—between our sins and our Sin-bearer. Also, what is the connection between Christ's saving work on our behalf and the benefit we receive from it?

The answers to such questions lie in part in how we understand the role of faith in justification, and also in the crucial doctrine of penal substitution, both of which I shall return to shortly. But in order to grasp the theo-logic of justification, we must first establish the personal reality that makes the justification of sinners possible. Otherwise, the doctrine of justification itself becomes distorted and itself becomes difficult to justify.

The claim that justification is rooted in our union with Jesus Christ in his person and work is certainly not new. Luther and Calvin, the fountainheads of the evangelical theological tradition and the men to whom we rightly look for our understanding of justification, were insistent that justification comes about only because we are united to the Savior. As we noted at the end of the last chapter, Luther was fond of describing salvation in imagery pertaining to marriage: Christ the Bridegroom takes the bride's sins, death, and damnation so that she may share in his grace, life, and salvation. The marriage union is the

---

[4] Wayne Grudem, *Systematic Theology: An Introduction to Bible Doctrine* (Grand Rapids: Zondervan, 1994), 723. Grudem does not mention union with Christ in his chapter on justification, nor does he explicitly refer to justification in his chapter on union with Christ, leaving the insightful reader to wonder what the connection might be.

prerequisite, so to speak, for sharing in any of Christ's benefits, justification included. In other words, for Luther, justification is grounded in the believer's union with Christ through faith:

> Therefore faith justifies *because* it takes hold of and possesses this treasure, the present Christ. . . . Therefore the Christ who is grasped by faith and who lives in the heart is the true Christian righteousness, *on account of which* God counts us as righteous and grants us eternal life.[5]

And again:

> But so far as justification is concerned, Christ and I must be so closely attached that He lives in me and I in Him. What a marvelous way of speaking! Because He lives in me, whatever grace, righteousness, life, peace, and salvation there is in me is all Christ's; nevertheless it is mine as well, by the cementing and attachment that are through faith, by which we become as one body in the Spirit.[6]

Luther's doctrine of justification has often been misunderstood. In an effort to stress his affirmation that justification is legal and imputative in nature, many have assumed that it is also a synthetic declaration that takes into account no prior relationship of the believer with the *person* of Christ (perhaps fearing that a prior relationship with Christ would threaten the forensic nature of Luther's affirmation). But this misses Luther's point in a rather profound and momentous way. Luther understood the believer's union with Christ in the most profoundly real and intimate sense, and he maintained that it is precisely because of this union that the believer is justified.[7] Justification is, for Luther, more than a bare legal declaration that takes no account of a shared intimacy with Christ. It is rather a declaration of forgiveness and righteousness that *depends* on such intimacy. This does not, at least for Luther, threaten the forensic nature of God's justifying verdict—our justification rests wholly on Christ's merits, for God justifies no

---

[5] Martin Luther, "Commentary on Galatians (1535)," *Luther's Works*, 55 vols., gen. ed. Jaroslav Pelikan (St. Louis: Concordia Publishing House; Philadelphia: Fortress Press, 1955–1975), Vol. 26, 130 (emphasis added).

[6] Ibid., Vol. 26, 167–68.

[7] On this point, see Paul Louis Metzger, "Mystical Union with Christ: An Alternative to Blood Transfusions and Legal Fictions," in *Westminster Theological Journal* 65 (2003), 201–13; Marcus Johnson, "Luther and Calvin on Union with Christ," in *Fides et Historia* 39 (2007), 59–77.

one on account of an inherent goodness or moral quality. However, he conceived of the connection between sinners and Christ's righteousness in personal terms. To anticipate a point I will make below, Luther grounded the forensic/judicial elements of justification in a personal/participatory reality: in justifying us, God does in fact take into account the presence of the indwelling Christ.

Calvin followed Luther closely on this point. In fact, we notice in Calvin a heightened emphasis and clarity on the necessity of being incorporated into Christ in order to benefit from his saving work, justification included.[8] A quotation from Calvin's *Institutes of the Christian Religion* that we considered in the introduction makes this point well:

> First, we must understand that as long as Christ remains outside of us, and we are separated from him, all that he has suffered and done for the salvation of the human race remains useless and of no value to us. Therefore, to share in what he has received from the Father, he had to become ours and to dwell within us . . . for, as I have said, all that he possesses is nothing to us until we grow into one body with him.[9]

Calvin also said:

> But we define justification as follows: the sinner, *received into communion with Christ*, is reconciled to God by his grace, while, cleansed by his blood, he obtains forgiveness of sins, and clothed with Christ's righteousness as if it were his own, he stands confident before the heavenly judgment seat.[10]

Calvin unfolds his teaching on justification in the sphere of the person of Jesus Christ and our union with him. The benefits of Christ's saving work are received only insofar as Christ himself is received. Thus, justification for Calvin, as for Luther, is a legal benefit of a personal reality; God justifies us because we are joined to Jesus Christ by Spirit-wrought faith.

---

[8] Alister McGrath writes, "Calvin is actually concerned not so much with justification, as with incorporation into Christ (which has, as one of its necessary consequences, justification)" (*Iustitia Dei: A History of the Christian Doctrine of Justification*, second edition [Cambridge: Cambridge University Press, 2002], 225). McGrath's words may be somewhat less than judicious—Calvin is very much concerned with justification—but his point on the whole is accurate.

[9] Calvin, *Institutes*, 3.1.1.

[10] Ibid., 3.17.8 (emphasis added).

This way of framing justification is also evident in a number of the works of the most important theologians and confessions/catechisms that belong to the Reformation tradition. For instance, we see it in Calvin's successor, Theodore Beza (1519–1605):

> But we understand that we are justified by faith because it embraces Him who justifies us, i.e., Jesus Christ, in such a way that it unites and knits us together with Him to be partakers of all the goodness which He has—He, who being granted and imputed to us, is fully sufficient to make us perfect and accepted as righteous before God.[11]

It is also clear in the writing of the Puritan William Ames (1576–1633), whose theological influence on early American theology was immensely significant: "For by the same grace with which he called Christ to the office of mediator and the elect to union with Christ, he accounts those who are called and believing, justified by the union."[12]

We also see this understanding in perhaps the most important of the Reformed catechisms, the Heidelberg Catechism (1563). Throughout, the Heidelberg makes clear that none of what Christ has accomplished can become ours unless we are "partakers" of Christ, "implanted" or "ingrafted" into him by faith. For example, Question 20 asks, "Are all men, then, saved by Christ as they have perished in Adam?" The catechism then answers, "No, only those who by true faith are ingrafted into Him and receive all His benefits."[13] We also find it in the similarly influential Westminster Larger Catechism (1647).[14]

These few examples show that while the Reformed tradition, broadly speaking, highlighted the immense importance of justification, it did not do so apart from the recognition that justification is to be understood in the broader context of union with the One who is our justification.

---

[11] Beza's Confession of 1560, cited in James T. Dennison Jr., *Reformed Confessions of the 16th and 17th Centuries in English Translation: Vol. 2, 1552–1566* (Grand Rapids: Reformation Heritage Books, 2010), 254.

[12] William Ames, *The Marrow of Theology*, trans. John D. Eusden (repr., Grand Rapids: Baker, 1997), 162. Ames's compendium of theology, originally written in 1623, became standard and even required reading for undergraduate students at Harvard and Yale. Ames' understanding of salvation is suffused with the notion of union with Christ. See especially Book 1, sections 24–31.

[13] Ibid., 774.

[14] For instance, see Questions 65 and following. Robert Letham writes, "The Catechism then goes on to place the whole process of salvation in this life, from justification onward, under communion with Christ" (*The Holy Trinity: In Scripture, History, Theology, and Worship* [Phillipsburg, NJ: P&R, 2004], 473). The Westminster Confession of Faith and the Shorter Catechism, while they do not omit this point altogether, are far less clear, it seems to me.

JUSTIFICATION ONLY "IN CHRIST"

In framing justification in this way, the Reformed tradition followed a clear line of biblical teaching that locates the benefits of justification "in Christ." Romans 8:1 tells us that "there is therefore now no condemnation for those who are *in Christ Jesus*." We read in 1 Corinthians 1:30 that it is because of God that we are "*in Christ Jesus*, who became to us wisdom from God, righteousness and sanctification and redemption." Clearer still may be the teaching of Philippians 3:8–10, where Paul makes clear that the righteousness we so desperately need is secured only as we "gain Christ" and are "found in him." These passages and others serve to establish the point that while justification most certainly must be understood in forensic terms—a verdict of acquittal resulting from the forgiveness of our sins and the imputation of Christ's righteousness—justification is founded upon, and has its cogency, only as we view it as the result of being united to the One who secured our acquittal.

In light of this, it is easier to see why it was so important to describe the *nature* of union with Christ before describing the *benefits* that flow from that union. In chapter 1, I showed that our saving union with Christ is a participation in him, through whom we share in his relation to the Father through the Spirit. This union is the most real and personal of all unions, a union described in the most intimate ways in Scripture, and which we justly describe as vital, organic, personal, and profoundly real. It is through this union, which eclipses merely legal and moral descriptions, that we enjoy any of that which Christ has accomplished in our flesh for our salvation. Thus, to be justified before God, we must be united to Christ in this way, and this union must precede our justification in terms of causal priority. This is how the Reformers spoke of the relationship between union with Christ and justification—as a mysterious but nevertheless profoundly real "cementing, ingrafting, implanting, conjoining, flesh-union" with/into Christ, who is the reality of which justification is an inevitable consequence.

I believe this is what the Westminster Larger Catechism is saying when it describes union with Christ as follows:

Q. 66. What is that union which the elect have with Christ?
A. The union which the elect have with Christ is the work of God's grace, *whereby they are spiritually and mystically, yet really and inseparably, joined to Christ as their head and husband*; which is done in their effectual calling. (emphasis added)

The catechism goes on to describe the benefits of salvation, including justification, as manifestations of this spiritual, mystical, real, and inseparable union with Christ our Husband. The union, as it is described here, is definitely more than merely legal, for it is described in realistic, personal terms (with forensic benefits).

It is certainly confusing, then, when we read the following excerpts from Louis Berkhof's *Systematic Theology*, one of the most widely used and influential Reformed textbooks in the twentieth century:

> This (mystical) union may be defined as *that intimate, vital, and spiritual union between Christ and His people, in virtue of which He is the source of their life and strength, of their blessedness and salvation.* That it is a very intimate union appears abundantly from the figures that are used in Scripture to describe it.[15]

Here, Berkhof describes salvation as sourced in an "intimate, vital, and spiritual" union with Christ. On the other hand, just a few pages further on, he seems to contradict what he has asserted by writing the following:

> The mystical union in the sense in which we are now speaking of it *is not the judicial ground, on the basis of which we become partakers of the riches that are in Christ.* It is sometimes said that the merits of Christ cannot be imputed to us as long as we are not in Christ, since it is only on the basis of our oneness with Him that such an imputation could be reasonable. *But this view fails to distinguish between our legal unity with Christ and our spiritual oneness with Him, and is a falsification of the fundamental element in the doctrine of redemption, namely, of the doctrine of justification.* Justification is always a declaration of God, not on the basis of an existing condition, but on that of a gracious imputation— a declaration which is not in harmony with the existing condition of the sinner. The judicial ground for all the special grace which

---

[15] Louis Berkhof, *Systematic Theology* (1938; repr., Grand Rapids: Eerdmans, 1996), 449 (emphasis added).

we receive lies in the fact that the righteousness of Christ is freely imputed to us.[16]

Regarding these excerpts, two points are of special interest to this chapter: (1) Berkhof rightly asserts that the union between Christ and his people is intimate, vital, and spiritual (following the Scriptures, Reformers, and confessions), and that it is "in virtue of which" union that Christ is the source of his people's "blessedness and salvation." So, this union that he describes in the first paragraph above in personal, life-giving, and intimate terms is the *source* of salvation. This assertion is consistent with what I have argued in this chapter. However, (2) he goes on to write, in the second paragraph above, that justification is certainly *not* the result of this mystical union with Christ, for such an understanding fails to reckon with the "fundamental element" in redemption (justification), which cannot by its nature be the result of any existing condition of the sinner—apparently not even an intimate, vital, spiritual, personal union with Jesus Christ, which he has just written is the source of our salvation.[17] This strikes me as enormously confusing and as out of step with Luther, Calvin, and the bulk of his own tradition. In an apparent effort to clarify matters, Berkhof, in classic federalist fashion, then distinguishes between a legal oneness with Christ, of which justification is the subject, and a spiritual/mystical oneness with Christ, of which every benefit, except justification, is apparently the subject. Berkhof sees the spiritual/mystical union as a threat to the forensic nature of justification, so justification becomes the judicial ground for the spiritual/mystical union.

At this point, questions immediately surface: What are the biblical grounds for speaking of two unions with Christ that are not otherwise forced upon the text by assuming the priority of justification? Is our saving union with Christ that we read of in Scripture capable of being differentiated in this way? If there is a "legal union with Christ" and a "spiritual/mystical union with Christ," and the former grounds the latter, what exactly is "union with Christ" that cannot

---

[16] Ibid., 452 (emphasis added).

[17] Similarly, "Since the believer is 'a new creature' (II Cor. 5:17), or is 'justified' (Acts 13:39) only in Christ, *union with Him logically precedes both regeneration and justification by faith*, while yet, chronologically, the moment when we are united with Christ is also the moment of our regeneration and justification" (ibid, 450, emphasis added).

otherwise be reduced to either justification or the results of justification? According to Berkhof's understanding, union with Christ ceases
to be an independent, constitutive reality in which Christ himself
is the source of every saving benefit.[18] In other words, is union with
Christ an independent, personal, profoundly real actuality? Or is it
just a concept that allows us to break salvation down into its constituent parts? Berkhof seems to speak two ways on the matter—of a
"mystical" union that is the source of salvation, and of a legal union
that grounds a mystical union—but ultimately prefers to privilege
justification (or legal unity with Christ) as the central redemptive
reality. In so doing, he seems to have lost, or at least obscured, the
insights of the Reformers (and of many of the confessional docu-
ments of his tradition) that privilege vital, personal, intimate, spiritual union with Christ as the central redemptive reality, of which
justification is a consequence.[19]

A move such as Berkhof makes contributes to a kind of soteriological abstractionism and reductionism in which salvation becomes
dominated by merely legal notions, causing the person of Christ and
our very real union with him to fade into the background.[20] Berkhof
and his successors would have done better to retain the vital, personal,
and profoundly real nature of our union with Christ and insist that
one of the benefits of such a union is that Christ is our legal substitute
and righteousness. This would not only retain the best insights of the
Reformed evangelical tradition, but also avoid the less-than-desirable
results that inevitably follow, as I will explain below.

---

[18] William B. Evans argues persuasively that Berkhof's soteriology is the logical conclusion of a federal
theological trajectory, epitomized by Charles Hodge, in which union with Christ "ceases to function
as an umbrella category unifying all of salvation." Union with Christ is simply reduced to justification
(legal union with Christ) and sanctification (mystical union with Christ) without remainder (*Imputation
and Impartation: Union with Christ in American Reformed Theology*, Studies in Christian History and Thought
[Eugene, OR: Wipf & Stock, 2000], 236–37). Obviously the importance of the person of Jesus Christ is
(unintentionally) minimized in this type of soteriological understanding.

[19] And also Jonathan Edwards: "What is real in the union between Christ and his people, is the founda-
tion of what is legal; that is, *it is something really in them, and between them*, uniting them, that is the ground
of the suitableness of their being accounted as one by the Judge" ("Justification by Faith Alone," in *The
Works of Jonathan Edwards* [New Haven, CT: Yale University Press, 1957–2009], 19:156, cited in Robert
W. Caldwell, *Communion in the Spirit: The Holy Spirit as the Bond of Union in the Theology of Jonathan Edwards*,
Studies in Evangelical History and Thought [Eugene, OR: Wipf & Stock], 132).

[20] One sees a similar soteriological construction in the recent works of Michael Horton and J. V. Fesko,
who follow Berkhof in grounding vital, personal union with Christ in justification. Both assert, with
Berkhof, that union with Christ is foundational to salvation, but then essentially subordinate it to
justification, indicating that they see union with Christ as reducible to sanctification. See Horton, *The
Christian Faith: A Systematic Theology for Pilgrims on the Way* (Grand Rapids: Zondervan, 2011), 588–89, 591,
649; Fesko, *Justification: Understanding the Classic Reformed Doctrine* (Phillipsburg, NJ: P&R, 2008), 276–280.

FAITH AND JUSTIFICATION

In chapter 1, I described the nature of our union with Christ under the conviction that the nature of the union provides insight into the nature of the benefits that flow from it. This also holds true with regard to the relationship between faith and justification. In chapter 1, I noted that union with Christ comes about through faith, though not on any meritorious grounds of faith. The theo-logic of the Reformation confession *sola fide* is not that faith itself is saving, but that faith joins us to Jesus Christ, who *is* our salvation. Thus, strictly speaking, we are not saved because we believe, but because we are united to Christ through faith. The same logic applies to the insistence in evangelical soteriology that sinners are justified by faith alone. This insistence, of course, is an echo of the apostle Paul's teaching in Romans 3 and other passages (Gal. 2:15; 3:2) that justification is received apart from works of the law, apart from our own righteousness—it is received only by those who have faith in Christ. We cannot justify ourselves, for justification is a gift that is received through faith. Faith thus operates to protect the completely gratuitous character of justification, which takes place not by works but through faith.

But how do we avoid the possible objection that faith is itself a work of its own kind, a type of religious disposition that is pleasing to God and so deserves his recognition? Could not faith be construed as possessing intrinsic, justifying merit?

The Reformers sought to oppose this objection at every turn. They did so by insisting that faith justifies only because faith unites us to Christ, through whom we are justified:

> As I have said, faith grasps and embraces Christ, the Son of God, who was given for us. . . . When he has been grasped by faith, we have righteousness and life.[21]

> Now, what is our purpose in discussing faith? Is it not that we may grasp the way of salvation? But how can there be saving faith except in so far as it engrafts us into the body of Christ?[22]

---

[21] Luther, *Works*, Vol. 26, 177.
[22] Calvin, *Institutes*, 3.2.30.

> Therefore we justly say with Paul, that we are "justified by faith" alone. . . . However, to speak more clearly, we do not mean that faith itself justifies us, for it is only an instrument with which we embrace Christ our righteousness. . . . And faith is an instrument that keeps us in communion with Him in all His benefits, which, when they become ours, are more than sufficient to acquit us of our sins.[23]

> Therefore, because faith apprehends Christ our righteousness and attributes all to the praise of God in Christ, in this respect justification is attributed to faith, chiefly because of Christ whom it receives, and not because it is a work of ours; for it is the gift of God.[24]

We are justified, therefore, not because faith happens to be a religious quality that God finds worthy of justification, but because faith is the instrument through which we apprehend Jesus Christ, and therefore apprehend life, forgiveness, and righteousness in him.

This truth is reflected in many places in Scripture, perhaps most clearly in John's Gospel, where Jesus claims over and over again that *he* is the source and substance of that which he offers us (John 1:4, 16; 4:13–14; 6:22–58; 8:12; 11:25–26; 14:6; 15:5; 20:30–31). Indeed, John explicitly tells us that the purpose of his Gospel is that people may believe that "Jesus is the Christ, the Son of God, and that *by believing you may have life in his name*" (20:31). The same theology of faith appears throughout Paul's writings, where we see faith as nearly synonymous with life in Christ, acting as a kind of entry point into that life (Gal. 3:25–27; Col. 2:12, 20; 2 Cor. 13:5; Eph. 1:13; 3:17).[25] What is more, the whole tenor of Scripture points to Jesus Christ as the only One who is truly *faithful*. God is not looking for sinners who have a kind of faith that is a suitable replacement for Christ's faith and faithfulness. Rather, in Thomas F. Torrance's words: "We in faith flee from our own acts even of repentance, confession, trust and response, and take refuge in the obedience and faithfulness of Christ. . . . That is what it means to be justified by faith."[26]

---

[23] Belgic Confession (1561), Article 22: "Our Justification Through Faith in Jesus Christ," in Dennison, *Reformed Confessions*, Vol. 2, 437.
[24] The Second Helvetic Confession (1566), Chapter 15: "Of the True Justification of the Faithful," in ibid., 840.
[25] See Herman Ridderbos, *Paul: An Outline of His Theology* (Grand Rapids: Eerdmans, 1975), 232–33.
[26] Thomas F. Torrance, *Theology in Reconstruction* (London: SCM Press, 1965), 160.

The Forgiveness of Sins: The Passive Obedience of Christ

I stated in the definition at the beginning of this chapter that justification in Christ consists of two aspects: the forgiveness of sins and the imputation of Christ's righteousness. These are distinguishable aspects of justification, but they are an inseparable unity in the person and work of Christ. Over the course of Jesus's incarnate existence, he lived, died, and was resurrected in our humanity and for our salvation. His human existence was a vicarious existence in which he became what we are so that he might reconcile us to God in a life of total obedience and faithfulness before the Father. His vicarious obedience for us was both a *passive* obedience (from the Latin *patior*: "to suffer, endure"), in which he bore the penalty for sin in our place, and an *active* obedience, in which he lived a perfectly faithful, righteous life in our place.[27] The former is essentially a negative concept and is associated with forgiveness, the *removal* of sins, while the latter is essentially positive and is associated with imputation, the *attribution* of righteousness. Our subject in this section is the forgiveness of sins, and to describe this aspect of justification I turn to the obedience of Jesus in his crucifixion.

Evangelicals have traditionally understood Christ's atoning death on the cross in terms of penal substitution—the biblical teaching that God gave himself in the person of his Son to suffer instead of us the death, punishment, and curse due to fallen humanity as the penalty for sin.[28] In order for us to be "in the right" before God, our sin, and the associated death, punishment, and curse, had to be atoned for. This is precisely what Christ did when he assumed our humanity and sin into his person and subjected himself to rejection (Isa. 53:3), humiliation (Luke 22:63–65), and crucifixion (Phil. 2:8; 1 Peter 2:24), in which he bore the wrath of God against sin (Rom. 5:8–9) and the condemnation of death (Rom. 8:1–3; Gal. 3:13). He did all of this so that our sins would be removed "as far as the east is from the west" (Ps. 103:12), and he did it as the Sinless One in our place, that we might be the "righteousness of God" (2 Cor. 5:21).

---

[27] John Murray is right to point out that this distinction may be overly fine in that Jesus's entire obedience at every stage is simultaneously active and passive. See *Redemption Accomplished and Applied* (Grand Rapids: Eerdmans, 1955), 20–21. The distinction is useful, however, in understanding the two aspects of justification.

[28] This is the definition I cited earlier from Steve Jeffrey, Michael Ovey, and Andrew Sach, *Pierced for Our Transgressions: Rediscovering the Glory of Penal Substitution* (Wheaton, IL: Crossway, 2007), 103.

However, to say that Christ is our "substitute" in this horrific and glorious work is not to say that Christ is thereby removed from us in his work. As I attempted to show in chapter 2, the incarnation demands that Christ took *our humanity* under the conditions of sin to the cross. His substitutionary crucifixion was no mere representation, but rather a substitutionary identification with our estranged existence. Christ's sacrificial death *alone* is the sufficient payment for our sin, and yet it was our humanity he bore in his person on the cross. Christ died *for us*, in our place, but he also crucified us *with him*, taking us with him to the cross and the grave (Romans 6). If penal substitution is not to dissolve into a legal fiction, we must hold to the reality of the union of God and humanity in the incarnate Word of God.

At this point, our saving union with Christ is particularly helpful. When we rightly insist that the passive obedience of Christ is the ground by which our sins are forgiven, we must not imply that the forgiveness we receive is achieved in a merely extrinsic or abstract way, as if we were not bound up with Christ in his crucifixion. To be sure, Christ and Christ only is the satisfaction for our iniquity; he alone is "the propitiation for our sins" (1 John 2:2). But amazingly, as Paul describes it time and again, when we were included in Christ through faith, we were "baptized into his death" (Rom. 6:3), were "united with him in a death like his" (Rom. 6:5), died "with Christ" (Col. 2:20), were "crucified with him" (Rom. 6:6; Gal. 2:20), and were "buried with him" (Col. 2:12). In a truly remarkable convergence between Christ's work "for us" (accomplished redemption) and "in us" (applied redemption), Paul tells us that in union with Christ believers participate in Christ's death on their behalf.[29]

Let us be clear: Paul never suggests that we are co-redeemers in Christ's passive obedience. Yet let us be equally clear that our identification with Christ is more than "virtual." The doctrine of penal substitution protects the truth that only Christ, and he in our place, is the full and sufficient atonement for sin; he is the One who bears the penalty and suffers. But it does not and should not imply that Christ is atonement *apart* from us, as if his incarnation was the assumption

---

[29] This amazing truth grounds the significance of the sacrament of baptism, in which believers are given a clear picture of their union with Christ in his death and, therefore, his resurrection life (see chapter 8).

of a hypothetical human flesh divorced in reality from our own. He bore us in him as he subjected himself to the rejection, humiliation, suffering, and death that accompanied his crucifixion. We enjoy the perpetual benefits of this as we are united to Christ through faith: he is our complete and total justification before God.

It becomes evident again that the way we conceive of justification is predicated on how we think of the nature of our union with Christ. If we conceive of this union in merely or primarily federal/legal terms, we face the ever-present danger of reducing the penal-substitutionary, vicarious humanity of Jesus Christ to a merely forensic mechanism. We risk reading the assertions that we have "been crucified with," "died with," and been "buried with" Christ as mere "as ifs"—God thinks of us "as if" we had been identified with Christ. While this may reflect a Christ who *represents* us, it fails to reflect the One in whom we *participate* personally. Justification then becomes dislodged from an actual union with Christ and loses its grounding in reality.

On the other hand, if we begin with a union that is vital, personal, and profoundly real, we are then able to resolutely affirm the significance of the legal aspects of penal substitution without losing the reality of which they are a part. The relation between the passive obedience of Christ, the forgiveness of sins, and the believing sinner can thus be expressed as follows: by virtue of our union with Jesus Christ, we are incorporated into the (sin-bearing, guilt-negating, wrath-absorbing, death-defeating, curse-annulling) crucifixion, death, and burial of Jesus Christ, through which our sins are forgiven and we are freed from the sentence of guilt, condemnation, and death which stood against us. Under this definition, none of the crucial forensic significance of Christ's passive obedience *for us* is lost, and yet we ground it in the reality of Christ's vicarious identification *with us*.

There is a further advantage of viewing Christ's passive obedience/penal substitution in this participatory, and therefore also forensic, way. We may begin to see that there have been others in the history of the church who, in affirming the substitutionary nature of Christ's death, affirmed something similar in different words, even if they did not always frame their understanding of the atonement in primarily forensic fashion, as we tend to do. Overly extrinsic, forensic conceptions of penal substitution and justification may blind us to the theological resonance we have with the church at all times and in all places. Penal substitution, in other words, has a historical pedigree that extends back well before the Reformation, as long as we are willing to see that substitution does not exclude participation, and vice versa.[30]

The Imputation of Righteousness:
The Active Obedience of Christ

It would be tempting, given the incredible benefits that come to us because of Christ's passive obedience, to imagine that this alone is sufficient to account for our justification before God. But, shockingly, the good news about justification is bigger and more wonderful than even that. There is a good reason why the Reformed evangelical tradition has followed Calvin in asserting that justification consists "in the remission of sins *and* the imputation of Christ's righteousness."[31] This *and* reflects a recognition that Christ's obedience in our flesh is not exhausted by his suffering and death on the cross, but extends to include the whole course of his incarnate life and resurrection. The cross is indispensable to a proper understanding of justification, but it is not wholly sufficient to explain it. Christ's passive obedience shows us that our sins are truly forgiven in him, but his active obedience shows us that we are the beneficiaries of the whole course of his obedient, faithful, holy life. Torrance notes:

> This mutuality of Christ's active and passive obedience is important for it means that in our justification we have imputed to us not only the passive righteousness of Christ in which, in suffering *his* death on the cross, he satisfied and atoned for sins, but the active righteousness of Christ in which he positively fulfilled the Father's will in an obedient *life*. In other words justification means not simply the non-imputation of our sins through the pardon of Christ, but positive sharing in his human righteousness. We are saved therefore not

---

[30] Two recent works have chapters that document this: *Pierced for Our Transgressions*, chapter 5; Anthony C. Thiselton, *The Hermeneutics of Doctrine* (Grand Rapids: Eerdmans, 2007). Thiselton writes: "Over against any tendency to play down the substitutionary nature of the death of Christ as a sacrifice 'for our sins' (albeit alongside the themes of representation, identification, and participation), the subapostolic and early Patristic writings are striking in their repetition of this core understanding" (355).
[31] Calvin, *Institutes*, 3.11.2 (emphasis added).

only by the death of Christ which he suffered for our sakes but by his vicarious life which he lived for our sakes.[32]

The distinction between the passive and active obedience of Christ is thus not meant to artificially divide them, but to explain the fullness of Christ's person and work for our justification.

This means that in our reading of the four gospels, we need not wait until the passion narratives to extol the riches of our justification. After Jesus assumed our human nature, he lived his entire life of faithfulness, obedience, prayer, holiness, love, self-giving, and humility (and much more besides) for us and for our justification. In our union with him, we share in his perfectly righteous *life*. As the last and life-giving Adam, Jesus overcame temptation, whereas Adam and we did not (Luke 4:1–13); Jesus obeyed the Father, whereas Adam and we did not (Luke 22:42); Jesus fulfilled the law, whereas Adam and we did not (Matt. 5:17); Jesus prayed, whereas Adam and we did not (Luke 22:44–46); Jesus loved his enemies, whereas Adam and we did not (Luke 22:50–51); and Jesus trusted the Father, whereas Adam and we did not (John 11:40–42). The list could go on indefinitely. The point, in sum, is that the Word of God joined himself to human flesh to "fulfill all righteousness" (Matt. 3:15), not for his own sake but for us and for our salvation. And in a truth almost too amazing to imagine, we confess that we are joined to Christ in his righteousness—the righteousness of Christ is imputed to us.

The doctrine of imputation is founded upon a number of key verses that convey, in one way or another, that justification includes the attribution of righteousness—none other than Jesus Christ's. Paul writes, "And because of him [God]you are in Christ Jesus, who became to us wisdom from God, righteousness and sanctification and redemption" (1 Cor. 1:30). Christ became (among other things) righteousness to us, for God placed us "in Christ." For this reason we say that Christ's righteousness is ours; we share in what belongs to him.[33] His righteousness is therefore regarded as ours; it is imputed.

---

[32] Thomas F. Torrance, *Incarnation: The Person and Life of Christ* (Downers Grove, IL: IVP Academic, 2008), 81.

[33] See David E. Garland, *1 Corinthians*, Baker Exegetical Commentary on the New Testament (Grand Rapids: Baker, 2003), 79; Anthony C. Thiselton, *The First Epistle to the Corinthians*, New International Greek Testament Commentary (Grand Rapids: Eerdmans, 2000), 193.

Perhaps even clearer is Paul's teaching in his epistle to the Philippians:

> But whatever gain I had, I counted as loss for the sake of Christ. Indeed, I count everything as loss because of the surpassing worth of knowing Christ Jesus my Lord. For his sake I have suffered the loss of all things and count them as rubbish, in order that I may gain Christ and be found in him, not having a righteousness of my own that comes from the law, but that which comes through faith in Christ, the righteousness from God that depends on faith. (3:7–9)

The "gain" to which Paul refers, which he now counts as loss, is more than his ethnic pedigree; it is also the law-keeping blamelessness that he imagined at one point was worthy of a righteous position before God. He discards this "righteous" life before God as "rubbish" in order that he may "gain Christ and be found in him." Why? So that he may have a righteousness that is found only through faith and that is in Christ—that is, so that he may have Christ's righteousness. Peter T. O'Brien writes:

> The righteousness Paul now has, and will have when he is found in Christ perfectly, is of a different order: it is that status of being right with God which comes as his gift (cf. Rom. 3:21). Its basis is Christ's faithfulness, that is, his unflinching obedience to the Father's will and to his loving purposes of salvation through suffering and death.[34]

There is, further, Paul's statement that Jesus Christ "was delivered up for our trespasses and raised for our justification" (Rom. 4:25). What does Jesus's resurrection have to do with our justification? As Richard B. Gaffin Jr. points out, the resurrection of Christ is the vindication of his righteous life and death. Christ identified himself with us in order to bear the guilt of our sin. He became a curse and was made subject to the condemnation of the law unto death, so that "consequently, his being raised on account of our justification identified him with us in the justifying verdict inevitably attendant on the righteousness which he established for us (better, which he established for himself

---

[34] Peter T. O'Brien, *The Epistle to the Philippians*, New International Greek Testament Commentary (Grand Rapids: Eerdmans, 1991), 392.

as he was one with us) by his obedience unto death."[35] Another way to put this is that our justification is a participation in Christ's own resurrection-justification, in which he was released from the verdict of condemnation and his righteous obedience was supremely vindicated. In our union with the resurrected Jesus, we share in the vindication and affirmation of Christ's life and death.

The doctrine of the imputation of Christ's righteousness, or active obedience, has occasioned some controversy of late even among some Reformed and evangelical scholars. Perhaps the two most prominent examples are Robert Gundry and N. T. Wright, both of whom question whether the imputation of Christ's righteousness can be supported biblically and/or theologically. While Gundry argues that the Bible gives us no warrant for speaking of imputation in this way,[36] Wright's argument is a bit more nuanced. In the main, he questions whether referring to (what he sees) as the Reformed doctrine of the imputation of Christ's righteousness is necessary or even redundant:

> Here we arrive at one of the great truths of the gospel, which is that the accomplishment of Jesus Christ is *reckoned* to all those who are "in him". This is the truth which has been expressed within the Reformed tradition in terms of "imputed righteousness", often stated in terms of Jesus Christ having fulfilled the moral law and thus having accumulated a "righteous" status which can be shared with all his people. As with some other theological problems, I regard this as saying a substantially right thing in a substantially wrong way, and the trouble when you do that is that things on both sides of the equation, and the passages which are invoked to support them, become distorted.[37]

A response to those who either question or deny that justification involves what has been historically termed the imputation of Christ's

---

[35] Richard B. Gaffin Jr., *Resurrection and Redemption: A Study in Paul's Soteriology*, second edition (Phillipsburg, NJ: P&R, 1987), 123.

[36] Robert Gundry, "The Nonimputation of Christ's Righteousness," in *Justification: What's at Stake in the Current Debates*, ed. Mark Husbands and Daniel Treier (Downers Grove, IL: IVP, 2004).

[37] From N. T. Wright, "Paul in Different Perspectives: Lecture 1: Starting Points and Opening Reflections," accessed June 27, 2011, from www.ntwrightpage.com. For comments similar to this or relevant to this, see Wright's *Justification: God's Plan & Paul's Vision* (Downers Grove, IL: IVP Academic, 2009), 46, 158, 231; *What Saint Paul Really Said: Was Saul of Tarsus the Real Founder of Christianity?* (Grand Rapids: Eerdmans, 2005), 98–99. I do not have the space to fully engage Wright here, but allow me to say that while I find his work generally very helpful, his rejection of the classical doctrine of imputed righteousness is, regrettably, based on a caricature. Wright would have done well to have retrieved his own tradition, as we shall see below.

righteousness may take several helpful avenues.[38] It seems to me that those who question imputation—and some of those who attempt to defend it against its detractors—do so on the basis of a caricature of the doctrine. Specifically, if the objection to the doctrine of imputation rests on the notion that Christ's righteousness is transferred mechanically and extrinsically *from* him *to* believers—that is, the "righteousness of Christ" is a quality or commodity that can exist apart from Christ's person—then I believe the objection is legitimate. Far too often, the doctrine of imputation is articulated or understood, even by those who embrace it, in an abstract or merely extrinsic way. This creates the impression that there is a *thing* we refer to as "Christ's righteousness," which can be reckoned to the believer's account with no regard to the believer's union with the righteous person of Christ. This is the implication, intentional or not, of understandings of the doctrine of justification that are not rooted in union with Christ at all or that ground justification in a merely legal/representative union with him. In both cases, the doctrine of the imputation of Christ's righteousness suffers distortion and is left open to some of the objections we have seen.

At the root of the objections to the doctrine, as well as the caricature of it, is a failure to understand the meaning of the term *imputation*. If by "the imputation of Christ's righteousness" we are asserting that God justifies us by an external transaction that does not take into account the union between believers and Jesus Christ, who *is* our righteousness, then we have failed to do justice to the term. If by *imputation* we mean that God regards us as merely legally united to Christ, and therefore credits Christ's righteousness to our accounts, then the term dissolves into a legal fiction and unreality: God "thinks of Christ's righteousness as belonging to us" even though the righteousness is not ours.[39]

However, the concept of imputation, as it was understood by Luther and Calvin, suffered neither of these faults. Because we have used

---

[38] See D. A. Carson, "The Vindication of Imputation: On Fields of Discourse and Semantic Fields," in *Justification: What's at Stake in the Current Debates*, 46–78; John Piper, *The Future of Justification: A Response to N. T. Wright* (Wheaton, IL: Crossway, 2007), esp. chapter 8. For other helpful works on justification and imputation, see Michael F. Bird, "Incorporated Righteousness: A Response to Recent Evangelical Discussion Concerning the Imputation of Christ's Righteousness in Justification," in *Journal of the Evangelical Theological Society* 47, no. 2 (June 2004), 253–75, and Brian Vickers, *Jesus' Blood and Righteousness: Paul's Theology of Imputation* (Wheaton, IL: Crossway, 2006), esp. chapters 5 and 6.

[39] Grudem writes: "When we say that God *imputes* Christ's righteousness to us it means that God *thinks* of Christ's righteousness *as belonging to* us. He 'reckons' it to our account" (*Systematic Theology*, 726, emphasis in original).

Calvin's definition of justification as a guiding point, let us begin with his understanding of imputation:

> Therefore, that joining together of Head and members, that indwelling of Christ in our hearts—in short, that mystical union—are accorded by us the highest degree of importance, so that Christ, having been made ours, makes us sharers with him in the gifts with which he has been endowed. *We do not, therefore, contemplate him outside ourselves from afar in order that his righteousness may be imputed to us but because we put on Christ and are engrafted into his body—in short, because he deigns to make us one with him. For this reason, we glory that we have fellowship of righteousness with him.*[40]

For Calvin, to be justified means to be justified *in Christ*, to be "engrafted" into him and therefore to be "sharers with him," and to have "fellowship" with him in his righteousness. Notice that imputation rests on an indwelling of Christ, a mystical union through which we are "engrafted into his body." It is "for this reason" that we can refer to the imputation of Christ's righteousness. This intimate, personal "joining together" explains why imputation is what it is.[41] It seems that for Calvin the righteousness of Christ inheres in his person; it has no independent existence outside of him. Hence, it is necessary that we be truly joined to him in order to benefit from that righteousness. Thus, imputation is hardly an external transaction; rather, it is a sharing in the righteousness of Christ. It is undoubtedly his righteousness alone, but we share that righteousness because we are made one with him.[42]

Luther spoke in much the same way. Imputation for him is also a concept rooted in a personal identification with Christ:

> Here it is to be noted that these three things are joined together: faith, Christ, and acceptance or imputation. Faith takes hold of Christ and

---

[40] Calvin, *Institutes*, 3.11.10 (emphasis added).

[41] It is curious that Horton, who so appreciates Calvin, can say, "Not even Christ's indwelling of the believer can be the basis for justification, but merely his active and passive obedience on our behalf" (*The Christian Faith*, 611). This appears to run counter to Calvin's point, but does explain why Horton relies on a merely legal union with Christ as the foundation of salvation.

[42] Richard B. Gaffin Jr. interprets Calvin's view as follows: "Here Christ's righteousness imputed is alien or other in the sense that it is his doing, his obedience, not ours. But in another sense, in union with him, it is not alien at all. Union brings justification as a forensic fellowship, a sharing in Christ's righteousness, and it does so by imputation" ("Justification and Union with Christ," in *A Theological Guide to Calvin's Institutes: Essays and Analysis*, ed. David Hall [Phillipsburg, NJ: P&R, 2008], 265).

makes him present, enclosing him as the ring encloses the gem. And whoever is found having this faith in the Christ who is grasped in the heart, him God accounts as righteous. This is the means and merit by which we obtain the forgiveness of sins and righteousness. "Because you believe in me," God says, "and your faith takes hold of Christ, whom I have freely given to you as your Justifier and Savior, therefore be righteous." Therefore God accepts you or accounts you righteous only on account of Christ, in whom you believe.[43]

Notice that God accepts the one who has faith as righteous *on account of the present Christ.* There is no separation of Christ from his righteousness; acceptance or imputation depends on a unity with the Righteous One. This may seem, at first glance, to transgress the notion, articulated by the Reformers, that the righteousness of Christ by which we are justified is *extra nos* ("outside of us"), that it is an "alien" righteousness because it does not originate in us and is not intrinsic to us—God, in other words, justifies us because of the righteousness of *another*, not because we are inherently righteous. This truth is basic to Reformed evangelical theology and needs to be recovered, retained, and defended—which is precisely the function of the term *imputation*. The term is meant to protect the fact that the righteousness by which we are justified is properly Christ's, not ours. He alone is the Righteous One, and righteousness is found in none other.

The righteousness of Christ is "alien" in the sense that it is not an achievement of ours. But Christ himself is not "alien" to us or *extra nos*. Rather, he makes us one with him so that we may share in *his* righteousness. The concept of imputation is meant to express a forensic aspect of a personal reality. J. I. Packer expresses this in his typically clear manner:

> God declares [believers] to be righteous, because he reckons them to be righteous; and he reckons righteousness to them, not because he accounts them to have kept the law personally (which would be a false judgment), but because he accounts them to be united to the one who kept it representatively (and that is a true judgment). For Paul union with Christ is not fancy but fact—the basic fact, indeed,

43 Luther, *Works*, Vol. 26, 132.

in Christianity; and the doctrine of imputed righteousness is simply Paul's exposition of the forensic aspect of it.[44]

The Dangers of Abstracting Justification from Union with Christ

Evangelicals have always maintained that justification is at the heart of the gospel, and so it is. Without the forgiveness of sins and the imputation of Christ's righteousness, the gospel would cease to be truly good news. That justification is indispensable to the gospel should not mean, however, that it constitutes the entirety of the gospel. Justification is, in fact, derived from a more "basic fact," as Packer puts it. When justification, or any other benefit of salvation for that matter, is removed from the more basic reality of our union with Christ, it suffers distortions that open it up to questions and objections for which only union with Christ is the answer. As Anthony Thiselton has written, "Being in Christ is the horizon of understanding within which the various 'problems' associated with justification by grace through faith alone become simply questions that receive intelligible answers."[45]

I opened this book by warning of the danger of what I called "soteriological reductionism." By this I mean that it is possible, with even the best of intentions, to reduce salvation to an impersonal reality, which involves an "objectification" of Christ in which his benefits begin to eclipse his person. This danger may be especially acute with the doctrine of justification when it is defined or understood apart from our union with the incarnate, crucified, resurrected, living Jesus Christ. Regrettably, justification is sometimes expressed as the primary and fundamental reality of salvation, as if salvation is itself justification—"to be "saved" is more or less the same as "to be justified." But this way of conceiving of justification can hardly be the case. There is no justification without participation in the Justified One. To be clear,

---

[44]J. I. Packer, "Justification," in *Evangelical Dictionary of Theology*, ed. Walter A. Elwell (Grand Rapids: Baker, 2001), 596. The Puritan Thomas Boston understood it similarly: "From this union with Christ results a communion with him in his unsearchable riches, and consequently in his righteousness. . . . Thus the righteousness of Christ becomes [man's]; and because it is his by unquestionable title, it is imputed to him; it is reckoned his in the judgment of God, which is always according to truth" (*Human Nature in Its Fourfold State* [Carlisle, PA: Banner of Truth Trust, 1964; repr., 1989], 288).
[45]Thiselton, *The Hermeneutics of Doctrine*, 349.

there is no salvation *without* justification, but salvation in its essence is Jesus Christ, not one of his benefits.

We do not solve this reductionism by insisting that our justification is dependent on a merely "legal union with Christ." This kind of soteriological construction gets us closer to the truth—justification in Christ is indeed forensic in nature—but it suggests that the basic reality of salvation is a legal transaction or association in which the benefits of Christ's life, condemnation, death, and resurrection are merely matters of divine bookkeeping. The living, personal reality of Jesus Christ falls from the picture, and we are left with a gift but bereft of the Giver. As a study of historical theology tells us, when justification is "objectified" or dislodged from Christ in this way, we tend toward either antinomianism or moralism, and toward the inevitable and unnecessary debates that follow.[46]

A related and equally problematic result of abstracting justification from union with Christ is the tendency to distort the very nature of justification. Justification is, by classical Protestant definition, a *declaration* of righteousness for the one who is in Christ. Justification is conceptually distinguished from sanctification by its forensic nature, and it is crucial that we make this distinction if we are to remain evangelical and Protestant. Justification is not about God *making us righteous*, it is about God *declaring us righteous*. This declaration rests not on our holiness or transformation (the subject of sanctification), but on the merits of Christ's life and death that are imputed to us. This is the theological and pastoral essence of the doctrine. Justification simply *must not* be confused with sanctification.

It may strike us as rather strange, then, when we read in the works of theologians who are Reformed, evangelical, and Protestant that "sanctification is the inevitable *effect* of the justifying verdict," that "sanctification is the *effect* of justification," or that "the legal aspect of our union with Christ is the *ground* of the transformative aspect of our

---

[46] Protestant church history has been beset by perennial debates attempting to navigate the poles of antinomian and moralist emphases. This is due, no doubt, to what Evans refers to as a "bifurcated soteriology" or a "bifurcated union with Christ." In soteriologies such as these, the unity of salvation is destroyed and it becomes impossible to hold together justification and sanctification (see Evans, *Imputation and Impartation*, 260). The most recent example is the late twentieth-century "Lordship Salvation" controversy in which the participants seemed to be wrangling over how to relate the benefits of Christ, as if they could be isolated from him.

union."[47] This kind of language is confusing because if justification "effects," "grounds," "produces," "brings in its wake," or "actualizes" sanctification, in what way is this different from saying that justification "includes" sanctification? This way of stating the relation between justification and sanctification begins to blur the line between a Protestant understanding of justification, in which God *declares* the sinner righteous, and a Roman Catholic understanding, in which God *makes* a person righteous. To assert that justification effects or produces sanctification appears to obscure the material principle of the Protestant doctrine of justification by implying that justification contains *transformative* realities.

The great comfort and assurance that the doctrine of justification provides the church lie precisely in the fact that our acceptance with God is secured by God's *forensic declaration* of our right standing. The fact that justification is a forensic reality, not a transformative reality, is all-important. This, I believe, all evangelical Protestants would resolutely affirm. Why, then, do many theologians in the tradition, who otherwise rightly insist on the forensic nature of justification, go on to claim that justification "produces" or "effects" sanctification—effectively making justification something *other* than justification?

The answer, in short, is that when justification is removed from the larger, more basic, personal reality of whom it is a part (Jesus Christ), and is made to carry the whole weight of salvation, one must deduce from *it*, rather than from *him*, how to think of Christ's benefits. Thus, a "legal union with Christ" is made to perform the saving and sanctifying work that only Jesus Christ himself can be to us; justification is forced to be more than it *is*. But justification is not meant to carry that burden. Rather than saying that justification produces sanctification, it would be better for us to say instead that *Jesus Christ himself* in our union with him is our justification, and that *Jesus Christ himself* in our union with him is our sanctification.[48] Justification is one

---

[47]The first two quotes are from Horton, *The Christian Faith*, 611. The other is from Fesko, *Justification*, 277. Horton and Fesko, whose works cited here are both otherwise valuable, are hardly the only examples. They are following in a federalist tradition that so prioritizes justification ("legal union with Christ") that every other benefit of salvation, including personal/spiritual/vital/actual union with Christ, is subordinated to it. Berkhof writes, "The judicial ground for all the special grace which we receive lies in the fact that the righteousness of Christ is freely imputed to us" (*Systematic Theology*, 452).

[48]See chapter 4 for an elaboration on the assertion that Christ is himself our sanctification.

benefit of being united to Christ that must be carefully distinguished from sanctification, another benefit of being united to Christ. Sanctification is an "effect" of our union with Christ, not an "effect" of our justification.[49]

D. A. Carson has written that "if we speak of justification or of imputation . . . apart from a grasp of this incorporation into Christ, we will constantly be in danger of contemplating some sort of transfer *apart* from being included in Christ, *apart* from union with Christ."[50] We would be in danger, in other words, of contemplating the transfer of a quality rather than intimacy with a person.

Conclusion

The intention of this chapter was to situate the great doctrine of justification in relation to our incorporation into Christ. I sought to do so not merely to protect justification from possible distortion, but also so that we might better learn to marvel at our justification in Christ. And marvel we should. No other benefit of our union with Christ so resolutely assures us that we have present and everlasting peace with God; no other benefit so lays the axe to the root of legalism and moralism (even in the church); no other benefit is quite so comforting to the troubled conscience; no other benefit shows more clearly than justification that salvation is truly, wholly, and perfectly the unmerited free gift of God's grace in Christ Jesus.

---

[49] This is not at all to say that the doctrine of justification is not significant to the Christian life. It most certainly is. Justification provides the church the assurance that she is forever in the right with God, an assurance that is enormously significant for the church's pursuit of holiness. I am pointing out that it is not justification *per se* that produces transformed lives, but rather the sanctifying work and person of Jesus Christ.

[50] Carson, "The Vindication of Imputation," 72.

4

SANCTIFICATION IN CHRIST

For those whom he foreknew he also predestined to
be conformed to the image of his Son, in order that
he might be the firstborn among many brothers.

ROMANS 8:29

I am the vine; you are the branches. Whoever
abides in me and I in him, he it is that bears much
fruit, for apart from me you can do nothing.

JOHN 15:5

In evangelical theology, the doctrine of sanctification has enjoyed little of the status or attention afforded the doctrine of justification. Whereas justification is often equated with salvation itself, sanctification is sometimes pushed to the periphery of our understanding of soteriology, as if it were an afterthought in God's redemptive plan. We tend to rejoice in the fact that God *declares us righteous* in Christ, forgiving our sin and imputing Christ's righteousness to us, assuming that this wonderfully good news constitutes the whole of our salvation. But in this rejoicing, it is easy to neglect or overlook the fact that God is also *making us holy* in Christ, that the gospel of our salvation is incomplete without God's glorious work of sanctification (from the

Latin *sanctus + facere*: "to make holy; to set apart"). In other words, we often fail to appropriately and appreciatively rejoice in the good news that Christ is both our righteousness *and* our holiness. Thus, while justification is often equated with "the gospel," sanctification is often equated with "the Christian life" or the "spiritual disciplines," suggesting that sanctification has at least been terminologically, if not conceptually, divorced from salvation.

So, in an attempt to provide holiness with a soteriological "home," sanctification is sometimes thought of as our *response* to the saving work of Christ rather than as an integral part of that work. Similarly, we often conceive of our holiness as rooted in our attempt to manifest our gratitude to God for forgiveness, rather than as a manifestation of our new life in Christ.[1]

I cannot help wondering, further, whether the parsing of the person and work of Christ in conceptions such as these is reflected in the similar parsing of the persons of the Trinity in the familiar phrase "Jesus saves us and the Spirit sanctifies us" and similar refrains. This idea may strike some as theologically tidy, but it is barely biblical. Jesus Christ does not "hand over" the work of sanctification to the Spirit and absent himself after he has "saved" us; Jesus Christ *is* our salvation, and therefore our sanctification, *through the Spirit.*

Finally, and most problematic of all, is the notion that sanctification is essentially an optional exercise reserved for spiritually mature Christians, for those who graduate from "believer" to "disciple." This notion suggests that there are Christians who are not experiencing the sanctifying power of Christ's death and resurrection in their lives.

Notions such as these—which are an almost inevitable consequence of an objectified view of salvation—convey the impression that one benefit of Christ, such as justification, is available to us apart from another, such as holiness. This is a sure indication that Christ's

---

[1] One often hears comments like this: "Christ saves us, and we respond to that salvation in obedient gratitude." John Piper's caution against the "debtor's ethic" is relevant here: "The debtor's ethic has a deadly appeal to immature Christians. . . . The Christian life is pictured as an effort to pay back the debt we owe to God. The admission is made that we will never fully pay it off, but the debtor's ethic demands that we work at it. Good deeds and religious acts are the installment payments we make on the unending debt we owe God. . . . God wants us to be grateful to Him for what He has done, but He doesn't want us to thank Him by thinking it is our duty to try and work for Him, paying Him back." (*Brothers, We Are Not Professionals* [Nashville: B&H, 2002], 34).

work has been severed from his person and rendered a soteriological smorgasbord for our selective taking.

I would point to two factors that may help explain why sanctification has a somewhat ambiguous and peripheral status in our understanding of salvation. The first is a failure to reckon fully with the comprehensive effects of our sin condition. In chapter 2, we noted the widespread agreement among evangelical Reformed theologians that there is twofold catastrophe resulting from our union with Adam: (1) we are declared guilty and condemned to death, and (2) our nature is corrupted or depraved. Justification is the triumphant gospel answer to the former problem: we are declared righteous in Christ. If this were all that our condition required as a solution, we might well rest satisfied that justification exhausts the gospel. But there is the remaining problem of our depravity; we have corrupted natures that seek out, and take pleasure in, sin. The biblical doctrine of sanctification makes clear that God has made provision for this aspect of our fallen condition as well, and it too is part of the salvation we experience in Christ. God not only declares us righteous in Christ, he also makes us righteous in Christ. Sanctification tells us that God will not leave us in our polluted, depraved condition, for he has promised us that he *has* healed us, and *will* heal us, in Jesus Christ. God's beneficence extends to every area of our brokenness, and this is good news indeed!

The second, and more decisive, reason for the lack of clarity on sanctification is what I have referred to as a tendency toward soteriological reductionism. When we parcel out Christ's benefits in abstraction from the wholeness of his saving person, we are bound to have difficulty relating one benefit to another. We may even begin to imagine that one of Christ's benefits—for instance, justification—makes the others superfluous or redundant: "If we are justified, what is the urgency or necessity of sanctification? If we are already forgiven, are we not already saved?" Again, this kind of soteriological reductionism implies that salvation is something like a smorgasbord, where we choose that which most suits our tastes. But, blessedly, God knows that we are beggars, not choosers. He has given us, and is giving us, *everything* that we truly need, and he has done so by uniting us to Jesus Christ, who is our "righteousness and *sanctification* and redemption"

(1 Cor. 1:30). To be in union with Christ is to experience *all* that he is to us in the utter fullness of his saving person.

To experience all that Christ is to us means that we are not only forgiven and accounted righteous in him, but that we are made holy in him; in our union with Christ, he sanctifies us. Thus, sanctification is not merely a byproduct of salvation, it is part of what it means to be saved. In other words, there is no such thing as being saved without being sanctified, precisely because Jesus Christ cannot be other than who he is to us, namely our righteousness and our holiness. To be in union with him is to be crucified, buried, and risen with him—to participate in the sanctifying power of his death and resurrection in our very lives. Indeed, God has predestined us to the end that we might be transformed into the image of Jesus Christ, the embodied holiness of God. This is what sanctification is all about.

As a foundation for what follows, I define sanctification thus:

> Sanctification is that benefit of our union with Christ in which God, through the power and presence of the Holy Spirit, delivers us from our depraved natures by transforming us into the holy image of Jesus Christ through our participation in his death and resurrection.

The chapter will unfold by first explaining how sanctification is rooted in our union with Jesus Christ, and how this helps us to properly locate sanctification in the gospel. Second, it will explore the richness of sanctification in terms of its definitive and progressive aspects. To be sanctified, in other words, means that we are both *already* (definitively) sanctified in Christ and *continually being* (progressively) sanctified in Christ. Third, it will demonstrate that sanctification consists in our conformity to and transformation into the image of Jesus Christ. This means that sanctification can never be confused with moralism, and neither can it be reduced to a life of gratitude or imitation. It is, rather, God forging us into the likeness of Christ through our participation in his death and resurrection. Finally, the chapter will conclude with a section about what it means to say that we are called to participate in our sanctification. Here I look at the means that God uses, and that we are therefore called to use, as he transforms us into the likeness of his Son.

Union with Christ and Sanctification

In order to re-establish sanctification as an integral part of the good news of our salvation in Christ, let me first remind you of the basic thesis of this book: the central reality of our salvation is that through faith, by the power of the Holy Spirit, we enter into a vital, personal, and profoundly real union with the incarnate, crucified, resurrected Savior, Jesus Christ, through whom all the blessings of salvation flow to us. In light of this, we should ask: Is sanctification one of the blessings we receive in our union with Christ? Do we have good biblical reason to say that Jesus Christ is our sanctification or that we are sanctified "in him"?

An excellent place to begin answering these questions is 1 Corinthians 1:30, where Paul tells us that because of God we are "in Christ Jesus, who became to us wisdom from God, righteousness and sanctification and redemption." Of the many blessings that Christ is to us, one is sanctification. Especially worthy of note in this passage is the assertion that Jesus "became to us . . . sanctification," a phrase that suggests that he is more than merely our *sanctifier*—he is himself our *sanctification*.

Although it may at first be difficult to imagine how or why Jesus "became" sanctification to us if he was already perfectly holy, we should remember that he took on our human nature in order to present us holy before the Father: "For their sake I consecrate [or "sanctify"] myself, that they also may be sanctified in truth" (John 17:19). Thomas F. Torrance refers to this as the self-sanctification of Christ in the incarnation:

> The holiness of the church is derived from God through Jesus Christ, through his self-sanctification or self-consecration in life and death on our behalf. He sanctified himself in the human nature he took from us, that we might be sanctified through the Word and truth of God incarnated in him.[2]

Again, this understanding points to the significance of the incarnation. Christ is uniquely our sanctification because in him alone the sanctification of our human nature has taken place by union with his

---

[2] Thomas F. Torrance, *Atonement: The Person and Work of Christ*, ed. Robert T. Walker (Downers Grove, IL: IVP Academic, 2009), 386.

divine life. What unholy humanity so desperately needs is union with the Sanctified One. As Anthony Hoekema has aptly put it, "If Christ is indeed our sanctification, we can only be sanctified through being one with him."[3]

A cluster of biblical passages further establishes that sanctification is one of the salvific blessings of being united to Christ. Paul designates believers as "those sanctified in Christ Jesus" (1 Cor. 1:2). This designation takes a number of similar forms throughout his letters: "the saints" (2 Cor. 1.1), "the saints . . . in Christ Jesus" (Eph. 1:1), "the saints in Christ Jesus" (Phil. 1:1), "the saints and faithful brothers in Christ" (Col. 1:2), and those "sanctified . . . in the name of the Lord Jesus Christ" (1 Cor. 6:11). It is axiomatic for Paul that those joined to Christ are indeed the sanctified ones. It could hardly be any other way if Jesus has become sanctification to us (1 Cor. 1:30). There is no other way in which we can have sanctification, or become sanctified, than through and in Christ.

Our sanctification in Christ derives from the newness of life we have in him. We read that we are created anew in Christ: "Therefore, if anyone is in Christ, he is a new creation. The old has passed away; behold, the new has come" (2 Cor. 5:17). To be in Christ is to have a newness of life founded in him. In Ephesians 2:10, we find that "we are [God's] workmanship, created in Christ Jesus for good works, which God prepared beforehand, that we should walk in them." Our new life, our holiness and sanctification, and our good works are all bound up with our being "in Christ." It is no wonder, then, that Paul can write that God has predestined us "to be conformed to the image of his Son" (Rom. 8:29).

Paul's teaching on being sanctified in Christ is surely an echo of what he heard from his Savior, perhaps something very similar to the striking words we find in John's Gospel:

> Abide in me, and I in you. As the branch cannot bear fruit by itself, unless it abides in the vine, neither can you, unless you abide in me. I am the vine; you are the branches. Whoever abides in me and I in him, he it is that bears much fruit, for apart from me you can do nothing. (15:4–5)

---

[3] Anthony Hoekema, *Saved by Grace* (Grand Rapids: Eerdmans, 1989), 62.

This passage is perhaps the clearest of all the biblical teachings that our "fruit-bearing," which I take to be an integral part of what it means to be sanctified, comes about as a result of our being grafted into Jesus Christ, who is the source of our holiness. Apart from him, there is no possibility of our bearing fruit, for we are totally dependent on his life-giving nourishment.

Even if Martin Luther will forever be associated with the doctrine of justification by faith alone, his comments on this passage show that he also had a robust doctrine of sanctification by faith alone:

> My holiness, righteousness and purity do not stem from me, nor do they depend on me. They come solely from Christ and are based only in Him, in whom I am rooted by faith, just as sap flows from the stalk into the branches. Now I am like Him and of His kind. Both He and I are of one nature and essence, and I bear fruit in Him and through Him. The fruit is not mine; it is the Vine's.[4]

Luther's words nicely summarize the teaching of Scripture on the relationship between union with Christ and sanctification, which relationship I wish to emphasize here. One of the benefits we receive in being joined to Jesus Christ is a newness of life through which we bear holy and righteous fruit. Sanctification therefore is not an addendum to salvation, and neither is it a quality of life that we can bring into existence, anymore than we can forgive our own sins or impute to ourselves Christ's righteousness. Sanctification, like any other soteriological blessing, is a direct result of being joined to Christ in the glorious fullness of who he is.

This does not mean that we cannot, or should not, distinguish between the benefits we receive in Christ. We cannot and should not blur the distinction, for instance, between justification and sanctification; they are distinguishable benefits of being joined to Christ that bless us in unique ways. The same goes, as we shall see in the next chapter, for the blessing of adoption. Adoption should not be confused with either justification or sanctification, for it has its own unique privileges. Being joined to Christ does not make of salvation a mass of

---

[4] Martin Luther, in *Luther's Works*, 55 vols., gen. ed. Jaroslav Pelikan (St. Louis: Concordia Publishing House; Philadelphia: Fortress Press, 1955–1975), Vol. 24, 226.

indistinguishable blessings. It helps us to see, rather, that Christ himself is the sum of all blessings to us. Thus, when we are united to him, we receive *all* that he is to us, never one blessing without the others.

The implications of this for how we think of sanctification are immensely significant. To put it as starkly as possible, there is no such thing as a Christian who is not sanctified in Christ, because Christ is himself our sanctification. We can no more fail to be sanctified in Christ than we can fail to be justified or adopted in him.[5] Trying to separate justification from sanctification, John Calvin argued, is like trying to separate the heat of the sun from its light. The benefits of the sun can certainly be distinguished (they perform different functions), but they just as certainly cannot be separated; the one always accompanies the other.[6] The same goes for the benefits of the Son: justification and sanctification can be distinguished (they perform different soteriological functions), but they cannot be separated; the one always accompanies the other. The reason they cannot be separated, Calvin argued, is because that would be equivalent to dismembering Christ:

> Although we may distinguish between them [justification and sanctification], Christ contains both of them *inseparably in himself*. Do you wish, then, to attain righteousness in Christ? You must first possess Christ; but you cannot possess him without being made partaker in his sanctification, because *he cannot be divided into pieces.* . . . Since, therefore, it is *solely by expending himself* that the Lord gives us these benefits to enjoy, he bestows both of them at the same time, the one never without the other. Thus it is clear how we are justified not without works yet not through works, since in our sharing in Christ, which justifies us, sanctification is just as much included as righteousness.[7]

Here Calvin paints a graphic word picture that clearly communicates the fullness of sharing in Christ. If we share in him, we share in all that is his, because Christ's saving benefits cannot be divorced from his person. Conversely, if we do not share in him, we share in nothing

---

[5] The Scottish Confession of 1560 is clear on this point: "For this we most boldly affirm, that it is blasphemy to say that Christ Jesus abides in the heart of those in whom there is no spirit of sanctification" (Article XIII) (cited in James T. Dennison Jr., *Reformed Confessions of the 16th and 17th Centuries in English Translation: Vol. 2, 1552–1566* [Grand Rapids: Reformation Heritage Books, 2010]).

[6] John Calvin, *Institutes of the Christian Religion*, ed. John T. McNeill, trans. Ford Lewis Battles, Library of Christian Classics, Vols. 20–21 (Philadelphia: Westminster, 1960), 3.11.6.

[7] Ibid., 3.16.1 (emphasis added).

that is his, because "he cannot be divided into pieces." The primary gift we receive in salvation is not this or that benefit; it is Jesus Christ in the fullness of his saving person.

As I noted in the previous chapter, evangelical Protestant thought has been marked by perennial debates over the relationship between justification and sanctification. The debates stem from an ambiguity about the relationship of Christ's saving benefits to his person, a fissure between christology and soteriology. Such debates are sure to continue unabated so long as Christ's benefits are thought of as separable from his person and so long as salvation is thought of as primarily something other than union with him.

MORTIFICATION AND VIVIFICATION

Among the reasons it is important to view the saving blessing of sanctification in the matrix of union with Christ is because doing so allows us to capture the full force of the biblical teaching that our sin-polluted existence is overcome through our participation in the death of Christ (mortification) and the resurrection of Christ (vivification). Christ assumed our flesh into his existence; thus, when we are joined to him, we are crucified, buried, and raised with him (Gal. 2:20; Eph. 2:6; Col. 2:12). In the previous chapter, we saw the benefits of this identification with Christ in terms of justification. When we are identified with him in his death and burial, our sins are forgiven and we are freed from condemnation. Likewise, when we are identified with him in his resurrection, we are vindicated and declared in the right. But we must not miss that the benefits of this identification with Christ in his death and resurrection extend also to our sanctification. In our union with him, Christ's death and resurrection are the redemptive realities through which the dominion of sin is overcome in us and we are restored to newness of life. In other words, his death and resurrection are not to be thought of as merely historical events. They have present operative effects in the lives of those united to him.

Paul drives this point home in Romans 6, where he responds incredulously to an imaginary interlocutor who suggests that continual sinning by those who are justified might furnish the occasion for God to serendipitously manifest his grace: "Are we to continue in sin that grace may abound? By no means!" (vv. 1–2a). Paul's incredulity is directed toward an apparently fundamental misunderstanding of the reality of salvation and its far-reaching, existence-altering effects: "Do you not know that all of us who have been baptized into Christ Jesus were baptized into his death? We were buried therefore with him by baptism into death, in order that, just as Christ was raised from the dead by the glory of the Father, we too might walk in newness of life" (vv. 3–4).

It is important to note what Paul does *not* say in order to appreciate what he *does* say. In response to the absurd notion that God's free grace in justification provides the possible occasion for continual sin, Paul does not say, "Do you not know that we all owe God a debt of gratitude for the fact that he has justified us freely in Christ?" Neither does he say, "Do you not know that our justification produces in us the effect of sanctification?" No, Paul's answer stretches back to a more all-encompassing reality: our participation in the death, burial, and resurrection of Christ. The questioner has not understood what it means to be united to Christ.

Paul's extended answer encompasses essentially two main points. The first is that by being united with Christ in his death, "we know that our old self was crucified with him in order that the body of sin might be brought to nothing, so that we would no longer be enslaved to sin" (v. 6). The second is that by being united to Christ in his resurrection, we are enabled to "walk in newness of life" and to live as "alive to God in Christ Jesus" (vv. 4, 11). Our participation in Christ's death sets us free from the enslavement of sin, and our participation in his resurrection makes us alive to God in righteousness: "Paul makes it clear, by the sequence in this paragraph, that we can live a holy life only as we appropriate the benefits of our union with Christ."[8]

Because it is a given for Paul that believers are united to Christ in his death and resurrection, his incredulity is perfectly understandable. He is not expressing the hope that believers might respond to God's grace in obedient gratitude or that God's freely justifying grace might provide an incentive to lives of holiness. Rather, he is insisting

---

[8] Douglas J. Moo, *The Epistle to the Romans*, New International Commentary on the New Testament (Grand Rapids: Eerdmans, 1996), 391.

on the more fundamental, inescapable reality that believers are the present beneficiaries of the sanctifying effects of Christ's death and resurrection.[9]

A similar grounding of sanctification in the death and resurrection of Christ occurs in the book of Colossians. After establishing in 2:12–13 that we have in fact been buried and raised with Christ, Paul writes:

> If then you have been raised with Christ, seek the things that are above, where Christ is, seated at the right hand of God. Set your minds on things that are above, not on things that are on earth. For you have died, and your life is hidden with Christ in God. When Christ who is your life appears, then you also will appear with him in glory. Put to death therefore what is earthly in you:sexual immorality, impurity, passion, evil desire, and covetousness, which is idolatry. (3:1–5)

Again, notice that the *reality* of our participation in Christ's death and resurrection is the ground for the actual holiness of our lives (cf. 2:20). Paul is no instructor in morals or teacher of virtue; his conviction regarding the righteous lives of Christians rests in our incorporation into Christ, from whose death and resurrection flow the power for holiness. Indeed, Paul's exhortations to holiness originate in his conviction that believers have already died and risen with Christ. Thus, he does not enjoin us to "live holy lives because Christ has died and has risen," but to "live holy lives because you have already died and been raised with Christ!"

The significance of Christ's death and resurrection, usually relegated to discussions of justification, needs to be recovered as the primary paradigm for understanding sanctification as well.[10] Intriguingly,

---

[9]The interpretation of Romans 6 by many commentators has suffered (in my view) from a failure to see that Paul does not refer his readers back to their justification to explain their sanctification, but back to their union with the crucified, resurrected Christ. As important as justification is to Paul's thinking in general, and to his letter to the Romans in particular, the more basic soteriological category for Paul is union with Christ.

[10]Calvin taught that sanctification consists of two parts, mortification and vivification: "Both things happen to us by participation in Christ. For if we truly partake in his death, 'our old man is crucified by his power, and the body of sin perishes' (Rom. 6:6), that the corruption of original nature may no longer thrive. If we share in his resurrection, through it we are raised up into newness of life to correspond with the righteousness of God" (*Institutes*, 3.3.9). Calvin's successor, Theodore Beza, taught similarly that sanctification is a direct result of the indwelling Christ, through whom we experience mortification, burial, and resurrection (see Beza's Confession of 1560, in Dennison, *Reformed Confessions*, Vol. 2, 260–61). Not surprisingly, the Heidelberg Catechism ties together the renewal of our nature with our participation in Christ's death and resurrection (Questions 43 and 45). Again, not surprisingly, we read the following in the Westminster Confession of Faith, Chapter 13: "They, who are once

there are some conceptual similarities between justification and sanctification that bear pointing out, and that might prove helpful in thinking
through the theo-logic of sanctification. As I noted earlier, justification
consists of both a negative aspect, namely, the remission of sin and
condemnation through the death of Christ (Rom. 8:1), and a positive
aspect, namely, the declaration of righteousness through Christ's life
and resurrection (Phil. 3:9). Sanctification may be thought of similarly.
It would be fair to say that sanctification consists of both a negative
aspect, the putting to death of our sin and sin-nature through the death
of Christ (Rom. 6:6; Gal. 2:20; Col. 3:3–5), and a positive aspect, ris-
ing to newness of life and holiness through the resurrection of Christ
(Rom. 6:4, 11; Col. 3:1; Phil. 3:10). This way of conceiving the matter may
provide a useful paradigm for appreciating the expansive, sanctifying
effects of our union with Christ in his death and resurrection.

THE ROLE OF THE HOLY SPIRIT

If I were following conventional theological wisdom for a chapter on
sanctification, I would have highlighted the role of the Holy Spirit by
now. Conventionally, the work of Christ is highlighted in doctrines
related to atonement, salvation, and justification, whereas the work of
the Spirit is emphasized in the doctrine of sanctification. It is customary to think of Jesus as the Savior and the Spirit as the Sanctifier. While
there is no doubt that the role of the Spirit in the sanctification of the
church is crucial, I think the popular conception needs to be refined.
The role of the Spirit in sanctification needs to be precisely defined
lest we begin to imagine that his work somehow eclipses or replaces
the work of Christ in our sanctification. Jesus does not send the Spirit
to the church in order that she might become holy in Jesus's absence.
Rather, Jesus sends the Spirit in order that he, through the Spirit, *might
be present as her holiness.*

---

effectually called, and regenerated, having a new heart, and a new spirit created in them, are further
sanctified, really and personally, *through the virtue of Christ's death and resurrection,* by His Word and Spirit
dwelling in them" (in Philip Schaff, ed., *Creeds of Christendom, Vol. 3: Evangelical Creeds* [Grand Rapids,
Baker, 1966], 629, emphasis added). In the Westminster Larger Catechism, Question and Answer 75,
the Spirit is said to apply the death and resurrection of Christ to God's people in their sanctification.
What *is* surprising is the relative difficulty one encounters in finding other authoritative sources that
clearly articulate sanctification in such a manner. More often than not, even in otherwise excellent
works, sanctification (or good works or holiness) is said to come from "faith" or the Spirit, with little
or no mention of the fact that sanctification is the work of Jesus Christ for us and in us by the power
of his death and resurrection.

Thus, the principal significance of the Spirit in sanctification is to mediate the presence and power of Jesus Christ, who is our sanctification. The reason for this, as we saw in chapter 1, is that our union with Christ occurs through the power and indwelling presence of the Holy Spirit—the Spirit brings us into communion with the Holy One. The indwelling Holy Spirit is the "Spirit of Christ" (Gal. 4:6; Phil. 1:19). Paul elaborates on this point in Romans 8:9–11:

> You, however, are not in the flesh but in the Spirit, if in fact the Spirit of God dwells in you. Anyone who does not have the Spirit of Christ does not belong to him. But if Christ is in you, although the body is dead because of sin, the Spirit is life because of righteousness. If the Spirit of him who raised Jesus from the dead dwells in you, he who raised Christ Jesus from the dead will also give life to your mortal bodies through his Spirit who dwells in you.

The Holy Spirit is vital to the holiness of believers because by his presence we are assured of the presence of the holiness of Christ, through whom we are dead to sin and alive to God.

The relationship between the Holy Spirit and Jesus Christ in our sanctification has been admirably captured by John Murray:

> It is as the Spirit of Christ and as the Spirit of him who raised up Christ from the dead that the Holy Spirit sanctifies. We may not think of the Spirit as operative in us apart from the risen and glorified Christ. The sanctifying process is not only dependent upon the death and resurrection of Christ in its initiation; it is also dependent upon the death and resurrection of Christ in its continuance. It is by the efficacy and virtue which proceed from the exalted Lord that sanctification is carried on ... it is by the Spirit that this virtue is communicated.[11]

The role of the Spirit as sanctifier is not diminished by this view. On the contrary, the Spirit's role is brought to its full glory. As Jesus taught us in John 14, he sends the Spirit to dwell in us in order that we might be in Christ and he in us (cf. Eph. 2:22; 3:16–17). What greater honor could be accorded the work of the Spirit than this? We should go on to stress that the existence of the church herself is dependent

---

[11]John Murray, *Redemption Accomplished and Applied* (Grand Rapids: Eerdmans, 1996), 147–48.

on her communion with the Lord, brought about by the power and presence of the promised Spirit, who blesses the church with the inexhaustible riches of Christ. Through the Spirit we are baptized into Christ and become members of his body, equipped to love and serve each other in holiness with the gifts of Jesus Christ that come by the Spirit (Eph. 4:11; 1 Corinthians 12). The church reflects the image and holiness of Christ in the world through her participation in the Spirit of holiness who is the Spirit of the Lord Jesus Christ (2 Cor. 3:18).

> [The Holy Spirit] only is the Spirit of holiness, he only the Spirit of truth; and therefore it is only through his presence and power in the church that it partakes of the holiness of Jesus Christ. . . . Because the church is the body of Christ in which he dwells, the temple of the Holy Spirit in which God is present, its members live the very life of Christ through the Holy Spirit, partaking of and living out the holy life of God. Therefore their personal holiness and all the qualities of the divine life and love found in their lives, are the fruits of the Holy Spirit.[12]

The role of the Holy Spirit in the sanctification of believers needs to be emphasized, but never in a way that suggests that the Spirit is an alternative or substitute for the presence of Jesus Christ, who not only is our sanctification, but through whose death and resurrection believers find the power and efficacy of their death to sin and newness of life.[13] The Holy Spirit is so very crucial to our sanctification because it is through his empowering presence that we are sanctified *in* Christ Jesus, who sanctifies the church and will present her "to himself in splendor, without spot or wrinkle or any such thing, that she might be holy and without blemish" (Eph. 5:26–27).

Definitive and Progressive Sanctification

Theologians, in an attempt to distinguish between justification and sanctification, have often maintained that while justification is a once-

---

[12] Torrance, *Atonement*, 386–87.
[13] Karl Barth asks, "Why is it that he is the Holy Spirit *per definitionem*? . . . The answer is staggering in its simplicity. He is the Holy Spirit in this supreme sense—holy with a holiness for which there are no analogies—because He is no other than the presence of Jesus Christ Himself" (*Church Dogmatics*, IV.2, cited in Andrew Purves and Charles Partee, *Encountering God* [Louisville, KY: Westminster John Knox, 2000], 47–48).

for-all completed action, sanctification is marked by its progressive nature; it is an ongoing process of overcoming sin.[14] There is some truth in this assertion, particularly regarding justification, yet the truth is more complex and wonderful than that.

As we pay attention to the biblical witness to our sanctification, we find that it has two aspects: it is both a definitive, once-for-all reality, and also a progressive, ongoing, lifelong process. Murray is frequently cited on this matter: "It is a fact too frequently overlooked that in the New Testament the most characteristic terms that refer to sanctification are used, not of a process, but of a once-for-all definitive act."[15] In order to gain a properly comprehensive view of the benefit of sanctification, it is important that we pay close attention to both of these aspects, for together they tell us something very important about what it means to be sanctified in Christ. The fact that our sanctification includes both a definitive aspect and a progressive aspect is best explained by the corresponding fact that our union with Christ is both definitive (we have been decisively united to Christ) and progressive (we are continually growing in our union with him). We have been irrevocably, indissolubly united to the whole Christ, and for that reason we continue to grow into the fullness of Christ throughout our lives.[16]

DEFINITIVELY SANCTIFIED IN CHRIST

Paul often addresses the church in a way that is initially surprising if we are prone to think of sanctification or holiness in merely progressive terms. As we noted above, he addresses believers as *already having been sanctified* in their present state (1 Cor. 1:2; 6:11). Believers are referred to as "saints" in Christ (Phil. 1:1; Col. 1:2; 2 Cor. 1:1) despite the persistent presence of sin in their lives. Many of us are conditioned to think of the sanctified state as the glorified condition of the believer in eternity, and to think of the designation "saint" as referring to one who has reached an elevated state of holiness achieved in a lifetime

---

[14] Millard J. Erickson writes, "Justification is an instantaneous occurrence, complete in a moment, whereas sanctification is a process requiring an entire lifetime for completion" (*Christian Theology* [Grand Rapids: Baker, 1998], 982).

[15] John Murray, *Collected Writings*, 2:277, cited in Hoekema, *Saved By Grace*, 203.

[16] It may be helpful, in this sense, to think of our salvation in terms of a marriage union. A marriage is both a definitive act of union *and* a union that ought to grow continually in intimacy, faithfulness, and self-giving.

of good works. But we repeatedly run into Paul's curious use of the past tense when referring to the sanctified state of believers and his startling habit of conferring sainthood on manifestly imperfect Christians.[17] How do we account for these apparent anomalies?

We can do so only by referring back to the reality Paul assumes has taken place in the life of every believer—that every Christian has been united to the Sanctified One, Jesus Christ, and in this union has mysteriously and truly been crucified, buried, and resurrected with him (1 Cor. 1:30; Rom. 6:3–5; Col. 2:12; 3:1). In this union, our sinful nature has been put to death and we have been raised with Christ to newness of life. Even as we were dead in our trespasses and sins, God "made us alive together with Christ—by grace you have been saved—and raised us up with him and seated us with him in the heavenly places in Christ Jesus" (Eph. 2:5–6). In order that we might be sanctified, God has definitively, decisively put our sinful nature to death in Christ's death and has given us new life in Christ's resurrection. Our sanctification in Christ is definitive in nature precisely because our union with Christ is definitive in nature; because we have already been united to Christ, we have already been sanctified in him.[18] Our holiness is bound up with his, and because he is the Holy One, we are by consequence the holy ones (saints) in him. We could no more be denied the status of having been sanctified in him than we could be denied the status of having been justified or cleansed in him: "But you were washed, you were sanctified, you were justified in the name of the Lord Jesus Christ and by the Spirit of our God" (1 Cor. 6:11).

What does it mean that we have been definitively sanctified in Christ? It means that believers have experienced an actual, decisive break with the power of sin through their participation in Christ's death, and have experienced an actual, decisive newness of life through their participation in his resurrection. We are "dead to

---

[17] When we reserve the title "saint" only for those whom we judge to be of exemplary holiness, or those whom we believe have "earned" the title by virtue of a lifetime of virtuous living, we do a serious injustice to the biblical teaching on sainthood.

[18] Hoekema refers to both objective and subjective sides of our definitive sanctification. Because we were included in Christ before the foundations of the world, there is a sense in which we objectively died and rose with Christ in his historical death and resurrection: "Christ must never be thought of apart from his people, nor his people apart from him." Subjectively, we experience the reality of this death and resurrection in our present lives when we appropriate Christ through faith by the power of the Holy Spirit (*Saved By Grace*, 204–5).

sin and alive to God in Christ Jesus" (Rom. 6:11). "Therefore, if anyone is in Christ, he is a new creation. The old has passed away; behold, the new has come" (2 Cor. 5:17). This means that those in Christ have an *actual* newness of life; they have experienced a transformation or renewal of their very persons through their death-dealing and life-giving union with Christ.

This does not mean that Christians do not and will not struggle with sin or that they have entered into a state of sinless perfection. Such ideas flatly contradict biblical teaching. But we must insist that being sanctified in Christ means that we truly are new creatures in him: "Believers, therefore, should see themselves and each other as persons who are *genuinely* new, though not yet *totally* new."[19] This actual, new, sanctified existence that we have in Jesus Christ is the basis for a continual life of progressive holiness that culminates in our full and entire sanctification when we are glorified with Christ.

PROGRESSIVELY SANCTIFIED IN CHRIST

To be progressively sanctified in Christ means that believers experience the gradual, continual benefits of having already been sanctified in him. This means, most importantly, that we are being continually transformed, through a process of lifetime growth and struggle, into the likeness of Jesus Christ. "And we all, with unveiled face, beholding the glory of the Lord, are being transformed into the same image from one degree of glory to another. For this comes from the Lord who is the Spirit" (2 Cor. 3:18).[20]

Why do we need continual, progressive transformation? It is because, as the Bible insists—and as our lives abundantly testify—we continue to struggle with and indulge our old sinful nature. We continue, inexplicably, to sin, despite the fact that we have been made holy in Christ. Indeed, if we should be brash enough to claim we have no sin, we only compound our sinfulness (1 John 1:8). Even after we are

---

[19] Ibid., 205 (emphasis in original). Hoekema makes an important distinction between positional and definitive sanctification. Some have held that our holiness in Christ is "positional," in that the holiness of Christ is imputed to the believer in a legal, judicial sense. But this seems to conflate sanctification with justification. Definitive sanctification, on the other hand, allows sanctification to remain sanctification—it insists that the believer is genuinely, actually transformed by being joined to Christ.
[20] Calvin called our gradual transformation into the image of Christ "the design of the gospel" (John Calvin, *Calvin's Commentaries* [Edinburgh: Calvin Translation Society, 1844–56; reprinted in 22 vols., Grand Rapids: Baker, 2003], 2 Cor. 3:18).

united to Christ, there remains within us a native desire to satisfy the passions of our fallen existence. In a titanic act of absurdity, we attempt to find life in the death-dealing corruption of our old existence in Adam. Wretched ones that we are! Who will deliver us from this body of death? (Rom. 7:24).

God already *has delivered us* by including us in Jesus Christ, through whom we already have died to sin and risen to new life. And God certainly *will deliver us* by completing what he began in us, transforming us more and more into the image of his Son (Phil. 1:6; Rom. 8:29). This gradual transformation in holiness happens only because, through the Spirit, we benefit more and more from our union with Jesus Christ and his holiness. We grow more and more into our Christ-existence. We are, therefore, to "grow up in every way into him who is the head, into Christ" (Eph. 4:15). This progress in holiness is the gradual destruction of our corrupt natures, a day-by-day, year-by-year, lifelong process in which God fulfills his promises in Christ Jesus to us: he will not leave us in our sin.[21]

Just as our definitive sanctification in Christ does not render our progressive sanctification redundant, neither does our progressive sanctification in Christ render our definitive sanctification unnecessary. Quite the contrary, for to think so would be to misunderstand the nature of our salvation in Christ. Just as we have already been united to Christ and so are justified, sanctified, and adopted, so we grow in ever-increasing intimacy with him: we are continually being forgiven, growing in holiness, and more closely bearing his likeness as his children. He is, after all, the constant source of our nourishment—the bread of life, the living water, and the life-giving vine. Having been sanctified in our union with him, we are to continue to live out the implications of that sanctifying union; we are to live in the reality of having been crucified and resurrected in Christ:

> So you also must consider yourselves dead to sin and alive to God in Christ Jesus. *Let not sin therefore reign in your mortal body, to make you obey*

---

[21] I have always been comforted and encouraged by Calvin's insight on the progress of our sanctification: "In this way it pleases the Lord fully to restore whomsoever he adopts into the inheritance of life. And indeed, this restoration does not take place in one moment or one day or one year; but through continual and sometimes even slow advances God wipes out in his elect the corruption of the flesh" (*Institutes*, 3.3.9).

its passions. Do not present your members to sin as instruments for unrighteousness, but present yourselves to God as those who have been brought from death to life, and your members to God as instruments for righteousness. (Rom. 6:11–13)

The "therefore" in this passage is all-important, for it tells us that our progress in holiness is grounded in our already having been united with Christ in his death and resurrection; we are dead to sin and alive to God in Christ. A similar argument appears in Colossians 3, where we read that on account of our death and resurrection in Christ, we are to "seek the things that are above" and "put to death . . . what is earthly in [us]" (vv. 1–5). In sum, when we were included in Christ, we actually died to sin through his death and actually rose to new life in his resurrection. Thus, we are to die to sin and present ourselves as alive to God. God's plan of salvation is so wide and deep that he not only has made us new, but also is even now making us new through Christ.

We must insist, then, that sanctification is a work of God in Christ thought the Holy Spirit. God sanctifies us, for we cannot sanctify ourselves.[22] Does this mean that we effectively play no role in our sanctification? It does not. I shall say more below about what it means that we are called to be holy, that we are consistently exhorted to live holy lives, and about how we are to pursue holiness. Let it suffice for now to say that God actively involves our whole persons in responsible participation in his act of making us holy. We are not called to make ourselves holy; we are called to live out the holiness he is working in us. And this, too, is our salvation: "Therefore, my beloved, as you have always obeyed, so now, not only as in my presence but much more in my absence, work out your own salvation with fear and trembling, for it is God who works in you, both to will and to work for his good pleasure" (Phil. 2:12–13).[23]

---

[22] As John Webster asserts, "The sanctifying Spirit is *Lord*; that is, sanctification is not in any straightforward sense a process of cooperation or coordination between God and the creature, a drawing out or building upon some inherent holiness of the creature's own. Sanctification is *making* holy. Holiness is properly an incommunicable divine attribute; if creaturely realities become holy, it is by virtue of election, that is, by a sovereign act of segregation or separation by the Spirit as Lord" (*Holy Scripture: A Dogmatic Sketch* [Cambridge: Cambridge University Press, 2003], 27, emphasis in original).

[23] This leads me to recall Torrance's refrain: "'All of grace' does not mean 'nothing of man', but the very reverse, the restoration of full and authentic human being in the spontaneity and freedom of human response to the love of God" (*The Mediation of Christ* [Colorado Springs, CO: Helmer and Howard, 1992], 95).

Sanctification Means Reflecting the Image of Christ, Not Moralism

God is performing a beautiful re-creative act when he sanctifies us in Christ Jesus. To get to the heart of this amazingly good news, we must return to the beginning. The creation of humankind is accompanied by these sublime words: "So God created man in his own image, in the image of God he created him; male and female he created them" (Gen. 1:27). The fact that humans were created as images of God himself is the most blessed honor accorded humankind.[24] While there has not been widespread agreement about what exactly this image consists of,[25] theologians in the orthodox Christian tradition have resolutely affirmed two things: humans were created in the image of God, and that image in humans has been distorted or even lost. It is in this distortion that the great tragedy of sin lies. In our fallen state, we no longer truly reflect the image of God; we are something less than what we were created to be—we are less than authentically human in our self-contradiction. We witness the horrifying effects of the distortion or loss of the *imago Dei* ("image of God") on the first pages of the Old Testament and throughout the course of human history.

Amidst this tragedy of broken images—and the resultant bloodshed and deceit, faithlessness and shattered lives—a most extraordinary thing begins to be said about the One who bears our flesh:

> And the Word became flesh and dwelt among us, and we have seen his glory, glory as of the only Son from the Father, full of grace and truth. (John 1:14)

> He is the image of the invisible God, the firstborn of all creation. (Col. 1:15)

> He is the radiance of the glory of God and the exact imprint of his nature. (Heb. 1:3a)

---

[24] Herman Bavinck highlights the important idea that "a human being does not *bear* or *have* the image of God but . . . he or she *is* the image of God" (*Reformed Dogmatics*, Vol. 2 [Grand Rapids: Baker, 2004], 554–55). This means, first, that the image is not some virtue in God but God himself who is the archetype of man, and, second, that nothing in the human being is excluded from the image of God; the image extends to the whole person.

[25] See Anthony Hoekema, *Created in God's Image* (Grand Rapids: Eerdmans, 1986), 33–65, for an excellent historical overview.

If anything were good news to those of us who dwell in bodies of flesh, surely it would be this: someone exists among us who is the perfect image of God, and he is the Son of God and God himself; furthermore, he dwells in our flesh and is inviting us to partake of him and be united to him. Is it possible that God, in his mighty, patient, gracious, creative, and (literally) self-giving love, is actually re-creating us through Jesus Christ in order that we might truly be the blessed images of God again? It is, for that is exactly what God tells us: "For those whom [God] foreknew he also predestined to be conformed to the image of his Son, in order that he might be the firstborn among many brothers" (Rom. 8:29).

To restore us to the *imago Dei* we were originally created to be—to restore us to our authentic humanity, in other words—God himself *became that which he created.* In the incarnation, God disclosed himself perfectly through the Son; Jesus Christ is the fully human being, the perfect image of God. To restore us to our blessed state of true humanity, God joined us to his true image, and so we begin again to be who we were created to be. And this astounding, breathtaking turn of events lies at the root of our holiness: the essence and goal of our sanctification is reflecting the image of Jesus Christ.

We must firmly and vigorously reject, therefore, all notions of sanctification that can be reduced to "morality" and "ethics," which notions are usually nothing more than self-styled righteousness. We also must reject, with equal firmness and vigor, the notion that God is pleased with our "moral goodness" or "virtuous character." God, quite frankly, is not interested in *our* morality or virtue; he is interested in our reflecting *his* holiness. In fact, he contests our ability to determine right from wrong and good from evil.[26] That is why sanctification is not, at bottom, a matter of psychology, physiology, or sociology (although it may involve any or all of these); it is a matter of *christology.* To put it another way, sanctification is not a matter of constructing ethical systems for the improvement of us or of our society; it is our

---

[26] "But the serpent said to the woman, 'You will not surely die. For God knows that when you eat of it your eyes will be opened, and you will be like God, knowing good and evil'" (Gen. 3:4–5); "And a ruler asked him, 'Good Teacher, what must I do to inherit eternal life?' And Jesus said to him, 'Why do you call me good? No one is good except God alone'" (Luke 18:18–19). Christians do well to speak of "holiness" rather than "morality."

participation in the holiness of Jesus Christ, who is "the exact imprint" of God's nature. God is re-making us into his image, and he is doing so by uniting us to the One who *is* that image. Our sanctification is too precious, and sin is far too serious, to be hijacked by superficial notions of morality.[27]

In sanctification, we come face to face with the awe-inspiring reality that we are being "transformed . . . from one degree of glory to another" and that "Christ is [being] formed in [us]" (2 Cor. 3:18; Gal. 4:19). Of the many crucial ramifications of this reality, the following are a sample:

(1) *Sanctification is a work of God.* The primary reason that sanctification transcends moralism is that, while we may be able to achieve our moral programs, sanctification is *received*, not *achieved*. Our new life in Christ and all it entails—our re-creation, the crucifixion of our sinful nature, our definitive holiness—is *given* to us in our union with the Firstborn of all creation (Col. 1:15). We cannot *become* those who we *are not*. This is why the exhortations toward holiness in the New Testament are not exhortations to *achieve* holiness; they are exhortations to *live out* the holy existence we already have: "If then *you have been raised with Christ*, seek the things that are above, where Christ is, seated at the right hand of God. Set your minds on things that are above, not on things that are on earth. *For you have died*, and your life is hidden with Christ in God. When Christ who is your life appears, then you also will appear with him in glory" (Col. 3:1–4). We are not enjoined to make ourselves holy; we are enjoined to be who we already are in our union with the Righteous One. "It is a remarkable sentiment," Calvin wrote, "that believers live out of themselves, that is, they live in Christ; which can only be accomplished by holding real and actual communication with him."[28]

This does not mean that the Christian life is one of quietism, pas-

---

[27] The distinction I am making here between morality and holiness is exemplified by the fact that the religious/moral leaders of Jesus's day (and ever since) were blind to the fact that Jesus was the embodiment of perfect holiness—they even thought he was demonic! This should give us pause: What was the moral/religious standard to which they were subjecting Jesus? As my *doktorvater*, Victor Shepherd, is fond of pointing out, the opposite of evil is not good; the opposite of evil is God. Good and evil are not philosophically generated ethical abstractions. Rather, they are theologically generated (or, better, divinely revealed) personal, relational categories. There is no knowledge of good and evil apart from knowing God—there is only morality, which is usually nothing more than self-styled righteousness. No wonder, then, that so many were offended at the Son of God.

[28] *Commentaries*, Gal. 2:20.

sive resignation, and waiting on God to do what we cannot. The Scriptures allow for no such misconception. Believers are commanded in the clearest possible terms to pursue holiness at all times and with all of their persons. But that is just the point: holiness is commanded for people who have been united to the Holy One, who have experienced the death and resurrection of Jesus Christ (Eph. 4:20–24). There is no passive resignation here, for we have been re-created to live in the power and freedom of Christ himself, and thereby to overcome our distorted images. John Williamson Nevin has captured this "passive activity" well:

> The Christian is not called, either before or *after* his conversion, to *form an independent holiness for himself*; but only to receive continuously the stream of life that flows upon him from Christ. . . . And still this absolute *passivity* is at the same time the highest *activity*; since Christ works, not *without* the man, but in the *very inmost depths of his being*, infusing into the will itself the active force of his own life.[29]

Neither can the sanctified Christian life be thought of, as it often is, as our response to God's grace rather than as God's grace itself. Such an idea leaves us in the precarious position of conjuring up incentives for holy living that simply cannot bear the weight of what God is doing in our lives. For instance, while it is true that Christians are to exhibit gratitude for God's grace—thankfulness is indeed the proper posture of the saints—gratitude is not the foundation for our sanctification. After all, sanctification is itself something to be grateful for, and our consistent ingratitude is a state that needs sanctification! Even the imitation of Christ, a holy discipline in its own right, is not the sincerest form of flattery where God is concerned. Imitating Christ is not a way that we secure our holiness before God; it is the way we reflect our existence in Christ and as God's beloved children (Phil. 2:1–5; Eph. 4:32–5:2).[30]

---

[29]John Williamson Nevin, *The Mystical Presence: A Vindication of the Reformed or Calvinistic Doctrine of the Holy Eucharist*, American Religious Thought of the 18th and 19th Centuries, Vol. 20 (New York: Garland, 1987), 235 (emphasis in original).

[30]We do not imitate Christ in order to first become like him; we imitate Christ because we are in him. For Luther, Christ is always a gift to be received before he is an example to be followed, and that order is crucial: while Christ's example may be important, "this is the smallest part of the gospel, on the basis of which it cannot yet even be called gospel. For on this level Christ is of no more help to you than some other saint. His life remains his own and does not as yet contribute anything to you. In short this mode (of understanding Christ merely as example) does not make Christians but only hypocrites. . . . The chief article and foundation of the gospel is that before you take Christ as an example, you accept

(2) *Sin is a self-contradiction in the Christian life.* When sanctification is understood as God's act of re-creating us into his image through our union with Christ, we begin to see why sin in the church is handled (or should be handled) with deadly seriousness. Paul and John do not soft-pedal sin as if it were a mere moral lapse; they think of it as a contradiction of our existence. If we moralize sin, we will inevitably trivialize it, and having trivialized it, we will inevitably dismiss its seriousness altogether. We do more than transgress the law in our sin; we transgress the reality of our existence in Christ. We "de-create" what God has created and is creating.[31]

This explains the intense pastoral incredulity and exasperation we see in both apostles when they are confronted by habitual, blatant sin. They take for granted that believers have actually been united to Jesus Christ and have new life in him: "Do you not know that your bodies are members of Christ? . . . Do you not know that your body is a temple of the Holy Spirit within you?" (1 Cor. 6:15, 19); "Do you not know that all of us who have been baptized into Christ Jesus were baptized into his death?" (Rom. 6:3); "Do you not realize this about yourselves, that Jesus Christ is in you?" (2 Cor. 13:5); "No one who abides in him keeps on sinning" (1 John 3:6). Sin is horrific and incredible in the saints because it is an inversion of the reality that we have been re-created as holy images of God in Jesus Christ. We will never take sin seriously enough until we realize that it is an utterly absurd and outrageously foolish contradiction of reality.[32]

(3) *Sanctification involves suffering.* When sanctification deteriorates into the self-righteousness of morality, it leaves no room for the suf-

---

and recognize him as a gift, as a present that God has given you and that is your own. . . . Now when you have Christ as the foundation and chief blessing of your salvation, then the other part follows: that you take him as your example, giving yourself in service to your neighbor just as you see that Christ has given himself for you" ("A Brief Instruction on What to Look for and Expect in the Gospels," in *Works*, Vol. 35, 119–20).

[31] See Steve Jeffrey, Michael Ovey, and Andrew Sach, *Pierced for our Transgressions: Rediscovering the Glory of Penal Substitution* (Wheaton, IL: Crossway, 2007), 110–117.

[32] Cornelius Plantinga writes: "Sin is both wrong and dumb. Indeed, whenever the follies are playing, sin is the main event. Sin is the world's most impressive example of folly" (*Not The Way It's Supposed to Be: A Breviary of Sin* [Grand Rapids: Eerdmans, 1995], 121). Plantinga notes that in the Prophetic Books sin is viewed as outrageous folly, "like pulling the plug on your own resuscitator" (125). Barth provocatively refers to sin as an impossibility: "[Sin] has no basis. It has, therefore, no possibility—we cannot escape this difficult formula—except that of the absolutely impossible. How else can we describe that which is intrinsically absurd, but by a formula which is logically absurd? Sin is that which is absurd, man's absurd choice and decision for that which is not" (*Church Dogmatics*, ed. G. W. Bromiley and Thomas F. Torrance [Edinburgh: T&T Clark, 1966; repr., Peabody, MA: Hendrickson, 2010], 4/1, 410).

fering and cross-bearing of the Christian. The Christian life is a "cruciform life" by reason of its conformity to Christ, who bore the cross in his own body. To be in union with Christ is to live as members of his body, and thus to be conformed in suffering to his image. Christ's life was marked by suffering, cross-bearing, humiliation, and rejection, so the Christian should not be surprised (in fact, he may even find comfort) when his life also is marked by such trials. "Beloved, do not be surprised at the fiery trial when it comes upon you to test you, as though something strange were happening to you. But rejoice insofar as you share Christ's sufferings, that you may also rejoice and be glad when his glory is revealed" (1 Peter 4:12–13).[33] Paul also strikes the consistent note in his letters that his suffering and trials are a sharing in the suffering and death of Christ, and proof that he belongs to Christ and is reflecting Christ:

> For as we share abundantly in Christ's sufferings, so through Christ we share abundantly in comfort too. (2 Cor. 1:5)

> . . . always carrying in the body the death of Jesus, so that the life of Jesus may also be manifested in our bodies. For we who live are always being given over to death for Jesus' sake, so that the life of Jesus also may be manifested in our mortal flesh. (2 Cor. 4:10–11)

> . . . that I may know him and the power of his resurrection, and may share his sufferings, becoming like him in his death, that by any means possible I may attain the resurrection from the dead. (Phil. 3:10–11)

Suffering, persecution, trials, and rejection are marks of the Christian life because they marked Christ's own life. As Luther wrote:

> The holy Christian people are externally recognized by the holy possession of the sacred cross. They must endure every misfortune and persecution, all kinds of trials and evil from the devil, the world, and the flesh . . . by inward sadness, timidity, fear, outward poverty, contempt, illness, and weakness, in order to become like their head, Christ.[34]

---

[33] Of course, only Christ's death and suffering have atoning efficacy, but when we suffer in the name of Christ we are indeed sanctified.

[34] Luther, "On the Councils and the Churches," in *Works*, Vol. 41, 164. Luther believed that suffering was a true mark of the church.

While the world may applaud our moral aspirations, our sanctifying conformity to Christ may invite its derision. "If the world hates you, know that it has hated me before it hated you. If you were of the world, the world would love you as its own; but because you are not of the world, but I chose you out of the world, therefore the world hates you" (John 15:18–19). Christ's life and death are repulsive to the world because he perfectly reflects the holy image of God, and that image is an indictment of our perverted humanity. Just as God made himself known through the suffering, persecution, humiliation, and death of Christ, we can expect that God will continue to make himself known in the same way through Christ's body, the church.[35] His power is made perfect in weakness (2 Cor. 12:9). We are, after all, being transformed into the image of Christ.

Living in Light of Our Union with Christ

One of the greatest honors and blessings afforded the church is God's invitation and command to participate in his re-creative, transforming work in our lives. By joining us to Christ our sanctification, he liberates us to delight in his holiness and to image Christ in the world. To these ends, God has instituted various blessed means that we are called to employ as we grow up into Christ.[36]

(1) *Faith.* Faith is not only the instrument through which we initially grasp and appropriate Christ; it is also the means by which we continually enjoy his sanctifying presence. As Calvin put it, "Not only does [Christ] cleave to us by an indivisible bond of fellowship, but with a wonderful communion, day by day, he grows more and more into one body with us, until he becomes completely one with us."[37] As we grow in faith, we are transformed into the fullness of Christ (Col. 2:6–7; Eph. 4:11–13). Because sin is so firmly rooted in our failure to believe what we confess, sanctification is, in large part, a matter of bolstering our faith so that we have assurance of who we are in Christ and the conviction to live what we believe: "I believe; help my

---

[35] Startlingly, Paul writes, "Now I rejoice in my sufferings for your sake, and in my flesh I am filling up what is lacking in Christ's afflictions for the sake of his body, that is, the church" (Col. 1:24). We need to make room for this in our doctrine of sanctification.

[36] To this list we may have added many other sanctifying means, such as prayer, suffering, marriage, and self-denial.

[37] *Institutes*, 3.2.24.

unbelief!" (Mark 9:24). This is why the preaching of the gospel starts in the church.[38]

(2) *The written Word of God*. The church is nourished through the Word as we encounter Jesus Christ there, "clothed with his gospel."[39] Jesus prayed to the Father, "Sanctify them in the truth; your word is truth" (John 17:17). We study, meditate and reflect upon, and obey the Word, because "all Scripture is breathed out by God and profitable for teaching, for reproof, for correction, and for training in righteousness, that the man of God may be complete, equipped for every good work" (2 Tim. 3:16–17). By attentively hearing and reading the Word, we grow in our knowledge *of* (not merely *about*) Christ, and live out the purpose for which we were created in him: holiness (Eph. 1:4; 2:10). We receive Christ through his Word and continue to live in him through his Word: "Therefore, as you received Christ Jesus the Lord, so walk in him, rooted and built up in him and established in the faith, just as you were taught" (Col. 2:6–7).

(3) *The body of Christ*. As believers are united to Christ, they are simultaneously united to each other in a living, vital, organic fellowship (1 Cor. 12:12, 27). Our holiness is, therefore, wrapped up in the holiness of the other limbs and organs of Christ's body. Sanctification is no individual affair, for our holiness (and unholiness) is affected by, and affects, the holiness of the body (1 Cor. 5:6; 8:12). If our union with Christ is in fact a profoundly real, personal union, then it follows that our union with each other is the same. We grow in holiness *together*: "Rather, speaking the truth in love, we are to grow up in every way into him who is the head, into Christ, from whom the whole body, joined and held together by every joint with which it is equipped, when each part is working properly, makes the body grow so that it builds itself up in love" (Eph. 4:15–16). Our participation in Christ is where sanctification happens, and that participation is a bodily affair.[40]

(4) *The Lord's Supper*. Just as baptism is the sacrament through which we are included in the death and life of Christ,[41] so in the Lord's

---

[38] We must not overlook the fact that Paul was eager to preach the gospel to the *church* (Rom. 1:15), as well as to those outside the church.

[39] Calvin, *Institutes*, 3.2.6.

[40] See chapter 7 for a more extended discussion on the living reality of the church.

[41] See chapter 8 for an elaboration of this point.

Supper we continue to receive, and be nourished by, the crucified, resurrected Christ. Our participation in the body and blood of Christ is an ongoing participation in his holy presence (1 Cor. 10:16). This is so true that our failure to recognize the reality of this participation is a profaning of the body and blood of the Lord (1 Cor. 11:27–29). Just as we received (and receive) Christ through the preached Word, we continue to grow into him, and with each other, through the visible word, the Supper: "Therefore, let it be regarded as a settled principle that the sacraments have the *same office as the Word of God*: to offer and set forth Christ to us, and in him the treasures of heavenly grace."[42]

(5) *God's law*.[43] There is some confusion about the role of the law in the life of the Christian; some believers even dismiss the Ten Commandments as unnecessary or irrelevant to life in Christ. Such a position is not consonant with the evangelical Protestant tradition.[44] The law, to be sure, has been fulfilled in Christ and, as such, no longer stands against us as an indictment of our unrighteousness (Col. 2:13–14); Christ is our law-fulfilling righteousness (Rom. 3:21–24). However, we are freed from the death-dealing effects of the law through his death and resurrection so that we might live in the holiness of Christ. It is just here that we must remember that Christ is our sanctification, in part, because he is the fulfillment of the law (Matt. 5:17–18): *Christ himself is the embodiment of that law.* Our conformity to Christ is, thus, conformity to the law, which Christ loved (John 15:10) and the psalmists cherished (Psalms 1, 19, 119) precisely because the law is an expression of God's holy character. So the church, freed from the threats of the law, cherishes, follows, and loves God's law as a revelation of who God is.

Conclusion

Salvation is good news, not only because God justifies us in Christ, but also because he sanctifies us in Christ. To overcome our corrupt, sinful natures, God through his Spirit unites us to Jesus Christ—who

---

[42] Calvin, *Institutes*, 4.14.17 (emphasis added). See chapter 8 for further discussion of the living reality of the sacraments.

[43] For the sake of simplicity and brevity, I have equated the law of God with the Ten Commandments here.

[44] The catechisms of Luther, Calvin, Heidelberg, and Westminster (to name just a few) all contain expositions of the Ten Commandments, assuming the sanctifying function of the law in the life of the Christian.

is our sanctification—and includes us in his sin-destroying, life-giving death and resurrection. In and through the death and resurrection of Christ, we have already been made holy, and we are also being made holy, in order that we may be transformed into the very image of God himself, Jesus Christ. God calls us and commands us to participate in this astonishing, image-restoring, re-creative work by exercising our newfound freedom, power, and humanity in Christ.

5

ADOPTION AND SONSHIP IN CHRIST

For in Christ Jesus you are all sons of God, through faith.

GALATIANS 3:26

But to all who did receive him, who believed in
his name, he gave the right to become children of
God, who were born, not of blood nor of the will
of the flesh nor of the will of man, but of God.

JOHN 1:12–13

Jesus Christ is an inexhaustible fountain of blessing to us. When he gives himself to us that we might enjoy him, he is not only our justification—the One through whom we experience the forgiveness of sins and the fellowship of his righteousness—he is also our sanctification—the One through whom we are made holy and are transformed into his image. Yet he is the source of yet another blessing, one so amazing that it would be blasphemous to suggest if it were not true. In our union with Christ, the only begotten Son of God, we participate in what is most precious to him: his relationship with his Father. We are, in union with Christ, adopted into the family of God; we become the children, the sons and daughters, of the Most High God. The blessing of adoptive sonship answers another desperate need we have as sinners. Whereas justification (a forensic benefit) addresses the guilt and condemnation that accompanies sin, and sanctification (a transformative benefit) addresses the depravity and pollution of our nature, adoptive sonship (a familial benefit) addresses our estrangement and alienation from God.

J. I. Packer writes that adoption is "the *highest privilege that the gospel offers*: higher even than justification. . . . Adoption is higher, because of the richer relationship with God that it involves."[1] Donald Fairbairn suggests that, while it is true and important to speak of salvation in terms of justification and sanctification, "neither of these is the central aspect of the Christian life. Instead, forgiveness and becoming Christ-like flow from our participation in a relationship, from our becoming sons and daughters by adoption so as to share in the communion that the natural Son has with God the Father." This understanding of salvation, he asserts, was "widely represented in, and perhaps even the consensus of, the early church."[2] It is not widely known that John Calvin, too, regarded adoption as central to the gospel's benefits: "There are innumerable other ways indeed in which God daily testifies his fatherly love toward us, but the mark of adoption is justly preferred to them all."[3]

Given these testimonies, it is remarkable that the doctrine of adoptive sonship has been so neglected in the history of Christian thought. Packer goes so far as to write that "it is a strange fact that the truth of adoption has been little regarded in Christian history. Apart from two last-century books, now scarcely known . . . there is no evangelical writing on it, nor has there been at any time since the Reformation, any more than there was before."[4] Tim Trumper is right to say that "the time has arrived for our theology of adoption to catch up to our experience of it. It is our belief that a more comprehensive theology

---

[1] J. I. Packer, *Knowing God* (Downers Grove, IL: IVP, 1973), 206–07 (emphasis in original). Packer makes a distinction between adoption as the *highest* blessing and justification as the *primary* and *fundamental* blessing.

[2] Donald Fairbairn, *Life in the Trinity: An Introduction to Theology with the Help of the Church Fathers* (Downers Grove, IL: IVP, 2009), 10.

[3] John Calvin, *Calvin's Commentaries* (Edinburgh: Calvin Translation Society, 1844–56; repr. in 22 vols., Grand Rapids: Baker, 2003), John 17:23.

[4] *Knowing God*, 228. Tim Trumper writes, "[I]n perusing the literature one is not only staggered by the lack of attention adoption has received, but also by the silence about this inattention! As a matter of fact, adoption has rarely been thoroughly considered as a doctrine in its own right" ("The Metaphorical Import of Adoption: A Plea for Realisation. I: The Adoption Metaphor in Biblical Usage," in *Scottish Bulletin of Evangelical Theology*, 14, no. 2 [1996], 131). This regrettable omission has recently begun to be corrected by Trevor Burke, *Adopted into God's Family: Exploring a Pauline Metaphor* (Downers Grove, IL: IVP, 2006), and Robert Peterson, *Adopted by God: From Wayward Sinners to Cherished Children* (Phillipsburg, NJ: P&R, 2001).

of adoption cannot but have a positive effect on the deepening of our filial experience of salvation."[5]

The neglect of adoption in the soteriological understanding of the church is sorely lamentable, for our participation in the sonship of Jesus Christ is indeed basic to the New Testament gospel. From the biblical teaching on adoption, we learn that we are restored to a familial intimacy with God the Father, through which we are assured of his eternal fatherly care and provision, a love and indulgence that exceeds our imaginations. We learn that our relationship to God is so radically changed that we go from being "children of wrath" (Eph. 2:3) to his beloved sons and daughters, a relationship in which the Father vouchsafes to care for our every need. Perhaps even more amazing, we learn that by sharing in the Son we share in his rights as the Firstborn and only begotten Son of God—we are "heirs of God and fellow heirs with Christ" (Rom. 8:17). Our minds and hearts should surely stagger under the weight of this reality. It simply exceeds our comprehension.

All of this makes defining adoption concisely a rather difficult task. Nevertheless, here is my effort:

> Adoption is that benefit of being united to the Son of God through which we share in his sonship with the Father, become the beloved children of God, and enjoy all the privileges and rights of being included in God's family.

Distortions and Misunderstandings of Adoptive Sonship

The reasons for the general neglect of the doctrine of adoption in Christian history are hard to pinpoint. But we may point to two factors in relatively recent theological expression that have contributed to the church's lack of attention to this matter.

The first is that when adoption is treated in theological works (which is not a given), it is more often than not so assimilated into the doctrine of justification that it is eclipsed, obscured, or marginalized.[6] For instance, Louis Berkhof refers to adoption as a "positive

---

[5] Tim Trumper, "The Metaphorical Import of Adoption: A Plea for Realisation. II: The Adoption Metaphor in Theological Usage," in *Scottish Bulletin of Evangelical Theology* 15, no. 2 (1997), 114.

[6] Burke says, "The subsuming of adoption under justification allots a secondary role to the former, which has resulted in the theological integrity of adoption being compromised and the expression being relegated to a secondary position" (*Adopted into God's Family*, 24). Packer calls the treatment of adoption as a sub-section of justification "inadequate" (*Knowing God*, 187).

element of justification," and devotes one page of his approximately seven hundred-page systematic theology text to the topic.[7] Bruce Demarest calls adoption a "significant concomitant of justification," and gives it one page of approximately five hundred in a major work on soteriology.[8] These works are by no means alone. Anthony Hoekema, Millard J. Erickson, and Michael Horton similarly subsume adoption under justification and spill little ink about it.[9]

Why do so many Reformed evangelical theologians treat adoption under the auspices of justification? The answer is not simple, but perhaps one important reason can be found in the classic expression given to adoption in the Westminster Confession (one of the few confessions to explicitly mention adoption). It says:

> All those that are justified, God vouchsafeth, in and for his only Son Jesus Christ, to make partakers of the grace of adoption: by which they are taken into the number, and enjoy the liberties and privileges of the children of God; have his name put upon them; receive the Spirit of adoption; have access to the throne of grace with boldness; are enabled to cry, Abba, Father; are pitied, protected, provided for, and chastened by him as by a father; yet never cast off, but sealed to the day of redemption, and inherit the promises, as heirs of everlasting salvation. (Chap. XII)

We should be thankful to the framers of the confession for including adoption as a major aspect of soteriology, and for doing so with the beauty and simplicity of expression so characteristic of this work. I cannot help but wonder, however, whether the confession's inclusion of adoption under the benefit of justification consigned adoption to dwell in the shadows of justification. The "final papers" on adoption may have been signed here in 1646.[10]

Because adoption has mostly been seen in the light of justification,

---

[7] Louis Berkhof, *Systematic Theology* (1938; repr., Grand Rapids: Eerdmans, 1996), 515–16.

[8] Bruce Demarest, *The Cross and Salvation* (Wheaton, IL: Crossway, 1997), 376–77.

[9] Anthony Hoekema, *Saved by Grace* (Grand Rapids: Eerdmans, 1989), 185–87; Millard J. Erickson, *Christian Theology* (Grand Rapids: Baker, 1998), 974–78; Michael Horton, *The Christian Faith: A Systematic Theology for Pilgrims on the Way* (Grand Rapids: Zondervan, 2011), 642–45.

[10] Or, as Julie Canlis suggests, perhaps the demise of adoption occurred in tandem with the highly influential work of Continental theologian Frances Turretin (1623–87), "who subordinated adoption to justification in the *Theological Institutes* . . . dispossessing adoption of its true character for many years to come" (*Calvin's Ladder: A Spiritual Theology of Ascent and Ascension* (Grand Rapids: Eerdmans, 2010), 133.

adoption has been construed largely along legal, forensic lines. Most of the authors I cited above see adoption either primarily or solely in terms of a change in legal status. Erickson is characteristic here: "In the formal sense, adoption is a declarative matter, an alteration of our legal status."[11]

In this chapter, I will dispute the apparent consensus that adoption is an effect of justification and contend instead that it is best understood in relation to our union with the Son of God. There is no reason to contest that adoption has legal *elements*, but I will contest the claim that adoption is either founded upon or is in essence a legal notion. When adoption, or adoptive sonship, is relegated to the metaphors of the courtroom, the deeply personal and intimate reality of the doctrine can become lost to view.[12]

The second factor that may contribute to the indefinite position of adoption in evangelical soteriology is a tendency to make overly fine theological distinctions. Adoption is sometimes considered in distinction from the blessings of regeneration and of becoming the children of God. According to this view, adoption is confined to the Pauline corpus, where Paul specifically uses the term, while discussions of regeneration and "children of God" language are confined to the Johannine corpus. Trevor Burke frames this argument as follows:

> Thus regeneration, a Johannine term, delineates the imagery of *natural birth*. . . . Adoption, on the other hand, is a forensic term . . . and denotes a legal act or *transfer* from an alien family. . . . Thus Paul and John use two very different metaphors to express the way by which the Christian becomes a member of God's family.[13]

---

[11] *Christian Theology*, 975.

[12] Todd Billings suggests that the way to retain both the legal and relational elements of adoption is to recognize that only the act of *becoming* adopted is primarily forensic: "Theologians have often spoken about the act of *becoming adopted* as a forensic act, which is a valid point. . . . But the forensic sense of becoming adopted sons does not exhaust the meaning of Paul's metaphor, because the result of that act is that one is adopted to be a son or daughter of God, placed in the security of God's family, and given a new identity to live into in an eschatologically conditioned way. Some theologians have thus been too quick to assume that the meaning of 'adoption' is exhausted by the act of *becoming* adopted" (*Union with Christ: Reframing Theology and Ministry for the Church* [Grand Rapids: Baker, 2011], 20). Although Billings's points are to be commended, it is not clear to me that even *becoming adopted* is primarily a forensic act. Neither is it clear why a *forensic* act would have *transformative* results. It would be preferable to say that adoption is a result of *being* personally united to Christ, which union has both forensic and transformative results.

[13] Burke, *Adopted into God's Family*, 27. Burke later softens this distinction, it seems to me, when he asserts that adoption is "inextricably linked with and *dependent* upon Jesus' unique relationship to God as Son" (107). This is enticingly close to saying that adoption is dependent on union with the Father through the Son!—a preferable way to "reconcile" the linguistic differences in John and Paul.

This notion begs some questions. For instance, if the "metaphors" Paul and John use are so very different, did these two apostles have different conceptions about how we become members of God's family? Does Paul think of our familial relationship to God "forensically" while John thinks of it "naturally"? Does John, then, have a different understanding of what it means to say that we are the children of God than Paul does? Are Paul and John presenting disparate pictures of what it means to be included into the family of God? I think the answers to these questions are no.

I will assume in this chapter, based on a canonical reading of Scripture, that despite the nuances certainly present in their thought, Paul and John shared a basic, underlying conviction: we are included in God's family by virtue of being incorporated into God's own Son, Jesus Christ. It is only and ever through union with Jesus Christ that we can experience the blessing of being a member of God's family, or any other soteriological blessing for that matter. Thus, it would be better to say that the various ways in which God (and Paul and John) speaks to us of our familial restoration in Scripture (legal and relational) are expressions of the *same* reality: our participation in the Son of God and his relation to the Father. Only through and in Christ do we have "adoption as sons" (Rom. 8:15, 23; Gal. 4:5; Eph. 1:5), and only in and through Christ are we "born of God" (John 1:13; 1 John 4:7; 5:1) so as to become "children of God" (John 1:12; 1 John 3:1; 5:2).

The fact that God adopts us and we thereby become children of God is based in the reality of God's own relationship to his Son. It is not a reality that is derived from God *external* to himself—a category of blessing that God creates outside of the Father-Son relationship internal to his being—but an existence that is derived from within God's communal being as Father and Son. That is exactly what is so stunning about adoptive sonship—it is a sharing in the Son's own relationship to the Father: "He who loves me will be loved by my Father" (John 14:21). There is no adoption, no other way to be children of God, no experience of the fatherly love of God except through the Father's love for his only begotten Son. Underneath the nuance in the apostolic writings, the same basic reality is being expressed: we have become children of the Father through union with his Son.

These two contributing factors that help explain the relative neglect of adoption might be supplemented by a third, less demonstrable factor. Perhaps adoption is sometimes underplayed or muted because it expresses something almost *too* intimate, *too* personal, and *too* all-encompassing; perhaps we shrink from the claim that God is actually making on our lives when he adopts us. We tend to domesticate, blunt, and mute the unsettling aspects of the gospel. As Todd Billings has it, the fact that God (the King) wants us to be his very sons and daughters is simply too grand a notion:

> [A]doption by the King is *such* a radical notion, we resist it. We would rather have the occasional brush of God's presence, or a relic of his solidarity with us, so that God can be an appendage of *our* identity. But God wants more than that; he wants our lives, our adopted identity. By bringing us into the new reality of the Spirit, we can call out to God—Abba, Father—as adopted children united to Christ. Yet there are few things more countercultural than this process of adoption— losing your life for the sake of Jesus Christ, to find it in communion with the Triune God.[14]

Sharing in the Son's Relationship to the Father

In order to fully appreciate the blessing of adoptive sonship, we must recall the nature of our union with Christ. In chapter 1, I mentioned that the nature of this union determines how we view the redemptive blessings that flow from Christ. This has held true, I trust, with regard to justification and sanctification, and it holds true equally with regard to adoption. To conceive of our *adoption* in Christ as merely or primarily legal in nature—as a change of legal status—suggests that our *union* with Christ must be of a predominantly legal nature as well. That is not the case. Scripture describes our union with Christ in fundamentally personal, relational, intimate, and profoundly real terms, with attending legal elements and benefits. With this in mind, it becomes clear that the blessing of being the children of God is much more, though never less, than a legal affair. Because we truly become one with Christ, we truly share in his relationship with the Father, and so we really are the sons and daughters of God in him.

---

[14] Billings, *Union with Christ*, 18 (emphasis in original).

I noted in chapter 1 that our union with the Son is Trinitarian; that is, it is a union the Son brought about by the power of the Spirit and through which we are united to the Father. This is the theo-logic of salvation: we are restored to fellowship with God through the Son and by the Spirit. And this restoration is based on the great event of the incarnation of the eternal Son of God, in which he assumed our human nature and brought it into union with his divine nature. In this very important sense, our salvation is a participation in God's relational life—the eternal, life-giving bond of love between the Father, Son, and Spirit. Our restoration to fellowship with God, however, takes place in a distinctive way. It happens only as we are joined to the Son, and this reality forms the essence of our adoptive sonship. We become sons of God by being joined to *the* Son of God.

This familial note is clearest in the writings of the apostle John: "But to all who did receive him, who believed in his name, he gave the right to become children of God, who were born, not of blood nor of the will of the flesh nor of the will of man, but of God" (John 1:12–13). Being born as the children of God rests on our receiving the incarnate Word, "the only Son from the Father" (v. 14).

Later in John's Gospel, Jesus himself makes the point even more forcefully that our reception of him is a Trinitarian operation that involves us directly in the Son's unity with the Father:

> And I will ask the Father, and he will give you another Helper, to be with you forever, even the Spirit of truth, whom the world cannot receive, because it neither sees him nor knows him. You know him, for he dwells with you and will be in you. I will not leave you as orphans; I will come to you. Yet a little while and the world will see me no more, but you will see me. Because I live, you also will live. In that day you will know that I am in my Father, and you in me, and I in you. (John 14:16–20)

Through the presence of the indwelling Spirit, Jesus Christ comes to us and is one with us, *even as he is one with the Father.*

As we continue to read in this passage, we find that our being loved *by* Jesus and our loving *of* Jesus are bound up with the Father's love for his Son (v. 21). Further, we encounter the unfathomable statement that Jesus does not come to dwell with us by himself: "If anyone loves me, he will keep my word, and my Father will love him, and we will come to him and make our home with him" (v. 23). It seems that the relationship of love we have with Jesus includes a sharing in the love the Father has for his Son, so much so that the Father and the Son dwell within us. What could be more magnificent than this? Should we not be astonished at this thought?

Two chapters later, Jesus expounds further on this remarkable love when he reveals that the love of the Father abounds to us through our relationship to the Son: "In that day you will ask in my name, and I do not say to you that I will ask the Father on your behalf; for the Father himself loves you, because you have loved me and have believed that I came from God" (John 16:26–27). As we come to love and believe in the Son, we are included in the love the Father has for the Son. In other words, we come to share in the relationship of love between the Father and Son—we share in the privileges of Christ's sonship. This sublime truth is conveyed powerfully as Jesus prays to the Father for the disciples (and us) in John 17:

> I do not ask for these only, but also for those who will believe in me through their word, that they may all be one, *just as you, Father, are in me, and I in you, that they may also be in us,* so that the world may believe that you have sent me. The glory that you have given me I have given to them, *that they may be one even as we are one, I in them and you in me,* that they may become perfectly one, so that the world may know that you sent me and *loved them even as you loved me.* (vv. 20–23)

The italicized sections serve to highlight some important observations. The first is that we must resist the temptation to underinterpret this passage, as if it could be explained merely as a case of Jesus's wishful thinking for the unity of the church (a wish that seems to have gone unfulfilled if we consider the deep historical/denominational divisions in the church). Despite the many sermons we may have heard to the contrary, Jesus is not praying in the hope that the church might be unified in love (although his words most certainly have that implication). Rather, he is telling us what will in fact be the case: he will dwell in us, we will dwell in him, and we will together be in the Father and the Son. This passage, in other words, is not meant merely to provide material for reflection on ecclesiological unity after we have been "saved"; it is describing what it means to *be* saved, to be "the body of Christ."[15]

A second, related observation is that Jesus's prayer indicates in the clearest terms that becoming one with him involves becoming one with the Father, and indeed sharing in the unity the Son has with the Father, with the result that the Father loves us even as he loves the Son—"one of the most remarkable statements of the Gospel, given the enormity of God's love for his uniquely obedient Son."[16] We share in the Father's love for the Son precisely because we share in the Son's oneness with the Father: "To all who did receive him, who believed in his name, he gave the right to become children of God."

John expresses the truth of this filial benefit in other ways as well:

That which we have seen and heard we proclaim also to you, so that you too may have fellowship [Greek, *koinonia*][17] with us; and indeed our fellowship is with the Father and with his Son Jesus Christ. (1 John 1:3)

And we know that the Son of God has come and has given us understanding, so that we may know him who is true; and we are in him who is true, in his Son Jesus Christ. He is the true God and eternal life. (1 John 5:20)

If the church were to draw principally on the letters of John in formulating her soteriological understanding, we would be well within our rights to conclude that salvation, in its basic constitution, is a union with the Son of God through which the church shares in the Son's unity with the Father and enjoys the blessings of God's love for his Son. Salvation, in other words, is about our becoming God's beloved children: "See what kind of love the Father has given to us,

---

[15]The unity of the church is not predicated upon our attempts to secure it. The unity of the church is a given soteriological reality that is to be manifested in the life of the one church. I will expand on this point in chapter 7.

[16]Craig S. Keener, *The Gospel of John: A Commentary*, Vol. II (Peabody, MA: Hendrickson, 2003), 1063.

[17]The Greek word *koinonia*, usually translated "fellowship" in the New Testament, expresses something rather more personal and intimate than the English term suggests. It means something more like a living union with, or participation in, something or someone. See Gerhard Kittel and Gerhard Friedrich, eds., *Theological Dictionary of the New Testament*, 10 volumes (Grand Rapids: Eerdmans, 1965), Vol. 3, 789–809.

that we should be called children of God; and so we are" (1 John 3:1). However, at least in contemporary evangelical Protestant theology, the soteriological emphasis has been elsewhere.[18] We have tended to focus on (equally crucial) categories such as legal guilt and forgiveness.

This has not always been the case, however. As Fairbairn has shown, the early church fathers did in fact understand salvation primarily in terms of participating in the relationship between the Son and the Father, with its attending benefits.[19] If the soteriological musings of the church fathers sometimes seem strange to us, it may be because they were working out their soteriology in light of the great event of the incarnation of the Word of God. The incarnation tells us that the Word took on human flesh in order to incorporate us into his life. And, because Christ is the natural Son of God, when we are joined to him, we become adopted sons of God through him, truly and really sharing in his relationship to the Father through the Spirit.

If salvation is understood in terms of being united to the *person* of Christ, and Christ is indeed the natural Son of God, it is little wonder that the church fathers keyed in on the notion that salvation is about becoming the adopted sons of God through the natural Son of God.[20] This is why the protracted debates in the early church regarding the nature of Christ's person and his precise relation to the Father were so crucial. If Christ was not the natural Son of God, and therefore *not* God himself and *not homoousios* with the Father, if he was only human or only "like" God, then our hope of salvation is lost—we have no authentic connection with God![21] If, however, Christ was indeed the natural Son of God—God himself, *homoousios* with the Father—then in

---

[18] The words of Jonathan Edwards qualify such an assertion: "For, being members of God's own Son, they are in a sort partakers of his relation to the Father: they are not only sons of God by regeneration, but by a kind of communion in the sonship of the eternal Son" (Jonathan Edwards, *Works*, 19:593, cited in Robert W. Caldwell, *Communion in the Spirit: The Holy Spirit as the Bond of Union in the Theology of Jonathan Edwards*, Studies in Evangelical History and Thought [Eugene, OR: Wipf & Stock, 2007], 132).

[19] This is the thesis of his book *Life in the Trinity: An Introduction to Theology with the Help of the Church Fathers* (Downers Grove, IL: IVP, 2009).

[20] This may further explain why adoption has become a neglected doctrine. When union with Christ is not thought of as central to salvation, adoption may be obscured or lost to view.

[21] That argument, of course, works in the reverse as well: if Christ was not fully and authentically human, then salvation is lost on humanity. Hence the words of the Chalcedonian Creed (451): "We, then, following the holy Fathers, all with one consent, teach people to confess one and the same Son, our Lord Jesus Christ, the same perfect in Godhead and also perfect in manhood; truly God and truly man, of a reasonable [rational] soul and body; consubstantial [*homoousios*; "co-essential"] with the Father according to the Godhead, and consubstantial with us according to the Manhood" (cited in John H. Leith, *Creeds of the Churches: A Reader in Christian Doctrine from the Bible to the Present*, third edition [Louisville, KY: Westminster John Knox, 1982], 35–6).

our union with him we become sharers by adoption of what he is by nature. We may balk at the church fathers' use of terms such as *theosis* to describe salvation, but they did not mean by the term that Christians *become God*, but that Christians become participants in the divine life by being united to Jesus Christ, the true and natural Son of God. "The early church repeatedly insisted that Christ had to be none other than the natural Son of God in order to adopt us into God's family. The central feature of that adoption is that we share in the natural Son's fellowship with the Father and the Spirit, and only the natural Son could give us such fellowship."[22] In the words of the second-century church father, Irenaeus of Lyons:

> On what basis could we be sharers in adoption as God's sons? We had to receive, through the Son's agency, participation in him. The Word, having been made flesh, had to share himself with us. That is why he went through every stage of human life, restoring to all of them communion with God.[23]

Jesus's repeated invitations in the Gospel of John to receive him and partake of him—his insistence that *he* is the bread of life and the living water, that *he* is eternal life and the resurrection, that he and the Father are one, that we may be one with him and therefore one with the Father—all tell us that it is only *in him* that we have life, and that this life consists in our restoration to communion with God the Father. Our union with Christ has as one of its elemental consequences our sharing in his relationship to the Father: we are the children of God.

But John's Gospel is not alone in this emphasis. The apostle Paul also makes much of our adoption as sons through union with Jesus Christ.

Union with Christ and Adoption in Paul

The term *adoption* is sometimes used as a broad theological category to describe the New Testament teaching that believers have become chil-

---

[22] Fairbairn, *Life in the Trinity*, 155. Fairbairn includes a helpful discussion on the notion of theosis, 6–10. See also my discussion in chapter 1 of the present work on the difference between theosis and deification.

[23] Irenaeus, *Against Heresies*, 3.18.17, cited in Donald Fairbairn, "Patristic Soteriology: Three Trajectories," in *Journal of the Evangelical Theological Society* 50, no. 2 (June 2007), 295. Fairbairn's article and his book *Life in the Trinity* are highly recommended for evangelicals who wish to be acquainted with early church soteriology.

dren of God or sons of God. However, the term translated "adoption" in the New Testament is unique to Paul's letters. The Greek term is *huiothesia*, which Paul uses five times (Rom. 8:15, 23; 9:4; Gal. 4:5; Eph. 1:5). It is a compound of *huios* ("son") and *thesis* ("placing"), and could be literally rendered "placed as sons," although there is some disagreement among biblical scholars about how best to translate it.[24] Some of the disagreement revolves around whether Paul's use of *huiothesia* is indebted to the practice of adoption in the Roman culture in which he wrote; perhaps Paul was using a term with which his audience would have been familiar in order to build a conceptual bridge to his theological point. If so, then a better understanding of the Roman practice of adoption in the first century would lead us to a clearer understanding of how Paul used the term. This explains why many scholars assume that Paul's use of the term is legal or forensic in nature, reflecting the nature of the practice in the surrounding Roman culture.[25]

There may indeed be some merit in attempting to understand Paul's use of *huiothesia* against the cultural-linguistic backdrop of his day, but there is compelling reason to think that his use of the term was influenced far more by theological considerations than cultural ones.[26] In other words, when Paul speaks of Christians as "placed as sons," he has at the forefront of his mind our being placed in *the* Son, Jesus Christ. Paul's use of *huiothesia*, therefore, is better understood not in terms of the Roman cultural practice, marked by its legal nature, but by his core theological belief that Christians have been united to Jesus Christ, the true and natural Son of God, through which union we are said to be "adopted" as sons. As such, Paul is not "reaching" for cultural analogies as conceptual bridges to explain what it means that we are adopted by God; rather, he is working with a more basic theological notion: the Father-Son relationship that is intrinsic to God's own being, and which we come to share by incorporation into Christ.[27]

---

[24] See J. M. Scott, "Adoption, Sonship," in *Dictionary of Paul and His Letters*, ed. Gerald F. Hawthorne, Ralph P. Martin, Daniel G. Reid (Downers Grove, IL: IVP, 1993), 15–18.

[25] Ibid. Scott thinks there is insufficient evidence to establish a case for adoption as a legal metaphor.

[26] Burke recognizes the cultural influences at work in Paul's thinking without reducing his thought to those influences alone. Indeed, Paul's notion of adoption differs from his ancient social context precisely at the point of his insistence that adoption comes about through union with the Son of God (*Adopted into God's Family*, 123, 194–95).

[27] This does not mean that first-century Roman adoptive practices are absent from Paul's mind, but that Paul's thought is *rooted* in a reality that cannot be captured by the common cultural understandings of his time. As helpful as social, cultural, and linguistic studies of first-century Rome may be,

This means that Paul's understanding of our "sonship" in Jesus Christ is remarkably (and understandably) similar to John's. A brief look at the key passages ought to bear this observation out. A suitable place to begin is Ephesians 1:3–6:

> Blessed be the God and Father of our Lord Jesus Christ, who has blessed us *in Christ* with every spiritual blessing in the heavenly places, even as he chose us *in him* before the foundation of the world, that we should be holy and blameless before him. *In love he predestined us for adoption as sons through Jesus Christ*, according to the purpose of his will, to the praise of his glorious grace, with which he has blessed us *in the Beloved*.

The italicized portions of the text serve to emphasize the point that every spiritual blessing we receive from the Father, including our adoption as sons, takes place *in and through Jesus Christ*. This emphasis is consonant with what I have argued throughout, that Paul understands salvation, in all of its phases and features, as revolving around union with Christ. Adoption is no exception; it takes place "in Christ," "through Jesus Christ," and "in the Beloved." Union with Christ—understood here in its "predestinarian" phase and actualized through faith (as we shall see)—is the arena in which adoption takes place.

In fact, in all but one instance where Paul uses the term *huiothesia*, the context strongly suggests that he is thinking of adoption in terms of being included in Christ ("Son-placed"). For example, Romans 8:14–16 says:

> All who are led by the Spirit of God are sons of God. For you did not receive the spirit of slavery to fall back into fear, but you have received the Spirit of adoption as sons [*huiothesias*], by whom we cry "Abba! Father!" The Spirit himself bears witness with our spirit that we are children of God.

Three contextual clues suggest that Paul is thinking in terms of being included in Christ's sonship: (1) Paul attested earlier in the same chapter to Jesus's unique sonship (v. 3), (2) he asserted that it is through

---

Paul's thought is captured best by the inner logic of the gospel he preached: we know God the Father through incorporation into his Son.

"the Spirit of God" or "the Spirit of Christ" that we belong to Christ, and that he dwells in us (vv. 9–10), and (3) he is about to declare that God's ultimate purpose for believers is that they be "conformed to the image of his Son" (v. 29). Adoption is clearly couched in the context of Jesus's sonship and our participation in that sonship through his indwelling of believers by the Spirit. To have "received the Spirit of adoption" is thus to have benefitted from Christ's sonship through the Spirit of Christ. Perhaps even more telling is that the sons of God are enabled to cry to the Father in a way that echoes Jesus's own cry to his Father: "And he said, '*Abba, Father*, all things are possible for you. Remove this cup from me. Yet not what I will, but what you will'" (Mark 14:36).[28]

The relation of adoption to union with Christ is even clearer in our final passage, Galatians 4:4–6:

> But when the fullness of time had come, God sent forth his Son, born of woman, born under the law, to redeem those who were under the law, so that we might receive adoption as sons [*huiothesian*]. And because you are sons, God has sent the Spirit of his Son into our hearts, crying, "Abba! Father!"

This passage is similar to Romans 8 in that there is the evident priority of God's own Son in relation to the term *huiothesia*—we receive adoption only insofar as "God sent forth *his Son*"—and we find again the role of the "Spirit of his Son" in the witness to our adoption. Most important, however, in the verses immediately preceding, Paul has made clear how we become sons of God: "For in Christ Jesus you are all sons of God, through faith. For as many of you as were baptized into Christ have put on Christ" (Gal. 3:26–27). Evidently, then, adoptive sonship in Paul is best understood as a benefit of salvation that believers enjoy as they are united to Christ ("in Christ," "baptized into Christ," "put on Christ").

John Chrysostom (347–407), the preeminent fourth-century preacher and archbishop of Constantinople, thought Paul's assertion was awe-inspiring:

---

[28] Douglas Moo attributes the source of Paul's notion of sonship to the "unique sonship of Christ" (*The Epistle to the Romans*, New International Commentary on the New Testament [Grand Rapids: Eerdmans, 1996], 499). He adds, "We, 'the sons of God,' are such by virtue of our belonging to *the* Son of God" (ibid., 505).

Since [Paul] had said something great and remarkable, he also explains how one is made a son. "For as many of you as were baptized into Christ have put on Christ." Why didn't he say, "All of you who were baptized into Christ have been born of God," since that is the inference from showing that they were sons? Because what he says is more awe-inspiring. For if Christ is the Son of God and you put him on, having the Son inside yourself and being made like him, you have been made one in kind and form.[29]

Adoption is more than a legal metaphor. In Paul's thought, it conveys more than a mere legal transfer of rights or privileges to the adopted sons of God. All the rights and privileges of being the children of God are conveyed to us in our union with God's own Son, a union that Paul thinks of in the most intimate and profoundly real ways. In our union with the person of Christ in salvation, we share in his personal relationship to the Father and the glorious benefits that attend that relationship: we are co-heirs with Christ, we can cry to the Father as Jesus did, the Father loves us as he loves his own Son, the Father hears our prayers, and more. God does not just think of us *as if* we were his children; we *are* his children through our participation in his Son.

It is important to note that this does not mean that we are the sons of God in exactly the same way that Jesus is *the* Son of God; he alone is the true and natural son of God, the "firstborn of all creation" (Col. 1:15) and the "only begotten Son" (John 3:16). For this reason, there has been a consistent refrain in the history of the church asserting that what Christ is by nature we can become only by the grace of adoption:

Augustine: "[Paul] says *adoption* so that we may clearly understand that the Son of God is unique. For we are the sons of God through his generosity and the condescension of his mercy, whereas he is the Son by nature, sharing in the same divinity with the Father."[30]

Calvin: "To this name [only begotten] Christ has a right, because he is by nature *the only Son of God*; and he communicates this honor to us by adoption, when we are engrafted into his body."[31]

---

[29] John Chrysostom, "Homily on Galatians," cited in *Ancient Christian Commentary on Scripture, New Testament VIII, Galatians, Ephesians, Philippians*, ed. Mark J. Edwards (Downers Grove, IL: IVP, 1999), 51.
[30] Augustine, "Epistle to the Galatians," cited in ibid., 56 (emphasis in original).
[31] Calvin, *Commentaries*, John 3:16 (emphasis in original).

Heidelberg Catechism (Lord's Day 13): Q. 33. "Why is [Christ] called God's only-begotten Son, since we also are the Children of God?" A. "Because Christ alone is the eternal natural Son of God; but we are children of God by adoption through grace for his sake."[32]

Thomas Boston: "A third benefit flowing from union with Christ, is adoption. Believers, being united to Christ, become children of God, and members of the family of heaven. By their union with Him, who is the Son of God by nature, they become the sons of God by grace."[33]

These venerable sources are of the same mind, that adoption helps us to understand how we can truly become the children of God only in and through the natural Son of God. Adoption, thus, simultaneously protects the uniqueness of Christ's sonship while conveying to us a sense of the deep, personal intimacy involved in our union with him.

The parallel with the doctrine of justification might be instructive here: God justifies us (declares us righteous) because we share in the righteousness *of Christ* through our union with him. Similarly, God adopts us (declares us his children) because we share in the sonship *of Christ* through our union with him. Our righteousness and sonship are derived, not intrinsic; we benefit only by participation in what uniquely and properly belongs to the eternal Son of God. In both cases, God is declaring what is actually rather than virtually true of us, by reason of the fact that we are actually united to the person of Christ. Adoption may be said to preserve the distinction between Christ's sonship and ours, just as imputation preserves the distinction between Christ's righteousness and ours.[34] However, just as justification is no legal fiction, adoption is no legal metaphor. They both have legal benefits, to be sure, but they are rooted in a true, vital, organic, and profoundly real union with Jesus Christ. Adoption conceived in merely

---

[32] Cited in James T. Dennison Jr., *Reformed Confessions of the 16th and 17th Centuries in English Translation: Vol. 2, 1552–1566* (Grand Rapids: Reformation Heritage Books, 2010), 777.

[33] Thomas Boston, *Human Nature in Its Fourfold State* (Carlisle, PA: Banner of Truth Trust, 1964; repr., 1989), 292–93.

[34] Theologians in the federalist tradition have typically balked at speaking of a participation in the sonship of Christ, fearing that it trespasses upon the ontological relations among the members of the Trinity. Thus, John Murray has written, "In modern theology it is sometimes said that men by adoption come to share in Christ's sonship and thus enter into the divine life of the Trinity. This is grave confusion and error. The eternal Son of God is the only-begotten and no one shares in his Sonship, just as God the Father is not the Father of any other in the sense in which he is the Father of the only-begotten and eternal Son" (*Redemption Accomplished and Applied* [Grand Rapids: Eerdmans, 1955], 134). I beg to differ with Murray on this point and am hopeful that the parallel with justification may be helpful here.

legal ways would, in the end, leave us in a situation in which it would be more appropriate to say that we are the sons-*in-law* and daughters-*in-law* of God, or the brothers-*in-law* and sisters-*in-law* of Christ. I believe that the Bible says more: we are children of our heavenly Father by virtue of our union with his Son—we *really are* his children.[35]

The Order of Salvation

The doctrine of adoptive sonship raises some important questions about the order of the application of salvation. These questions typically have been addressed by what is called the *ordo salutis*, a Latin phrase employed by theologians to describe how the various benefits of salvation (such as those we have been discussing in this work) are related to one another. Berkhof defines the *ordo salutis* as follows:

> The *ordo salutis* describes the process by which the work of salvation, wrought in Christ, is subjectively realized in the hearts and lives of sinners. It aims at describing in their logical order, and also their interrelations, the various movements of the Holy Spirit in the application of the work of redemption.[36]

Every theological work aiming to describe salvation is based on a concept of how the benefits of salvation are ordered. Many of these works have specific chapters or sections devoted to the topic of the order of salvation.[37] But even those texts that do not devote a separate discussion to the *ordo salutis* imply an order by the way in which they arrange the benefits they discuss. If we peruse any systematic theological text, it quickly becomes evident that the author is deliberately presenting the application of salvation in one order or another. However, every Christian, not just the professional theologian, has explicit or implicit assumptions about how salvation is "ordered," about what is primary or secondary when it comes to the saving graces of Christ.

---

[35] The English word *adoption* is potentially misleading as a way of describing the intimacy of our familial relation to God. While an adopted child may indeed enjoy great physical and emotional closeness with his/her new siblings, we would never say of the adoptee that he or she is vitally, organically, or truly joined to natural sons or daughters, but only in a merely metaphorical sense. But we do, and should, say this of the one joined to Christ.

[36] *Systematic Theology*, 415–16.

[37] In addition to Berkhof, one may consult with profit Murray, *Redemption*, 79–87; Hoekema, *Saved by Grace*, 11–27; Demarest, *The Cross and Salvation*, 36–44.

And every Christian is bound to have questions about the interrelations of the myriad blessings of salvation we read about in the Bible.

This is a fitting place to discuss the order of salvation because this chapter has raised some of the very questions that an *ordo salutis* seeks to answer. For instance, when we speak of becoming the children of God by adoption, are we to conceive of adoption as taking place after we are justified or before we are justified? Can we be children of God *before* we are justified by him? We may ask similar questions of sanctification or justification: are we sanctified before or after we are justified? before or after we are adopted? Not only can these questions be multiplied with respect to other aspects of salvation, but there is the further question of how we are to relate these aspects to one another: are they causally, temporally, or logically related? (In other words, does faith cause justification, and does faith precede justification in time or merely logically?) Perhaps an even more important question for the frustrated beginning theological student is this: How important are our answers to these questions? Do the answers matter all that much?

The answer to the latter question is a very definite yes, but perhaps not for the reasons one might think. The first reason is that the Bible itself gives us indications that the plethora of saving benefits we experience are not an undifferentiated, unrelated mass. Although the Bible does not lay out an order of salvation in comprehensive or specific terms, there are clearly some aspects of salvation that "precede" or "follow" others. Many have taken Romans 8:30, for instance, as providing a foundation for an *ordo salutis*: "And those whom he predestined he also called, and those whom he called he also justified, and those whom he justified he also glorified." Other passages also suggest that salvation has an order, in at least some sense (John 3:3; 1 Cor. 1:30; 6:11; Gal. 2:15–16; Eph. 2:5–10).

The other reason why our understanding of the ordering of salvation matters is that the way in which we conceive of how salvation is ordered deeply influences, consciously or subconsciously, how we conceive of what (or *who*) salvation *is*, and vice versa. Our most basic understanding of salvation is reflected in the way we think and talk about how salvation "happens." I will elaborate on this point below.

The *ordo salutis* has been framed in various ways by various theologians with varying degrees of complexity.[38] Thinking through the way salvation is applied can be helpful in that, by doing so, we are reflecting on the manifold ways we are blessed by God. Distinguishing and recounting the various ways that God blesses us in Christ through the Spirit ought to lead us to an appreciation of the depth and beauty of salvation. An *ordo salutis* can also be helpful because it helps us to think through carefully—and learn to confess and prayerfully wonder at—the relations and distinctions among the benefits of Christ, so that we do not become theologically careless. It can help us to be clear about why we would not want to say, for instance, that sanctification is the cause of justification or adoption, for doing so would violate the truth that God loves and forgives us purely by a movement of his unmerited grace, not because he finds us to be holy. An *ordo salutis* also can help us to be clear about the difference between logical and temporal priority. For instance, on the one hand, we should affirm that faith precedes adoption logically but *not* temporally, and on the other hand, we should affirm that our election in Christ precedes justification both logically *and* temporally ("before the foundation of the world"). So, an *ordo salutis* can help us to consider, carefully and humbly, important distinctions among the saving benefits of Christ and how they are applied to sinners.

However, thinking in terms of an *ordo salutis* can also be unhelpful, obscuring our understanding of the nature of salvation. When the order of salvation is conceived of in a linear fashion, as the application of Christ's benefits in a logical or causal sequence of events, we run the risk of losing the forest (Christ himself) for the trees (his benefits). An order of salvation as traditionally conceived can convey the impression that the application of Christ's benefits (his work) is a mechanistic process by which we receive, in a logical sequence, a series of abstracted blessings that are applied apart from Christ's person. This impression is certainly not *intentional*, but may be conveyed nevertheless.

Consider, for example, the Reformed stalwart Berkhof, who prefaces his presentation of the *ordo salutis* with the caution that the ap-

---

[38] See Demarest, *The Cross and Salvation*, 36–40. Berkhof writes, "In view of the fact that the Bible does not specify the exact order that applies in the application of the work of redemption, there is naturally considerable room for a difference of opinion. And as a matter of fact the Churches are not all agreed as to the *ordo salutis*" (*Systematic Theology*, 417).

plication of the grace of God to the sinner is a "unitary process." Within this unitary process, however, various movements can be distinguished. While the Bible does not explicitly provide us with an exact order of salvation, he writes, "it offers us a sufficient basis for such an order."[39] After he notes how Reformed theologians have typically stressed that calling and regeneration precede the act of conversion (faith and repentance),[40] Berkhof then proceeds to offer his understanding of the majority Reformed view of the application of Christ's benefits:

> The discussion of faith naturally leads to that of justification, inasmuch as this is mediated to us by faith. And because justification places man in a new relation to God, which carries with it the gift of the Spirit of adoption, and which obliges man to a new obedience and also enables him to do the will of God from the heart, the work of sanctification next comes into consideration. Finally, the order of salvation is concluded with the doctrine of the perseverance of the saints and their final glorification.[41]

So, Berkhof's understanding of the order of salvation is: faith, justification, adoption, sanctification, perseverance, glorification. Even when we take into consideration his important qualification that salvation is a "unitary process," and that these soteriological distinctions are logical ones and not temporal (i.e., justification, adoption, and [definitive] sanctification take place simultaneously), it is still evident that Berkhof conceives of the application of the benefits in a *causal* sense. He writes that justification "carries with it the Spirit of adoption" and "obliges" one to new obedience (sanctification), and so functions as the *cause* of both adoption and sanctification.[42]

But we must ask, where in this order is any mention of the one

---

[39] *Systematic Theology*, 416.

[40] We are leaving aside the question of those acts of God that precede the application of Christ's benefits (e.g., election, calling, regeneration) in the interest of focusing more narrowly on the specific subjects covered in this book.

[41] *Systematic Theology*, 418. A similar order is followed by Murray (*Redemption*, 87). Curiously, while both Berkhof and Murray state elsewhere in their works that union with Christ is foundational in the application of salvation, their descriptions of the *ordo salutis* seem to obscure this point.

[42] Horton follows Berkhof in seeing the *ordo* as essentially forensically driven: "I am suggesting that we view all the items in the Pauline *ordo* as constituting one train, running on the same track, with justification as the engine that pulls adoption, new birth, sanctification, and glorification in tow. . . . This means that we never leave the forensic domain even when we are addressing other topics in the *ordo* besides justification proper" (*The Christian Faith*, 708).

basic soteriological reality that undergirds and allows for the application of these benefits: the application of Christ himself? Why present justification as logically preceding and including adoption when Christ is himself, in our union with him, the source and cause of both? Why are justification and adoption said to logically precede sanctification when Jesus Christ is also our sanctification in our union with him? Why say that justification "obliges" us to obedience when it is our participation in the crucified, resurrected Christ that sanctifies us? The answer seems to be that when our union with Christ is removed from a discussion of the order of salvation, Christ's benefits replace his person and are made to perform causally what Christ performs by joining us to him personally. The unintentional net effect is that salvation is conceived of as a series of benefits that lead to one another, benefits abstracted from Christ's person, suggesting that we could know the salvation of Christ from his benefits alone.

While Richard Gaffin appreciates the insights gained from historical reflection on the *ordo salutis*, he has noted this de-personalizing tendency in his own Reformed tradition:

> But it does seem fair to observe that a prevailing tendency down to the present has been to be preoccupied with the various benefits of Christ's work, and their interrelations, logical, causal and sometimes even temporal, *ordo salutis* in this sense. So that while Christ himself is certainly there, the danger is that, in matters of application, he fades, more or less, into the background. In effect, in some instances more than others, the focus has been, we may say, on *ordo* at the expense of *salutis*. . . . In concentrating on the various benefits of Christ's work or on one particular benefit, like justification, he, in his person and work, recedes into the background.[43]

An order of salvation conceived of in the traditional sense, while intending to exalt the work and benefits of Christ as applied to believers, may end up losing sight of the saving person of Christ. But Jesus Christ does not bestow his benefits in the abstract; he bestows *himself* to us, that we might enjoy who he is for us in all his saving graces. In

---

[43] Richard B. Gaffin Jr., "Union with Christ: Some Biblical and Theological Reflections," in *Always Reforming: Explorations in Systematic Theology*, ed. A. T. B. McGowan (Downers Grove, IL: IVP, 2006), 280.

our union with him, he is the cause of our justification, sanctification and adoption. And because it is Jesus Christ in the fullness of his person and work whom we receive in salvation, we receive all that he is to us simultaneously, never one benefit without the other.

We cannot divide the salvation we have in Christ into a linear, logically and causally related series of benefits without obscuring this point or, for that matter, without obscuring the benefits. "Union with Christ," writes Sinclair Ferguson, "must therefore be the dominant motif in any formulation of the application of redemption and the dominant feature of any 'order' of salvation."[44] The application of redemption is not a series of separate, causally related events, but rather distinct aspects of a single, all-encompassing reality. What makes the application of salvation a "unitary process" is not that God has decided to include one benefit along with another, but that in salvation God has included us in the one Jesus Christ. With this realization in mind, we are free to discuss his benefits in any *ordo* we wish, with no fear of confusing the benefits, and without the need to subsume one benefit underneath another.[45] Christ does more than "order" our salvation, and he is more than a giver of "gifts." The crucified, resurrected, living Jesus Christ *is* our salvation.

Conclusion

This truth is perhaps made clearest through the benefit of adoption. The Son's relationship to his Father is everything to him, for he has existed eternally in the intimate love of his Father. The love of the Father for his Son is the source of all love and the ground of all life. It is a love so extravagant that it overflowed into the creation of the world— God the Father created all things through and *for* his Son (Col. 1:16). In joining himself to us, the Son of God has signaled the re-creation of all things by opening up to us the love the Father has for him. He became one with us to make known the love the Father has for him.

---

[44] Sinclair B. Ferguson, "Ordo Salutis," in *New Dictionary of Theology*, ed. S. B. Ferguson and D. F. Wright (Downers Grove, IL: IVP, 1988), 480–81.

[45] It is important to note here that I am referring to the *application of redemption* in space and time. Some of the benefits of our union with Christ occur above and beyond time (our election in Christ, for instance). What further confounds orders of salvation that are conceived in linear, logical fashion is that many of the benefits of salvation are both received in our union with Christ through faith and yet await their consummation at his second advent (for instance, our sanctification, adoption, and even glorification).

But let us be perfectly clear—Jesus came to do more than preach *about* the Father's love for us; he came to make this love known *in us*:

> O righteous Father, even though the world does not know you, I know you, and these [those given to the Son by the Father] know that you have sent me. I made known to them your name, and I will continue to make it known, *that the love with which you have loved me may be in them, and I in them.* (John 17:25–26)

To be joined to Jesus Christ is to participate in the love the Father has for the Son. It means we now belong to God as his children, and the Father now loves us no less than he loves his only begotten. It is difficult to conceive of a greater benefit than this because it impossible to conceive of a love deeper than this. How incredible, then, is the doxology that pours forth from John's pen: "See what kind of love the Father has given to us, that we should be called children of God; and so we are" (1 John 3:1). Jesus Christ is our salvation because in him, and only in him, we share in the love that alone can be called eternal life.

6

PRESERVATION AND GLORIFICATION IN CHRIST

I give them eternal life, and they will never perish,
and no one will snatch them out of my hand.

JOHN 10:28

But our citizenship is in heaven, and from it we await
a Savior, the Lord Jesus Christ, who will transform
our lowly body to be like his glorious body.

PHILIPPIANS 3:20–21

We are accustomed, and even conditioned, to think of salvation in the past tense. This is reflected in the language we use to describe our salvation—"I have been saved"—and in the queries we direct to others—"When were you saved?" This use of the past tense indicates the way we conceive of salvation, for it reveals something we feel is basic to the good news of our salvation in Christ—that he has fully and objectively accomplished our salvation in his life, death, resurrection, and ascension, and that we have been made beneficiaries of his finished work through faith. We rightly insist, therefore, that salvation is not the product of a lifetime of moral achievement or the effect of years of gradual religious ascendancy. One of the wonderful aspects of the gospel is that it tells us we have *already* been united to Christ, we have *already* been justified in Christ, we have *already* been sanctified, adopted, and raised with and in Christ—through Christ, we are *already* beneficiaries of his glorious salvation. This completed aspect of the gospel provides Christians the assurance of their blessed and secure state, and on that assurance we rest our firm hope and conviction of things to come. Our use of the past tense, in other words, expresses a truth without which the gospel would cease to be truly good news. It is good news in large part because we *can* express it in the past tense.

This chapter, however, is about how salvation ought to be expressed in the present and future tenses as well. Our salvation in Christ is so comprehensive that, in addition to speaking of *having been* saved, we have biblical warrant to speak of the fact that we *are being* saved and *will be* saved in Christ—the present and future tenses of salvation are also integral to the gospel. There has been a tendency in evangelical theology to so stress the importance of the finished work of Christ that we lose sight of the ongoing work of Christ, through which he *is* saving us, and the yet-to-be-completed work of Christ, through which he *will* save us.[1] In an effort to accentuate the completed work of Christ, we often so "front-load" the gospel that we fail to incorporate other aspects of salvation with which we are less familiar or less comfortable, but that are no less decisive for what it means to experience salvation. When this happens, the gospel becomes truncated and we struggle to appreciate the richness and depth of our salvation in Christ. Thus, when Paul, for instance, tells us to "work out your own salvation with fear and trembling" (Phil. 2:12), that we were "created in Christ Jesus for good works" (Eph. 2:10), or that we have been predestined "to be conformed to the image of [God's] Son" (Rom. 8:29), we are sometimes at a loss to explain why this, too, is the gospel.

The present and future tenses of the gospel help us see the wonderful expanse of salvation, and to that end in this chapter I will describe two further benefits of being united to Christ: preservation and glorification.

To say that we are *preserved in Christ* means that once we have been joined to him, he continues to hold us close to him and promises to

---

[1] This may be explained, in part, by the tendency in evangelical soteriology to view justification as the primary motif of the gospel, as virtually synonymous with salvation.

never let us go. He unfolds the blessings of our union with him as he perpetually gives himself to us, that we may flourish, grow, and be blessed in an ongoing intimacy with him. He continues to mediate the blessings of which we have already partaken: though we are justified in Christ, he continues to uphold our justification through daily forgiveness and his everlasting intercession; though we are sanctified in Christ, we continue to grow into ever-increasing conformity to his image; and though we are adopted in Christ, we continue to grow into the maturity befitting the blessed sons and daughters of God.

To say that we are, and shall be, *glorified in Christ* means that our union with him will reach its full, final, and glorious climax as we are raised in our bodies to enjoy everlasting perfect communion with and likeness to Christ. As we come to the full realization of our glorification in Christ, the benefits of which we have already partaken, and which he has continually upheld and preserved, will be fully realized. Having been justified in Christ, we will be justified in him at the great day of judgment; we will know the completion of our sanctification—our perfect conformity to the image of Christ; and, as sharers in Christ's sonship, we will receive the full rights and blessings of the children of God. Indeed, Christ has saved us, is saving us, and certainly will save us.

Preservation in Christ

Let us begin with a definition of preservation in Christ:

> All those united to Christ will never be separated from him, and, being preserved by him, they will persevere in the enjoyment and manifestation of the abundant blessings of salvation in him.

The doctrine of preservation in Christ is another way of stating a teaching enshrined in the Reformed evangelical tradition: "the perseverance of the saints" (or of "true believers"). The terms *preservation* and *perseverance*, rightly understood, are both helpful for describing the biblical truth that our salvation in Christ is totally secure. *Preservation* highlights the Godward side of this truth: God will never lose or forsake those who belong to his Son. *Perseverance* highlights the manward side of this truth: those in Christ will never finally fail to endure in that salvation (they will stand firm to the end in faith).

John Murray and Anthony Hoekema prefer the designation *perse-verance of the saints*, as opposed to *preservation*, in order to guard against the notion that a believer is "secure as to his eternal salvation quite irrespective of the extent to which he may fall into sin and backslide from faith and holiness."[2] Murray, Hoekema, and others in the Reformed tradition are rightly concerned to guard against the notion of *eternal security*, understood as the belief that a Christian once saved is always saved without respect to a subsequent life of enduring faith and holiness in Christ. The perseverance of the saints is intended to highlight the truth that, while salvation is indeed totally secure, it is secure precisely because God enables and guarantees the perseverance of believers in faith and holiness: "Now it is God who makes both us and you stand firm in Christ" (2 Cor. 1:21, NIV1984). True believers, by God's grace, neither totally nor finally abandon the faith, and they stand firm in their faith to the end.

The Westminster Confession of Faith articulates the doctrine of perseverance as follows:

> They whom God has accepted in his Beloved, effectually called and sanctified by his Spirit, can neither totally nor finally fall away from the state of grace; but shall certainly persevere therein to the end, and be eternally saved. (17.1)

The emphases and safeguards that accompany the historic Reformed doctrine of perseverance are important, laudable, and should be retained. In my view, however, the term *preservation* is better suited to convey the truth that God infallibly secures the totality of our salvation in Christ. The definition I have provided above includes that which the doctrine of the perseverance of the saints aims to protect while simultaneously placing the emphasis where I believe the Bible does: we are *preserved* in Christ, and therefore we *persevere* in Christ. It emphasizes, in other words, the truth that God so preserves us in Christ that our lives actually reflect the effect of that preservation. This is because salvation is not an object or an abstraction—a gift that can be received and potentially ignored—but rather a participation in

---

[2] John Murray, *Redemption Accomplished and Applied* (Grand Rapids: Eerdmans, 1955), 154. See also Anthony Hoekema, *Saved By Grace* (Grand Rapids: Eerdmans, 1989), 236.

the living Christ and all of his blessings. Salvation in Christ, and the total security that accompanies that salvation, includes the believer's ongoing participation in Christ and his blessings. This does not mean that the saints do not fall into sin. It does mean, however, that God will never forsake those united to Christ, and therefore they will endure in the faith and holiness that are proper to that union. To put this another way, God is preserving us in a real, life-giving union with Christ, the blessings of which are necessarily manifest in the lives of those vitally united to him. Salvation would not be salvation if those united to Christ did not continue to live out the benefits of that saving union.

The advantage of using the phrase "preservation *in Christ*" over that of "perseverance *of the saints/true believers*" is twofold. First, it grounds the truth of God's infallible saving purpose in the underlying reality that secures it: our indissoluble union with Christ. Second, while it strenuously maintains that believers will indeed persevere in their faith, it locates that perseverance in the faithfulness of Jesus Christ, who will not fail to manifest himself and his blessings in those who belong to him. The union is indissoluble exactly because it is an actual, ongoing life *in the living Christ*, which he maintains by his continual presence and nourishment. This way of putting the matter emphasizes that the perseverance of the saints is inevitable due to the fact that salvation is a living, ongoing reality, a participation in Jesus Christ and his saving blessings. Believers endure in faith and holiness because Christ is faithful to maintain them in their faith and holiness, and this truth is inseparable from what it means to say that Christ *saves us*.[3]

I will explore this twofold reality by referring to (1) God's preservation of those he indissolubly joins to Christ and (2) the manifestation of that preservation in the lives of those united to Christ.

GOD PRESERVES US BY JOINING US
INDISSOLUBLY TO JESUS CHRIST

The gospel is full of inconceivably extravagant promises from our Father. He has given these promises to provide his children with the full

---

[3] Our preservation in Christ insures and demands our perseverance because salvation is far more like a marriage union than a Christmas present, the fidelity and fruits of which marriage are guaranteed and protected by the perfectly faithful Bridegroom, Jesus Christ.

assurance of his freely given, irrevocable love, and they are grounded in his steadfast, immovable, unchangeable faithfulness; what God promises he will infallibly bring to pass. And all the promises the Father makes are bound up inextricably in Jesus Christ, in whom they are fulfilled and completed: "For no matter how many promises God has made, they are 'Yes' in Christ" (2 Cor. 1:20, NIV1984). In order to bring to fruition all that he has promised us, God joins us indissolubly to the One in whom all the promises are contained, fulfilled, and secured. It is only in Christ that we benefit from any of God's lavish pledges.

Thus, the assurance believers have that God will infallibly save them, and that they will never cease to be saved, is rooted in their being joined to the Savior. The Father gives us to the Son, and it is the Father's will that the Son save us to the uttermost: "And this is the will of him who sent me, that I should lose nothing of all that he has given me, but raise it up on the last day. For this is the will of my Father, that everyone who looks on the Son and believes in him should have eternal life, and I will raise him up on the last day" (John 6:39–40). Our separation from Jesus Christ would mean nothing less than the failure of the Son to accomplish the Father's will. If any of those given to Christ were not to be preserved and resurrected, D. A. Carson writes, "it would be to the Son's everlasting shame: it would mean either that he was incapable of performing what the Father willed him to do, or that he was flagrantly disobedient to his Father. Both alternatives are unthinkable."[4]

Once joined to Christ, believers will never be separated from him. This is not because our grasp on Christ is so strong, but because his grip on us is unbreakable. We are not only perfectly and eternally preserved in Christ because his grasp is insuperable, but, should we need even greater assurance, Jesus tells us that his hold on us is undergirded by the invincible grasp of his Father: "I give [my sheep] eternal life, and they will never perish, and no one will snatch them out of my hand. My Father, who has given them to me, is greater than all, and no one is able to snatch them out of the Father's hand. I and the Father are one" (John 10:28–30). The Son and the Father have a common and

---

[4] D. A. Carson, *The Gospel According to John*, Pillar New Testament Commentary (Grand Rapids: Eerdmans, 1991), 291.

mutually re-enforcing grasp on those who belong to them. Indeed, we can say more: our preservation in Christ is anchored in the personal relations and purposes of the Father, Son, and Spirit. The Father gives us to his Son through his Spirit or, alternatively, the Spirit joins us to the Son, and through the Son to the Father (John 14:16–20). Only a breach in the common unity and will of the triune Godhead could sever us from Jesus Christ.

There is another important reason why we should insist on speaking of preservation *in Christ*. Because all of God's promises are contained and fulfilled in Christ, we are beneficiaries of these promises only insofar as we are included in Christ. If we are included in him, then we are *already* beneficiaries of all God's promises in him. The reason, in other words, that God infallibly preserves us in Christ is because we have already been made the benefactors of all that Christ has done in his person and work—God is accomplishing in us exactly what he has already accomplished in Christ, and God does not change his mind.

The clearest example of this is the fact that the Father has chosen and predestined us in Christ, having "blessed us in Christ with every spiritual blessing in the heavenly places" (Eph. 1:3). Our election in Christ guarantees that we will experience all the blessings that are already ours in him: "And those whom [God] predestined he also called, and those whom he called he also justified, and those whom he justified he also glorified" (Rom. 8:30). It is no wonder, then, that Paul can exclaim that nothing, absolutely nothing, is able to separate us from the love of God that is in Christ Jesus (Rom. 8:39). God will never cease to preserve us in Christ precisely because he has already blessed us in Christ. Because God has never contemplated us *outside of Christ*, he will never stop contemplating us *inside of Christ*.

When God joins us to Christ through faith, he is making real in our temporal lives what he has already decreed in his eternal will and accomplished in the incarnation, life, death, resurrection, and ascension of his Son. To be severed from the Son would require that the Father rescind what he has already decreed and accomplished. Every benefit that we have received from being united to Christ would have to be undone. Having already justified us in Christ, God would have to re-condemn us and repeal our participation in Christ's righteousness;

having already sanctified us in Christ, God would have to reverse our baptism into Christ's death, burial, and new resurrection life; having already adopted us in Christ, God would have to make us orphans; having already resurrected us with Christ and raised us in his ascension, God would have to lower us into death and cast us from the heavenly realms; and having already glorified us in Christ, God would have to terminate the end to which he appointed all of his blessings. In sum, having joined us to Christ, God would have to dismember the body of Christ.

For these reasons, Charles Haddon Spurgeon asserted, God cannot reject us any more than he can reject his own Son:

> Behold, he has put his people into the hands of his dear Son. He has even put us into Christ's body; "for we are members of his body, of his flesh, and of his bones." He sees us in Christ to have died, in him to have been buried, and in him to have risen again. As the Lord Jesus Christ is well-pleasing to the Father, so in him are we well-pleasing to the Father also; for our being in him identifies us with him. . . . Firmly believe that until the Lord rejects Christ he cannot reject his people; until he repudiates the atonement and the resurrection, he cannot cast away any of those with whom he has entered into covenant in the Lord Jesus Christ.[5]

GOD PRESERVES US IN THE LIFE AND
BLESSINGS OF SALVATION IN CHRIST

When we affirm that we are so preserved in Christ that we will never be separated from him, we should go on to insist that this infallible preservation infallibly manifests itself in the life of those joined to him. To be preserved in Christ means that we are maintained *in the living Christ*, not merely connected to his "work." It is the living Christ in whom we dwell and who dwells in us, and through whose life we are transformed into holy images of God. Thus, to say that we are preserved in Christ means that God continually administers and maintains the blessings of Christ to us in our union with him, and that these blessings have ongoing effects in our lives.

---

[5] Charles Haddon Spurgeon, "Perseverance in Holiness," in *Metropolitan Tabernacle Pulpit*, Vol. 35 (Pasadena, TX: Pilgrim, 1975), 547.

To be sure, God saves us in Christ by forgiving our sins once and for all and assuring us of eternal life. But salvation in Christ includes much more. We are also saved in Christ as we grow in faith, and therefore in our union with Christ, through Word and sacrament. We are saved in him as we are transformed into Christ's image, as we mature as God's children, as we are disciplined with his fatherly love, as we bear the cross of suffering, and as we obey and serve the Lord. In short, we are saved as we "grow up in every way into him who is the head, into Christ" (Eph. 4:15). The very first question of the Heidelberg Catechism (1563) frames this grand reality sublimely:

> **Q. 1. What is your only comfort in life and death?**
> A. That I am not my own, but belong with body and soul, both in life and in death, to my faithful Saviour Jesus Christ. He has fully paid for all my sins with His precious blood, and has set me free from all the power of the devil. *He also preserves me in such a way that without the will of my heavenly Father not a hair can fall from my head; indeed, all things must work together for my salvation. Therefore, by His Holy Spirit He also assures me of eternal life and makes me heartily willing and ready from now on to live for Him.*[6]

Notice the careful wording of the catechism: the believer is able to express complete confidence that she will never be separated from Christ, but salvation has an ongoing content that includes willingness and readiness to live for Christ. This is why Reformed theology has always insisted that salvation includes "the perseverance of the saints." This does not mean that believers are saved *because* they persevere in their faith—as if continually to merit God's grace—but that they persevere *as they are preserved by God's grace in Christ.* The saints indeed stumble in sin, and may sometimes even doubt that they truly belong to Christ, but they will never finally be overcome by sin or lose their assurance of God's fatherly care. The saints experience in their lives the faithfulness of Christ as they grow into his manifold blessings.

This is why a doctrine of "eternal security" that asserts that believers are eternally saved irrespective of the carnality of their lives,

---

[6] Cited in James T. Dennison Jr., *Reformed Confessions of the 16th and 17th Centuries in English Translation: Vol. 2, 1552–1566* (Grand Rapids: Reformation Heritage Books, 2010), 771 (emphasis added).

including the act of apostasy, is to be rejected strenuously.[7] Quite simply, this construal fails to take into account that the believer's eternal
security is grounded in his preservation *in the living, crucified, resurrected
Christ*, who will never fail to nourish his body. It is also typically reductionistic in its understanding of salvation, emphasizing that we
have been saved to the exclusion of the equally important truth that
we *are being* saved. The content of salvation, according to this view, is
reduced to, and is often synonymous with, what is referred to as the
"gift of eternal life," an abstraction that neglects the truth that Christ
is himself eternal life. The inevitable result is a doctrine of "eternal
security" that vitiates the good news that God continually imparts the
very life of Christ to his children. When Christ promises us eternal
life, he is promising more than a gift to be redeemed when we die—a
"get-out-of-jail-free" card, as it were. He is promising us a life in and
with him that begins when we receive him, manifests itself throughout our lives, and necessarily wells up into eternal blessedness (John
4:14; 15:1–8; 1 John 5:18–20).

Contrary to the rather crass notion of "once saved, always saved,"
the doctrine of preservation in Christ insists that the one who is united
to Christ (is saved) inevitably experiences the manifold benefits of that
union (is being saved). Christ gives us *himself* in salvation, and because
he is the crucified, resurrected, living Son of God, salvation means a
participation in his death, resurrection, and life. This means we not only
receive the benefit of justification through this union, we also receive
the benefit of sanctification. Sanctification, as we have seen, means not
only that we *have been made* holy in Christ, but that we *are being made*
holy in him—and this because we have been crucified and resurrected
with him. In fact, the very design of our predestination in Christ is that
we will "be conformed to the image of [God's] Son" (Rom. 8:29). We
are told, further, that we were created in Christ Jesus "for good works,
which God prepared beforehand, that we should walk in them" (Eph.

---

[7]Charles Ryrie asserts that a Christian may be so carnal as to be an evildoer, thief, murderer, and even
apostate, and still remain confident as to his eternal security (*So Great Salvation* [Wheaton, IL: Victor
Books, 1989], 65, 141). Ryrie is often misunderstood as if he had no room for the necessity of spiritual
growth in the life of the believer. This is not so. However, his understanding of salvation, it appears to
me, is so objectified—salvation is a "gift" we receive rather than a union with the Giver—that nothing
could conceivably count against the gift of salvation once it is received. I maintain, on the contrary, that
there *is* evidence that counts against the genuineness of one's profession of faith because salvation is a
living relationship (Romans 6; 1 Cor. 5:1–5; John 15:1–17; 2 Cor. 5:5, 1 John 3:6; 5:18; Ephesians 5; etc.).

2:10). God is in the process of sanctifying us "completely. . . . He who calls you is faithful; he will surely do it" (1 Thess. 5:23–24).

The same is true of our adoption in Christ. We have *already* been adopted in Christ, constituted God's children, and assured of the rights therein. But the fact that we are God's children means that God *continually* acts as our loving Father, nourishing us and disciplining us so that we grow up into maturity in Christ: "For what son is there whom his father does not discipline? If you are left without discipline, in which all have participated, then you are illegitimate children and not sons" (Heb. 12:7–8). Adoption into Christ is no mere punctiliar status that guarantees a merely future blessing. Adoption ushers us into a living and abiding relationship with our Father through which he presently loves, nourishes, and forgives us, and in which we love, seek nourishment, repent, obey, and are forgiven (1 John; 2 Cor. 6:16–7:1).[8] To be preserved in Christ means that we necessarily continue to experience the abundant blessings we receive in union with him.

Preservation in Christ does not mean that those united to Christ are mere passive recipients of a salvation that transpires over our heads or behind our backs. God calls us through Christ into creaturely participation in our new lives; he calls us into participation in our very salvation. God so loves us that he re-creates us in Christ so that we may experience the power and freedom of being his obedient children. In a wonderful gospel paradox, believers are called to work out their salvation even as God works within them (Phil. 2:12–13). An important part of the way God preserves his children is by calling them to grow into their existence in Christ—to grow in faith, obedience, and love as they demonstrate whom they belong to. God manifests his fatherly care by admonishing and encouraging his beloved children to continue in their utter dependence on him, to set their eyes on Christ, and to follow him obediently. He knows that we are often unfaithful children, prone to leave the God we love in search of alternative loyalties. The hymn writer Robert Robinson memorably underscored our tendency to wander from the steadfast faithfulness of God in "Come, Thou Fount of Every Blessing" (1758):

---

[8] This truth can become obscured when adoption is subsumed under justification, suggesting that adoption is no more than a legal transfer of rights. See chapter 5.

O to grace how great a debtor daily I'm constrained to be!
Let Thy goodness, like a fetter, bind my wandering heart to Thee.
Prone to wander, Lord, I feel it, prone to leave the God I love;
Here's my heart, O take and seal it, seal it for Thy courts above.

God preserves us by binding our hearts to him through Jesus Christ. What is more, he keeps us bound to him through various God-ordained means, which we are exhorted to employ so that we may endure in his saving goodness and presence.[9] The most important means that God has instituted for our preservation is the ministry of Word and sacrament, through which we continue to hear, confess, and taste of his exorbitant goodness toward us in Christ, so enriched by the gospel that we have the confidence and courage to live as his holy children.[10] The ministry of Word and sacrament also exposes our sinfulness, teaching us to recognize and confess our sins so that we may live humbly and faithfully before our Father. God exercises his fatherly benevolence by admonishing us again and again in his Word to guard our hearts and stand firm in our faith. He has instituted this ministry of Word and sacrament in the church, the body of Christ his Son, as a way of mediating his saving and reconciling presence. We celebrate the preached and visible gospel in the church in a sacred space and time as we experience the intimacy he has created with us, and also with others joined to the same Lord Jesus Christ.

In living relation to other members of Christ's body, we come to experience the reality of God's redemptive work and presence in the world, fulfilling the great gospel mystery that we will all be made one in Christ. Our unity in Christ means that we will grow into Christ only as a body, each member of that body giving himself up to the others in mutual self-sacrifice and love; thus, we are preserved in Christ *as his body*.

Another means by which God preserves us is prayer. In prayerful confession and petition, we participate in the glorious privileges

---

[9] Bruce Demarest has cataloged twelve such means in *The Cross and Salvation* (Wheaton, IL: Crossway, 1997), 448–49.

[10] In our missionary zeal to proclaim the gospel to all nations, we sometimes overlook that the gospel is first of all for the church, and is the primary means through which we are nourished by Christ. As evidence of this, we may recall that it is from letters written to *churches* that we derive the content of the gospel. Additionally, we should remember passages such as Rom. 1:13–16, where we find Paul zealously desiring to preach the gospel to the *church* in Rome. The church's call to proclaim the gospel to the nations is predicated upon its continually being itself nourished by Christ through the gospel.

of being God's children through Christ. We call on God as our Father, knowing that we are so beloved by him that he will always hear us. Prayer is a way in which we are assured of God's love such that our trust in him is nourished and sustained, and we therefore endure in faith.

Indeed, all the means that God has instituted to preserve us in Christ are aimed at sustaining our faith. It was through faith, by the power of the Spirit, that we were once bound to Christ, and it is through faith that we continue to grow into him; God preserves us by transforming us into greater and greater intimacy with Christ: "Not only does [Christ] cleave to us by an indivisible bond of fellowship, but with a wonderful communion, day by day, he grows more and more into one body with us, until he becomes completely one with us."[11] Joined indissolubly to Christ, the church is maintained and nurtured in that union by the faithful Bridegroom who would no more cease to feed us than he would deny his very body (Eph. 5:29–30).

Our preservation in Christ, in the end, is necessary to maintain the most sublime and resplendent of all the gospel promises: one day, God assures us, we will be fully re-created in Christ and appear before our Father as the perfect images of his Son forevermore.

Glorification in Christ

Glorification is the final goal of our salvation, the summation and culmination of our union with Christ and the manifold blessings that come to us from that union. In fact, we may say that God's intention in joining us to the Savior has the express design of bringing that union to this glorious consummation. All that we already are in Christ—elect, called, justified, sanctified, adopted, preserved—is brought to full realization in the summation of God's redemptive purpose; our glorification is the "already/not yet" of our salvation made the glorious "now."

The unmistakable eschatological orientation of the manifold blessings of salvation in Christ is summed up in our end-time glorification. When we are glorified, the various verb tenses in which we express our salvation—we *have been* saved, we *are being* saved, and we *will be* saved—reach their climax. Finally, we *are* completely, perfectly saved.

---

[11] John Calvin, *Institutes of the Christian Religion*, ed. John T. McNeill, trans. Ford Lewis Battles, Library of Christian Classics, Vols. 20–21 (Philadelphia: Westminster, 1960), 3.2.24.

Salvation is not complete until we reach the end for which we were re-created in Christ: our full conformity, body and spirit, to the image of the Firstborn of all creation, the Firstborn from the dead. Glorification, writes Murray, "is the complete and final redemption of the whole person when in the integrity of body and spirit the people of God will be conformed to the image of the risen, exalted, and glorified Redeemer, when the very body of their humiliation will be conformed to the body of Christ's glory."[12] In this glorious work, God's creation purpose, "Let us make man in our image" (Gen. 1:26), converges with his re-creative purpose, "those whom he foreknew he also predestined to be conformed to the image of his Son" (Rom. 8:29). We will be the image of God again, fully, perfectly and finally the image of God in Christ.

Glorification, like every other benefit of Christ, is not to be thought of except in relation to Christ's person. Just as Christ *is* our justification, sanctification, and adoption, so he is our glorification. In order to participate in any of Christ's benefits, we must participate in *him*. Because we have been truly joined to him, we therefore participate not in a series of individualized instances of glorification but in the very glorification of Christ himself. Just as Christ is the justified and sanctified Son of God, so he is the resurrected, exalted, and glorified Son of God. Just as surely as we have been justified, sanctified, and adopted in Christ, we have been raised, exalted, and glorified in him (Eph. 2:6–7; Rom. 8:30). So, the glorification that we await is a participation in the glorified Christ to whom we have already been joined. We will become so fully and finally joined to him that the whole of our humanity will experience the full and final realization of his glorified humanity; we will become exactly who we were re-created in Christ to be. We will be perfectly blessed and sanctified human beings in a perfectly blessed and eternal communion with God. Glorification, then, can be defined as the final, complete, and eternal enjoyment of perfect union with Christ, through which all the benefits of his person and work are fully, completely, and eternally realized in us, and by which we experience blessed fellowship with God forever.

In one sense, glorification transcends description. It reduces the human being to stammering, as Spurgeon noted well: "As for me, I can-

---

[12] *Redemption*, 175.

not say that I will speak of the glory, but I will try to stammer about it; for the best language to which a man can reach concerning glory must be a mere stammering."[13] Our theological descriptions, however imperfectly articulated, may still allow us a window into the kinds of realities that are involved when all of the blessings of our union with Christ become fully, completely, and eternally realized in our perfected union with him. Let us consider the full realization of the blessings of incarnation, justification, sanctification, and adoption:

(1) *Incarnation.* When the eternal Word of God assumed human flesh, he became in his one person the union between God and man. He became what we are so that we might be reconciled to God. By being joined to the incarnate humanity of Jesus Christ through faith, we are restored to fellowship with God. The incarnate life of Jesus Christ is the life of humanity that he took into his life in order to redeem us for God, and is thus a vicarious human existence, a living out of all that we were created to be before God. When we are joined to him through faith, all that he accomplished for us in that incarnate life redounds to us. By assuming our humanity into existence with his divinity, he overcame the estrangement from God that marks and mars our fallen existence. As I noted in chapter 1, the most astounding result of our union with the incarnate Christ is that we participate in his union with his Father through the power of the Spirit, the most intimate of all unions (John 14:20; 17:20–27). Glorification, then, marks the goal of the incarnation, the final realization of the union between God and man, where believers experience communion with God forever.

As Jonathan Edwards maintained, in glorification, the saints are admitted into the eternal blessedness of the Trinitarian household of God:

> Christ has brought it to pass, that those who the Father has given to him should be brought into the household of God, that he and his Father and they should be as it were one society, one family; that his people should be in a sort admitted into that society of the three persons in the Godhead. In this family or household God [is] the Father,

---

[13] Charles Haddon Spurgeon, *Sermons*, 14:183–84, cited in Bernard Ramm's fine study *Them He Glorified: A Systematic Study of the Doctrine of Glorification* (Grand Rapids: Eerdmans, 1963), 8.

Jesus Christ is his own naturally and eternally begotten Son. The saints, they also are children in the family; the church is the daughter of God, being the spouse of his Son. They all have communion in the same Spirit, the Holy Ghost.[14]

(2) *Justification*. Those united to Christ through faith have already been justified in him. God has pronounced upon them the verdict of the final judgment that is to come because they have participated in the vindication of Jesus Christ in his resurrection. Yet all people, unbelievers and believers alike, still await this future judgment, when God will vindicate his righteousness: "For we will all stand before the judgment seat of God" (Rom. 14:10). God will fully manifest his righteousness—those found to be unrighteous will be eternally condemned, and those found to be righteous will know eternal commendation. Who, then, will God find to be righteous? Only those who have been united to Jesus Christ, the Justified.

So what does it mean for those united to Christ to experience the judgment seat of God? In that judgment, we will experience the effect of what has already been declared of us in Christ; those who *have been* justified *shall be* justified. "There is therefore now no condemnation for those who are in Christ Jesus" (Rom. 8:1). God's righteous judgment of those who have been united to Christ, having reached back to the cross, the resurrection, and our temporal existence, will be fully and universally manifest. And just as Christ was justified in his resurrection and raised to glorification, so those united to him have been and will be justified, resurrected, and raised to glorification: "And those whom he called he also justified, and those whom he justified he also glorified" (Rom. 8:30).

(3) *Sanctification*. Glorification in Christ involves our complete and final sanctification. While it is true that God has sanctified us by joining us to Christ, and that he is presently sanctifying us by conforming us to his image, God will yet fully sanctify us by completing in our glorification what he has begun in our sanctification: "And I am sure of this, that he who began a good work in you will bring it to completion at the day of Jesus Christ" (Phil. 1:6). Glorification is the consummation

---

[14]Jonathan Edwards, *Miscellanies* (No. 571), in *The Works of Jonathan Edwards*, ed. Ava Chamberlain, 26 volumes (New Haven, CT: Yale University Press, 1957–2009), 18:110.

of the promise that all who are elect by God in Christ shall be "holy and blameless before him" (Eph. 1:4) and "conformed to the image of his Son" (Rom. 8:29). When we come to participate in the glorification of Christ, our knowledge of him will be such that the whole of our persons, body and soul, will be transformed into his glorious image. In this, our humanity will be perfected in his glorified humanity, and we will become what we were re-created in Christ to be: the perfect image of God.

Very far from some versions of Platonism, which anticipate the flight of the soul from the "prison house" of the body, a proper understanding of glorification bids the church to await our *bodily* resurrection and perfection in Christ, "who will transform our lowly body to be like his glorious body, by the power that enables him even to subject all things to himself" (Phil. 3:21). When the bride of Christ is glorified, she will attain to the full measure of unity with her Bridegroom, and reach the end for which she has been kept holy. Even as the body of Christ is now "being transformed into the same image from one degree of glory to another" (2 Cor. 3:18), so in glorification Christ's body will be completely transformed into his glory. To be glorified means to have the weight of our sin-distorted existence so completely eradicated that the deepest of all human longings—communion with God—is forever satisfied.

(4) *Adoption*. Just as glorification reveals and fulfills our justification and sanctification in Christ, so it reveals and fulfills our participation in Christ's sonship. Already made the children of our heavenly Father, we will one day be like him and experience his full personal presence: "Beloved, we are God's children now, and what we will be has not yet appeared; but we know that when he appears we shall be like him, because we shall see him as he is" (1 John 3:2). The present blessings we experience as children are already too many to number and too deep to fathom. How, then, will we put into words what it will be like to have our Father personally and fully present to us—to know God fully even as we are fully known by him? Our words may fail us here, but we can be sure that we will experience the full blessing of participating in the Father's love for his only begotten Son, and that it will be glorious indeed.

Perhaps more astonishing still, Paul tells us that creation itself "waits with eager longing for the revealing of the sons of God." The renewal of creation, which has been subject to bondage and decay, is actually tied up with the freedom of the children of God, whose adoption will be fully manifest and realized in the redemption of our bodies (Rom. 8:18–23). The restoration of creation waits upon the bodily redemption of God's children, and so the freedom of God's children becomes the freedom of all creation. Glorification thus involves the full enjoyment, personally and bodily, of our adoptive sonship in Christ, in which we experience the exquisite freedom of God's fatherly benevolence and through which even the created order experiences liberation.

C. S. Lewis artfully and tantalizingly portrays this glorious state of affairs:

> What we have been told is how we men can be drawn into Christ—can become part of that wonderful present which the young Prince of the universe wants to offer to His Father—that present which is Himself and therefore us in Him. It is the only thing we were made for. And there are strange, exciting hints in the Bible that when we are drawn in, a great many other things in Nature will begin to come right. The bad dream will be over: it will be morning.[15]

Incarnation, justification, sanctification, and adoption are a few of the blessings we receive in Christ that, when brought to their full manifestation, tell us something about what it means to be glorified in him. But there are others. For instance, having already been made participants in Christ's resurrection, our bodies shall be raised from the dead and made glorious, imperishable, and powerful. Our resurrection-glorification will be an overcoming of our existence in the first Adam so that we may participate in the glory of the last Adam: "Just as we have borne the image of the man of dust, we shall also bear the image of the man of heaven" (1 Cor. 15:49). So, too, having already been made alive with Christ—raised with him in his ascension and "seated . . . with him in the heavenly places"—believers will experience the realization of this promise in the coming ages (Eph. 2:4–7).

---

[15] C. S. Lewis, *Mere Christianity* (San Francisco: Harper, 2001), 200.

Glorification, then, is the summation and realization of all the blessings and promises we have been given due to our inclusion in Christ. All that we are in him, all that we are being made to be in him, and all that we wait for in him will be manifest, completed, and actualized. We will be fully alive for the first time—gloriously, blessedly, and eternally alive in the Christ who is life in himself: "When Christ *who is your life* appears, then you also will appear with him in glory" (Col. 3:4). We will be holy and blameless, "without spot or wrinkle or any such thing" (Eph. 5:27), freed from our distorted, bound, compromised, and temporal existences into a restored, liberated, unimpaired, and eternal existence in Christ. As full and complete participants in Christ's life, we will experience the personal presence and intimacy of the Father and the Spirit; we will have been joined to the life of our triune God. When God accomplishes our glorification, we will be participants in that one stupendous act of union in which all things in heaven and earth will be reconciled to God through Christ, through whom and for whom all things were created. And the most precious and cherished of all created realities, the bride of Christ—"the fullness of him who fills all in all" (Eph. 1:23)—will come to enjoy the unbroken, unspoiled fullness of communion with her Bridegroom in the eternal bliss of the re-created cosmos.

We would do well to listen to Edwards's beautiful stammering:

> The end of the creation of God was to provide a spouse for his Son Jesus Christ that might enjoy him and on whom he might pour forth his love. And the end of all things in providence are to make way for the exceeding expressions of Christ's close and intimate union with, and high and glorious enjoyment of, him and to bring this to pass. And therefore the last thing and the issue of all things is the marriage of the Lamb. . . . The wedding feast is eternal; and the love and joys, the songs, entertainments and glories of the wedding never will be ended. It will be an everlasting wedding day.[16]

---

[16] *Miscellanies* (No. 702), in *Works*, 18:298.

7

THE MYSTERY OF THE CHURCH IN CHRIST

For no one ever hated his own flesh, but nourishes
and cherishes it, just as Christ does the church,
because we are members of his body.

EPHESIANS 5:29–30

And he put all things under his feet and gave him
as head over all things to the church, which is his
body, the fullness of him who fills all in all.

EPHESIANS 1:22–23

This chapter might strike some as out of place. Why a chapter on the church in a book about salvation? After all, the vast majority of books on soteriology written from an evangelical perspective do not deal with matters of ecclesiology. Presumably this is because the doctrine of salvation is thought to occupy a doctrinal arena of its own, capable of description and analysis in isolation from the doctrine of the church.

However, despite the pedagogical benefit of distinguishing soteriology from ecclesiology—tidy classifications can sometimes be helpful in learning theology—there is an important sense in which such a distinction needs to be challenged or nuanced. At times, theological distinctions that are meant to be helpful can be overdrawn, obscuring rather than illuminating the subject matter, and creating artificial separations between realities that ought to be held together. In other words, distinctions that are meant to be helpful can sometimes be misleading or distortive. One such case, with which this book has been particularly concerned, is the distinction that is often drawn in theology between christology (the person of Christ) and soteriology (the work of Christ), a distinction that may create the impression that these subjects can be studied in isolation from one another.

Similarly, the distinction between soteriology and ecclesiology (the doctrine of the church) needs careful qualification, lest we begin to think that salvation has nothing to do with the church. Therefore, I have written the final two chapters of this book to demonstrate the inherent connections between the person and work of Christ and the church, and to show why our understanding of salvation deeply and necessarily impacts our understanding of the church.

We are increasingly being told that there is a crisis in evangelical ecclesiology. Evangelicals themselves seem prepared to admit that our ecclesiology is rather thin, especially when compared to the Protestant Reformers or the church fathers. "When one thinks about evangelicals and what they hold dear," writes Bruce Hindmarsh, "one would be forgiven for not thinking immediately of the church." Even the phrase *"evangelical ecclesiology,"* he suggests, "is an oxymoron, like an 'honest thief' or 'airline food.'"[1] Simply put, evangelical theology is marked by its emphasis on the gospel, but it has no similarly robust theology of the church.[2]

The reasons for this admittedly troubling state of affairs are manifold and complex. Among the reasons often listed as contributing factors to this apparent crisis is the extraordinary denominational diversity in evangelicalism, which presumably prohibits a shared ecclesiological vision. Another is the intense individualism that pervades evangelical soteriology, wherein salvation is viewed primarily as a pri-

---

[1] Bruce Hindmarsh, "Is Evangelical Ecclesiology an Oxymoron? A Historical Perspective," in *Evangelical Ecclesiology: Reality or Illusion?* ed. John G. Stackhouse Jr. (Grand Rapids: Baker Academic, 2003), 15.
[2] Happily, several recent publications by and for evangelicals have begun to address this crisis in theologically and historically helpful ways. Cf. Brad Harper and Paul Louis Metzger, *Exploring Ecclesiology: An Evangelical and Ecumenical Introduction* (Grand Rapids: Brazos Press, 2009), and Mark Husbands and Daniel J. Treier, eds., *The Community of the Word: Toward an Evangelical Ecclesiology* (Downers Grove, IL: IVP, 2005). One need not agree at all points with what these books have to offer in order to benefit from some of their insights.

vate affair, the commencement and continuation of which is divorced from the communal reality of salvation. To these factors we could add the sentiment among many evangelicals that speaking of salvation and the church in the same breath sounds suspiciously "Roman Catholic," a presumed violation of our Reformational sensibilities.

This last point is especially important because of the irony involved. The Reformers, and many since in the Reformation tradition, had robust ecclesiologies precisely *because* of the connections they saw between salvation and the church. For them, the nature of salvation bore directly upon the nature of the church. If we may speak of the demise of evangelical ecclesiology, it might be because we have lost sight of this crucial connection. When the gospel is artificially divorced from the church, the church is bound to assume a secondary theological status. The way back from such a diminished ecclesiology is to recognize that the church is what it is because salvation is what it is. In Gary Badcock's words:

> There needs to be a recognition of the primal theological fact that the church is part of the *mysterion*, part of the gospel, rather than merely an accidental appendage that happens to be added to faith because we are social animals, or the like. It is not something theologically secondary, or derivative, but something theologically primary, and of the first importance. Such recognition ought not to be hard to encourage among evangelicals, because the theme is, after all, biblical.[3]

When we begin, consciously or not, to think of the church as an "artificial appendage" of, or as "theologically secondary" to, the gospel, it may just be because our (mis)understanding of salvation has led us there. One's understanding of salvation is bound to be reflected in one's understanding of the church, and it is difficult to frame a rich account of the church around a soteriology dominated by forensic, extrinsic, and individualistic notions.

But what if, in articulating our ecclesiology, we begin instead with an understanding of salvation that is inherently participatory and relational? What if, in other words, we begin with the notion that salvation means being united together in Jesus Christ as his body, that the

---

[3] Gary D. Badcock, "The Church as 'Sacrament,'" in *The Community of the Word*, 199.

church, far from being an appendage to the gospel, is a living image of the gospel itself? In this chapter, I will seek to explore such notions, allowing the reality of our saving union with Christ to penetrate into our understanding of the church. To do so, I will first explore how salvation and the church are derived from the same reality—how, in our union with Christ, salvation and the church are together the "mystery of the gospel." Second, I will examine the enigmatic Pauline phrase "the body of Christ." Although this phrase is typically interpreted in a purely figurative way, when it is viewed in light of our being joined personally to Christ, it has vast potential to shape our understanding of the nature of the church. Finally, I will consider, from a Reformational and evangelical position, the ways in which it would be both possible and important to affirm what so many of our forefathers in the faith affirmed: *extra ecclesiam nulla salus*, "outside the church there is no salvation."

A doctrine of salvation in which union with Christ is the central reality is able to yield an evangelical doctrine of the church that is theologically primary, one that accentuates rather than jettisons the gospel we hold so dear. This does not mean that evangelicals need to move away from Protestantism in the least, but it does mean, as D. G. Hart has put it, that we will need "to provide a rationale for the church that moves beyond the Christian ministry as a spiritual vitamin that supplements a healthy personal religious diet to an older rendering . . . which regarded the church as the very sustenance of Christian life, apart from which believers have no hope of salvation."[4] This chapter can by no means provide a comprehensive description of the church, but I hope it will provide biblical and historic avenues to an enriched evangelical ecclesiology. To do this, we must bridge the chasm between salvation and the church that has held sway in our theology for too long.

The Church as the Mystery of the Gospel

The great and profound *mysterion* that lies at the heart of the gospel— "Christ in you, the hope of glory" (Col. 1:27)—also lies at the heart of the church. And it lies at the heart of the church *because* it lies at the

---

[4] D. G. Hart, "The Church in Evangelical Theologies, Past and Future," in *The Community of the Word*, 40.

heart of the gospel. The mystery of Jesus Christ is simultaneously the good news of salvation and the good news of the church.

Paul uses the Greek word *mysterion* twenty-one times in his letters. His use of this term denotes a nuanced but ultimately cohesive reality that brings together what we often distinguish: salvation and the church. So important is this mystery to Paul that he indicates on several occasions that it is the very substance of his preaching of the gospel. The mystery of which he writes ultimately explains the innate connection between soteriology and ecclesiology. Therefore, we will examine his use of this term in some detail, noting the shades of meaning as well as the underlying unity.

The apostle uses the idea of the *mysterion* of the gospel to refer to at least five distinct but inseparable soterio-ecclesiological insights of astounding import, the most important of which, for our purposes, occur in the letters to the Colossians and Ephesians.

(1) *Christ.* The most fundamental, definitive referent of the mystery about which Paul writes is quite simply Christ himself. In Colossians, Paul declares it his purpose that the churches will "reach all the riches of full assurance of understanding and the knowledge of God's mystery, which is Christ, in whom are hidden all the treasures of wisdom and knowledge" (Col. 2:2–3). Whatever else Paul refers to in his use of *mysterion*, the substance of the mystery is Christ, or the revelation of Christ in the fullness of his redemptive work and person (especially the cross; see 1 Cor. 2:1, 7). The redemptive purpose of God, previously hidden for ages and generations, has now been revealed—to the "rulers of this age" (1 Cor. 2:8), to "the rulers and authorities in the heavenly places" (Eph. 3:10), and to "the saints" (Col. 1:26)—and that mystery is Christ Jesus. The various applications of Paul's use of "mystery" boil down to the one essential revelatory reality of Jesus Christ. As the esteemed New Testament scholar Peter T. O'Brien has written: "Christ is the starting point for a true understanding of the notion of 'mystery' in [Ephesians], as elsewhere in Paul. There are not a number of 'mysteries' with limited applications, but one supreme 'mystery' with a number of applications."[5]

---

[5] Peter T. O'Brien, "Mystery," in *The Dictionary of Paul and His Letters*, ed. Gerald F. Hawthorne, Ralph P. Martin, Daniel G. Reid (Downers Grove, IL: IVP Academic, 1993), 623.

(2) *Indwelling.* Not only is the mystery Christ, it is also the mystery of the *indwelling* Christ: "To [the saints] God chose to make known how great among the Gentiles are the riches of the glory of this mystery, which is Christ in you, the hope of glory" (Col. 1:27). The mystery is not, therefore, Christ in the abstract, but Christ dwelling in his people. In Ephesians, Paul interprets the mystery of husband and wife becoming one flesh (Genesis 2) in relation to the union between Christ and his bride: "'Therefore a man shall leave his father and mother and hold fast to his wife, and the two shall become one flesh.' This mystery is profound, and I am saying that it refers to Christ and the church" (Eph. 5:31–32). The fact that Christ joins himself to his people so intimately that they may be called "one flesh" is integral to Paul's notion of mystery. Already we have here intimations of the inextricable connection between salvation and the church. As Christ dwells in us and as we are joined to him, we are at the same time the recipients of salvation *and* the ones who constitute his body, the church. We *are* the church precisely as we are joined to him for salvation.

(3) *Reconciliation and unity.* Mystery also means for Paul the reconciliation and uniting of all things in Christ. In a truly astounding revelation of the supreme lordship of Christ in the letter to the church at Ephesus, we read that not only are believers united and reconciled to Christ, but that *everything* in heaven and earth will be united in him. God is "making known to us the mystery of his will, according to his purpose, which he set forth in Christ as a plan for the fullness of time, to unite all things in him, things in heaven and things on earth" (Eph. 1:9–10). Thus, wrapped up in the mystery of Christ is his cosmic, eschatological headship over all things; there is nothing over which Christ will not be head. "Christ," O'Brien writes, "is the one *in whom* God chooses to sum up the cosmos, the one in whom he restores harmony to the universe. He is the focal point, not simply the means, the instrument, or the functionary through whom all this occurs."[6] This startling realization is made even more so by the declaration that the church, as Christ's body, is and shall be an essential part of Christ's cosmic redemptive headship (Eph. 1:22–23; Col. 1:17–18). In the full-

---

[6] Peter T. O'Brien, *The Letter to the Ephesians*, Pillar New Testament Commentary (Grand Rapids: Eerdmans, 1999), 111–12 (emphasis in original).

ness of redemptive time, God will bring all things together in Christ, who is head over his body, the church.

(4) *One body*. The mystery, which, as we have seen, is "Christ," "Christ in you," and the union and reconciliation of all things "in Christ," also means the uniting together of Jew and Gentile in one body:

> When you read this, you can perceive my insight into the mystery of Christ, which was not made known to the sons of men in other generations as it has now been revealed to his holy apostles and prophets by the Spirit. This mystery is that the Gentiles are fellow heirs, members of the same body,[7] and partakers of the promise in Christ Jesus through the gospel. Of *this gospel* I was made a minister according to the gift of God's grace, which was given me by the working of his power. (Eph. 3:4–7)

"This gospel" is both the announcement of the mystery of Christ and the means through which that mystery is realized: Jew and Gentile united together as the one body of Christ.[8] The preaching of the gospel unveils the mystery of God's manifold wisdom, and this unveiling takes place "through the church" (Eph. 3:10). Thus, the very fact of the existence of the church as Jew and Gentile, "members of the same body," is the revelation of the mystery of the gospel in Christ. The union of Jew and Gentile together in the one body of Christ is itself a witness to the gospel.

(5) *Gospel*. Furthermore, we see that the preaching of the gospel is the preaching of the mystery of Christ. Paul asks the church at Ephesus to pray for him, "that words may be given to me in opening my mouth boldly to *proclaim the mystery of the gospel*, for which I am an ambassador in chains, that I may declare it boldly, as I ought to speak" (6:19–20). To the church at Colossae he implores similarly: "At the same time, pray also for us, that God may open to us a door for the word, *to declare the mystery of Christ*, on account of which I am in prison" (Col. 4:3; cf. Eph.

---

[7] Paul uses the Greek word *syssoma* (translated here as "members of the same body"), which, as Frank Thielman tells us, "appears here for the first time in all known literature, and it is possible that Paul invented it" (*Ephesians*, Baker Exegetical Commentary on the New Testament [Grand Rapids: Baker, 2010], 205). Perhaps this mystery exceeds the boundaries of ordinary human language.

[8] "To sum up we may say that 'the mystery of Christ' is the complete union of Jews and Gentiles with each other through the union of both with Christ. It is this double union, with Christ and with each other, which is the substance of the 'mystery'" (John R. W. Stott, *The Message of Ephesians* [Downers Grove, IL: IVP, 1979], 117).

3:7; Rom. 16:25). Paul identifies his preaching of the gospel with the mystery of Christ as if to say that gospel preaching *is* the proclamation of this mystery.

What "mystery of the gospel" is Paul preaching exactly? What is so urgent and vital about this mystery that he identifies it with the gospel, for which he is willing to suffer in chains? We can be sure that Paul's understanding of the gospel invariably involved the proclamation of the death and resurrection of Christ for sinners, without which it could not have been gospel. Yet we can be equally sure that the gospel included more, in the sense that it included the *implications* of the death and resurrection of Christ. Given Paul's understanding outlined above, we can say that the "mystery of the gospel" is supremely the crucified and resurrected Christ, who indwells us and joins us to his body as his church, as part of a glorious, cosmic reconciliation of all things in him, demonstrated powerfully in the incorporation of Jew and Gentile into the one body of Christ, a reality so sublime it is to be preached at the risk of imprisonment or even death.

The "mystery of Christ" is thus inextricable from the "mystery of the gospel," and the "mystery of the gospel" is inextricable from the mystery that is the church. In this very important sense, the gospel mystery is the reality of the church united to Christ. The church is a resounding manifestation of God's redemptive purpose in Christ. Thus, the very existence of the church is a living witness to the gospel, and so cannot be divorced from it. Indeed, seen from the central soteriological reality of union with Christ, the church is far from a theological appendage to the gospel. On the contrary, the church is an essential aspect of the mystery of salvation. The soteriological reality of being joined to Christ is at one and the same time the ecclesiological reality of being joined to Christ. When we confess the saving mystery of Christ in us, we are confessing simultaneously the mystery of the church.

The Body of Christ

Surely the most provocative phrase used in the New Testament to describe the nature and reality of the church is "the body of Christ." At least it *would* be provocative if the phrase conjured up in our thoughts the reality to which it refers.

If Paul meant this phrase to indicate the profound reality of the church's actual participation in the incarnate, crucified, resurrected, ascended, glorified Jesus Christ, then we have here the most sublime expression of the nature of the church that can be imagined. The problem is that we have been told time and again that when Paul refers to the church as the body of Christ, he is speaking in merely figurative terms, or metaphorically.[9] This normally means that the language should not be pressed too far into reality; it is merely an instance of Paul's transferring the ideas derived from one kind of reality, a biological body, to another, the social functioning of the church. Thus, even if we can derive significant meaning from Paul's use of this phrase, he certainly does not intend us to understand him in any sense beyond the figurative: we are "like" the body of Christ, but not in any sense "really" the body of Christ. Paul's principal point is to engender in us a sense of our mutual dependence and an appreciation of the diversity of our gifts.[10] In other words, the church is to function as a body would, "so to speak."

The problem is not so much in identifying Paul's "body of Christ" language as metaphorical. Rather, the problem is with the way in which metaphors are typically understood. More often than not, the term *metaphor* is used in reaction against what are seen as overly literal or realistic interpretations of Paul's terminology.[11] The use of the term is commonly employed to downplay the (literal) reality of the comparison between the body of Christ and the church—as is evidenced by the tendency to refer to Paul's language as "purely" or "merely" metaphorical. The consequence is that a metaphor ends up functioning more like a simile, having a merely nominal or illustrative function, thereby implying that something is less than real. But surely this understanding does violence to the intention of a metaphor. After all,

---

[9] Note, for instance, the recent explanation from R. Y. K. Fung: "We may, therefore, with most recent Protestant interpreters, understand the body concept metaphorically, not literally and biologically or mystically" ("Body of Christ," in *Dictionary of Paul and His Letters*, 78). This explanation leaves one wondering what else is left to fill out the content of the "metaphor." Apparently, what Paul actually calls a "mystery" is not much of one.

[10] Wayne Grudem, *Systematic Theology: An Introduction to Bible Doctrine* (Grand Rapids: Zondervan, 1994), 859, is a fairly typical example of such a rendering.

[11] We will leave aside the complex question as to what constitutes a proper understanding of the term *literal*. Paul's language is certainly non-literal in the sense that Christ's body, localized in heaven, has a reality outside of the church. But this is far different than saying that his language is non-literal in the sense of "unreal." The term *literal*, in other words, is not precise enough in this case.

metaphors are linguistic devices intended to direct us to, not away from, the realities they denote.[12] There is a great difference between asserting that "the body of Christ" is metaphorical (which is technically proper) and the common (mis)understanding that associates a metaphor with a kind of figurative unreality, in which case "the body of Christ" functions as a mere simile that bears no realistic connection to the actual body of Christ to which it refers, and in which case the metaphor is an empty one.

Thus, the question is not whether Paul's language is metaphorical; rather, "the question is always how far into the realm of *being* the metaphor extends."[13] On the one hand, if we over-extend the metaphor into the realm of being, we may end up with a somewhat wooden identification of the church with Christ's body, such that the church is viewed as an extension of the incarnation. On the other hand, if we truncate the metaphor, we may end up divorcing the church from any actual connection with the life-giving flesh of Christ, which he assumed, and will forever maintain, for our salvation. It is this latter view—which is predominant among contemporary evangelicals, for whom the metaphor has become empty, a symbol of an unreality—that I wish to address in this section.

Part of what constitutes the so-called crisis in evangelical ecclesiology stems from an under-interpretation of the union that occurs between Christ and the church. In this underinterpretation, the essential nature of the church is lost to view. If the church is the body of Christ in a merely nominal or illustrative sense only, then what exactly is the reality of the church? Are we bound to say no more than that the church is a "voluntary association of like-minded believers" or that the church exists only on the strength of the shared faith experience and commitment of justified individuals? I believe that as evangelicals, we can and must say much more. I believe we can, together with our evangelical forefathers, confess that we are indeed—truly and actu-

---

[12] Andrew Perriman, in a highly instructive article on the use of metaphor, notes, "But there is no reason at all why a metaphor should not speak of a state of affairs that is real . . . the indirection that characterizes metaphor does not abrogate its semantic and referential functions, it merely renders them more complex" ("'His body, which is the church . . .' Coming to Terms with Metaphor," in *Evangelical Quarterly* 62, no. 2 [1990], 128).
[13] Gary Badcock, *The House Where God Lives: The Doctrine of the Church* (Grand Rapids: Eerdmans, 2009), 82 (emphasis in original).

ally—the body of Christ. And this mysterious reality constitutes the essential nature of the church. The church is what it is by reason of its union with the crucified, resurrected, living Lord Jesus Christ.

Interpretation of the "body of Christ" terminology rests, in large part, on the answer to this question: What is the nature of the union that the church has with Christ? The answer ought to determine how far into the realm of being we extend Paul's metaphor. If his understanding of the church's union with Christ is nothing more than a simile (a comparison of two distinct things), then we can assume with good reason that his "body of Christ" language is employed similarly. If, however, Paul's understanding of the church's union with Christ is more than this—that the church's union with her Savior is, in fact, profoundly real, intimate, organic, and vital; that it is an *actual* union with the incarnate person of Christ, *who has a body*—then we have reason to assume that Paul's body language is similarly realistic (a metaphor that explains a *reality*).[14] I have contended throughout this book that the way in which we understand the nature of our union with Christ ends up determining a great deal about how we understand the nature of salvation. I wish to suggest that the same applies to our understanding of the nature of the church. The way we conceive of salvation ought to determine the way in which we conceive of the church, because ecclesiology is simply the robust application of our christology and soteriology.

There are several reasons to believe that when Paul refers to the church as the body of Christ, he intends for us to understand his language realistically, though not in a crassly wooden fashion, to the end that we may freely confess that the church *truly is* the body of Christ.[15] First of all, we may recall that Paul's conception of the nature of the believer's union with Christ is exceedingly intimate and personal. When he refers to our being joined to Christ, he is referring to the living person of Christ who was crucified and resurrected for us. When Paul

---

[14] The term *metaphor*, it seems to me, is too often misunderstood as a comparison of two distinct objects or ideas, used merely for the purpose of illustration, which is in fact closer to the definition of a simile. But as I hope to show, when Paul refers to the church as the body of Christ, he is expressing metaphorically what is true in reality.

[15] As Robert Jenson so aptly puts it: "Of course the church is not an organism of the species *homo sapiens* and so not what we now will first think of as a human body. But Paul was not so ontologically inhibited as are we" ("The Church and the Sacraments," in *The Cambridge Companion to Christian Doctrine*, ed. Colin Gunton [New York: Cambridge University Press, 1997], 209).

proclaims the gospel mystery of "Christ in you," he is not employing a figure of speech merely to illustrate a powerful sentiment. He is declaring that we, the church, participate in the very person of Christ and therefore in the redemptive efficacy of his crucifixion and resurrection.[16] Paul goes so far as to declare that the mystery of our union with Christ is that we have been made "one flesh" with him (Eph. 5:31–32), a startling declaration if there ever was one. It is so startling, in fact, that we have often too hastily reduced this "profound mystery," as Paul calls it, to a linguistic flight of fancy without considering that biblical mysteries do not diminish realities but rather uphold and establish them. They humbly recognize the limits of human language without intending to detract from their reality. After all, the incarnation and the Trinity are certainly mysteries, but this does not mean that God took on flesh in a "figurative" sense, or that God is "metaphorically" one God in three persons. The incarnation and triune being of God are, rather, mysterious realities. The theologically orthodox procedure for deciphering biblical mysteries is to *assume the reality* of the mysteries and proceed to use biblically faithful language to describe realities that are ultimately ineffable.[17] To say, then, that our "one-flesh" union with Christ is a mere figure of speech (a "so to speak"), or to describe "body of Christ" language as "purely metaphorical," is to sell a mystery short.

The language Paul uses to describe our union with Christ is often strikingly graphic and "bodily": "Do you not know that your *bodies* are members of Christ himself?" (1 Cor. 6:15, NIV1984). Before we dismiss this language as merely illustrative or nominative, should we not first consider whether our union with Christ is so profoundly real and personal (and mysterious) that our persons participate in Christ, who also is an embodied person?[18] The same query should be applied to Paul's words in 1 Corinthians 10:16: "The cup of blessing that we bless, is it

---

[16] The reader may refer to chapter 1 for a more elaborate discussion of this assertion.

[17] We may be reminded, once again, of the words of Hilary of Poitiers: "We are compelled to attempt what is unattainable, to climb where we cannot reach, to speak what we cannot utter. Instead of the bare adoration of faith, we are under an obligation to entrust the deepest matters of faith to human language" (*De Trinitate*, 2.2, cited in *Nicene and Post-Nicene Fathers*, Second Series, Vol. 9, ed. Philip Schaff and Henry Wace [Grand Rapids: Eerdmans, n.d.]).

[18] As Paul J. Griffiths reminds us, Christian discourse about bodies should begin, not with *our* bodies, but with Christ's body: "Christ's body is, first, the most real of all bodies: it belongs to the second person of the Holy Trinity. . . . Among other bodies, it is this one that for Christians is of primary and unsurpassable significance, this one in terms of which all other bodies must be thought about and understood" ("Christians and the Church," in *Oxford Handbook of Theological Ethics*, ed. Gilbert Meilaender and William Werpehowski [Oxford: Oxford University Press, 2005], 400).

not a participation in the blood of Christ? The bread that we break, is it not a participation in the body of Christ?" Are we prepared to say that Paul's language here is just a "manner of speaking," that he might just as easily have made his point another way? If not, and if instead we maintain that Paul is referring to our true and mysterious participation in the body and blood of Christ, should it surprise us that he refers to the church as the body of Christ without qualification? Is it not just possible that Paul uses such language to assert the *reality* of the church's union with Christ without intending a strict, wooden identification of our localized human bodies with the localized human body of Christ? If so, then to describe the church as the body of Christ is to speak not merely in the realm of the "as if" or the "so to speak," but in that of reality and mystery.[19] In allowing this, we embark upon the humble exercise of allowing God's revelation to determine our thinking about reality without unnecessary or overly hasty recourse to philosophico-linguistic concepts to determine our confession of divine realities. When we confess the mysteries of the Christian faith, we are not explaining them but affirming and adoring them.

There is a second reason to suspect that "body of Christ" terminology is to be understood in a realistic way: the incarnation. The incarnation is at the heart of all Christian understanding because in it we see that God's redemptive intention is to join us to himself through Christ. Christ assumed humanity into existence with himself so that we might be joined to him. Robert Letham reminds us: "The basis of our union with Christ is Christ's union with us in the incarnation. We can become one with him because he first became one with us. By taking human nature into personal union, the Son of God has joined himself to humanity. He now has a human body and soul, which he will never jettison."[20] It is crucial to remember that Christ performed the truly extraordinary act of the incarnation by taking on *a real human body* in order to become one with us. The church's saving union with Christ through the Holy Spirit is founded on the fact of his taking our

---

[19] Scot McKnight's words are worth pondering: "Said another way, by receiving the metaphor into the soul, the soul learns the reality. Thus, we not only indwell the metaphor, the metaphor indwells us. The charitable, loving approach to metaphor is to let it have its way with us, and only by surrendering to it does it yield its truth" (*A Community Called Atonement: Living Theology* [Nashville: Abingdon Press, 2007], 36).

[20] Robert Letham, *Union with Christ: In Scripture, History and Theology* (Phillipsburg, NJ: P&R, 2011), 21.

human existence, which existence necessarily includes our bodies, into union with his person as God incarnate ("embodied"). In a very important sense, then, our union with Christ is a bodily union with the Christ who had, and has, a real human body.[21] This truth, Dietrich Bonhoeffer insisted, is fundamental to the gospel:

> Of his mercy God sends his son in the flesh, that therein he may bear the whole human race and bring it to himself. The Son of God takes to himself the whole human race bodily, that race which in its hatred of God, and in the pride of its flesh had rejected the incorporeal, invisible Word of God. Now this humanity, in all its weakness is, by the mercy of God, taken up in the body of Jesus in true bodily form. . . . The Body of Jesus Christ, in which we are taken up with the whole human race, has become the ground of our salvation.[22]

Our hope of bodily redemption, the only sort of redemption of which Scripture speaks, is predicated on the embodied existence of the eternal Word of God in the incarnation and resurrection. Without this bodily redemption, salvation could mean only a disembodied existence—which is expressly refuted in Scripture (especially 1 Corinthians 15)—with the result that salvation would cease to be the salvation of humans. Jesus Christ took the whole of our human existence into union with himself so that we might be joined to his person by the bond of the Spirit through faith. Unless we wish to jettison the truth of the incarnate person of Christ, we have every reason to insist that the church, in union with the incarnate Jesus Christ, is indeed joined to the very body of Christ, and so can truly be called the body of Christ. The fifth-century theologian Cyril of Alexandria wrote:

> So it is that the church is the body of Christ, and we are its members. For since we are all united to Christ through his sacred body, having received that one indivisible body into our own, our members are not our own but his.[23]

---

[21] In point of fact, Christ has the only truly and perfectly human body, as resurrected and glorified. Our bodies, broken and distorted as they are through the fall, are less than perfectly human. The good news is that our bodies will also be resurrected and glorified in Christ, and we shall then possess truly human bodies in him.

[22] Dietrich Bonhoeffer, *The Cost of Discipleship* (New York: Touchstone, 1995), 237.

[23] Cyril of Alexandria, *Commentary on the Gospel of John* 11.11, cited in *Ancient Christian Commentary on Scripture, New Testament IVb, John 11–21*, ed. Joel C. Elowsky (Downers Grove, IL: IVP Academic, 2007), 257.

To confess this mystery is not to so strictly identify the church as Christ's body as to lose the distinction between Christ and the church, as if Christ's existence is somehow exhausted in his church, as if Christ *is* the church without remainder. Thomas F. Torrance is right to point out the different uses of the phrase "body of Christ" in the New Testament:

> On the one hand it is used in a comprehensive sense to speak of the *whole Christ who includes the church* within his own fullness, the new man in whom the new race is concentrated, the true vine that includes the branches. In this sense Christ is the church, for he embodied himself in our humanity and as such gathers our humanity in himself into union with God. He identified himself with us, and on that ground claims us as his own, lays hold of us and assumes us into union and communion with him, so that the church finds its essential life and being only in him. Christ is the church, but it cannot be said that the church is Christ, for Christ is infinitely more than the church, although in his grace he will not be without it. Hence on the other hand, the New Testament uses the expression the body of Christ to relate him to the church in such a way that it is distinguished from him as *the body of which he is the head*, as the servant of which he is the Lord, and yet as his friend and partner upon which he freely bestows his royal inheritance as the Son of God.[24]

This distinction allows us to confess that the church is truly the body of Christ by reason of Christ's bodily assumption of our humanity and our union with him through faith—he "gathers our humanity in himself into union with God"—while simultaneously insisting that Christ's body is never circumscribed by the church, and neither is the church ever more than the body to its supreme Head, the Lord Jesus Christ. The church is, by reason of the incarnation, the body of Christ because the church is truly joined to Christ, who assumed our bodily existence into his own. To speak of the church as the body of Christ does not mean, however, that the church somehow exhausts or replaces Christ's body. Rather, the church *participates* in the one incarnate, crucified, resurrected body of Christ.

---

[24] Thomas F. Torrance, *Atonement: The Person and Work of Christ* (Downers Grove, IL: IVP Academic, 2009), 362.

A third reason to embrace the notion that the church is truly and even realistically the body of Christ is Paul's actual language. Evangelicals have been quick to classify his words in various ways that tend to depreciate the realities they express.

Take, for instance, Ephesians 1:22–23: "And [God] put all things under [Christ's] feet and gave him as head over all things to the church, *which is his body*, the fullness of him who fills all in all." If this passage is read straightforwardly, it does not self-evidently function as a simile, analogy, or illustration would, in which case the church would be described as being "like" Christ's body or said to operate in way that approximates the operations of a generalized body—whether a social, political, or human body.[25] Yet, following a peculiarly modern impulse, evangelicals assume that Paul's language must be interpreted in just such an illustrative fashion.

The problem with this type of interpretation is that the referent for "body" in the above passage is not some generalized notion of body, but the actual risen and ascended body of Christ (see v. 20): the church, Paul writes, *is this* (Christ's) body.[26] Paul is not asserting here that the church might best be described as an abstract human or political body; he is asserting that the church is "indeed," "in truth," or even "in fact" the body of Christ,[27] language that goes beyond the metaphorical (even rightly understood). So Paul is not using the notion of a body to illustrate proper ecclesial function, but asserting the reality of the mystery that we are "in Christ"—chosen, reconciled, made alive, raised, seated, created for good works, made one new man, indwelled, and even made one flesh *with and in Jesus Christ* (Eph. 1:4, 7, 13; 2:5, 6, 10, 15; 3:17; 5:30–32, to cite only a few passages). Unless we wish to make a "figure of speech" out of all that Paul says about the

---

[25] "Among Christians, however, the case is very different; for they do not constitute a mere political body, but are the spiritual and mystical body of Christ" (John Calvin, *Calvin's Commentaries* [Edinburgh: Calvin Translation Society, 1844–56; reprinted in 22 vols., Grand Rapids: Baker, 2003], 1 Cor. 12:12).

[26] The question here, of course, boils down to what Paul means by "is." One cannot help recalling the early Reformation eucharistic controversy over the "is" in Christ's words "this *is* my body." Ulrich Zwingli insisted that "is" is to be taken figuratively or symbolically. Martin Luther vehemently disagreed, as did Calvin after him. It seems that contemporary Protestantism leans heavily in a Zwinglian direction both sacramentally and ecclesiologically.

[27] Thielman has concluded that the Greek phrase *hetis estin to soma autou* is best translated "which is, in truth, his body." If this translation of *hetis* is correct, Thielman writes, "Paul wants to place special emphasis on his statement that the church is Christ's body: it is *indeed* his body" (*Ephesians*, 112). In this, Thielman is in agreement with Harold Hoehner, *Ephesians: An Exegetical Commentary* (Grand Rapids: Baker Academic, 2002), 290.

church's redemptive union with Christ, we would be better off maintaining the reality of the church as the body of Christ and confessing the mystery (as Paul does). The assumption that Paul is being merely illustrative or figurative risks losing the most profound ecclesiological reality.

The fact that Paul was willing to speak of the church as the body of Christ and "the fullness of Christ" struck Calvin as the very highest type of ecclesiology:

> This is the highest honour of the church, that, until he is united to us, the Son of God reckons himself in some measure imperfect. What consolation is it for us to learn, that, not until we are along with him, does he possess all his parts, or wish to be regarded as complete![28]

If we do not assume from the outset that the phrase "body of Christ" is merely illustrative or symbolic, and instead confess that Paul may be stating a reality that transcends the limits of language, how might we then read Colossians 1:24: "Now I rejoice in my sufferings for your sake, and in my flesh I am filling up what is lacking in Christ's afflictions *for the sake of his body, that is, the church*"? Is Paul merely being redundant here? Could he just as easily have left out "his body" and simply written "for the sake of . . . the church"? To put it another way, is Paul in this passage simply using "church" as a euphemism to avoid the potentially offensive identification of the church with Christ's actual body? Or is it rather, as Calvin says, that for Paul "there is so great a unity between Christ and his members that the name of Christ sometimes includes the whole body?"[29]

So great is this unity in Paul's mind, in fact, that we read the following in 1 Corinthians 12:12: "For just as the body is one and has many members, and all the members of the body, though many, are one body, *so it is with Christ*." We might expect at this point that Paul would have written, "so it is with the *body of Christ*," or perhaps, "so it is with *the church*." Instead, we read the surprising assertion "so it is with *Christ*." This strikes me as a decidedly strange way to begin a merely illustrative analogy. Paul has apparently so closely identified the church with

---

[28] Calvin, *Commentaries*, Eph. 1:23.
[29] Ibid., Col. 1:24.

Christ himself that the name of Christ is supposed to simultaneously invoke in us the reality of his church.[30]

One cannot help but recall here Paul's encounter with the risen Christ on the Damascus road, when Christ uttered the haunting words, "Saul, Saul, why are you persecuting *me?*" (Acts 9:4). This must have struck Paul as enormously strange, perhaps even mysterious, given that he was in the process of persecuting Christ's *followers.* Yet Christ so closely identified himself with his church that his charge against Paul was in the first-person singular. Jesus went on to say, "I am Jesus, *whom you are persecuting*" (v. 5). The enormously powerful impression this must have made on Paul may best explain why he would thereafter refer to the church, without qualification, as the body of Christ.

Extra Ecclesiam Nulla Salus?

The origin of the Latin phrase *extra ecclesiam nulla salus*, which means "outside the church there is no salvation," is commonly attributed to the early church father Cyprian. According to his view, Christ and his church are so closely joined that one cannot enjoy Christ and his salvation unless one is joined to Christ's church.[31] Closely connected to *extra ecclesiam nulla salus* is Cyprian's famous dictum, "You cannot have God for your Father unless you have the church for your mother."[32]

Most modern evangelical Protestants find such language suspicious, if not downright problematic. For many of us, these kinds of assertions suggest a kind of clericalism, institutional triumphalism, or an overly mechanized (often Roman Catholic) view of salvation that associates it with institutional church membership or sacramental practice. But besides the question of whether such understandings were what Cyprian intended, few evangelicals have sufficiently come to terms with the fact that many in the evangelical Protestant tradition have gladly affirmed this terminology:

---

[30] "In this, then, our consolation lies—that, as he and the Father are one, so we are one with him. Hence it is that his name is applied to us" (ibid., 1 Cor. 12:12).

[31] See S. L. Greenslade, trans. and ed., *Early Latin Theology*, Library of Christian Classics, Vol. 5 (Philadelphia: Westminster, 1956), 120–22; G. C. Berkouwer, *Studies in Dogmatics: The Church* (Grand Rapids: Eerdmans, 1976), 142.

[32] Cyprian, *On the Unity of the Catholic Church*, in *Early Latin Theology*, Library of Christian Classics: Ichthus Edition, trans. and ed. S. L. Greenslade (Louisville, KY: Westminster, 1956), 127–28.

Martin Luther: "The church is not wood and stone but the assembly of people who believe in Christ. With this church one should be connected and see how the people believe, live, and teach. They certainly have Christ in their midst, for outside of the Christian church there is no truth, no Christ, no salvation."[33]

John Calvin, echoing Cyprian: "For those to whom [God] is Father the church may also be mother. . . . Away from her [the church's] bosom one cannot hope for any forgiveness of sins or any salvation."[34]

The Westminster Confession of Faith: "The visible church . . . consists of all those throughout the world that profess the true religion; and of their children: and is the kingdom of the Lord Jesus Christ, the house and family of God, out of which there is no ordinary possibility of salvation." (25.2)

Surely there is a sense in which we do not want to affirm the *extra ecclesiam*—when it is interpreted to mean that salvation can be found by virtue of the mere association with or participation in the ecclesiological practices of a particularized institutional form of the church. This interpretation suggests that the church itself, rather than Christ, is the bestower of salvation, a view that was rightly rejected by the Reformers. However, given what I have argued thus far in this chapter, and elsewhere in the book, there are a number of important reasons why it would be entirely fitting for the evangelical church to heartily confess, in harmony with the historic Christian tradition, that "outside the church there is no salvation."

The first reason, as we have seen above, is that the proclamation of the gospel, the good news of salvation, is intimately bound up with the proclamation of the church. To proclaim the mystery of Christ includes the proclamation of the mystery of the church. To be joined to Christ (salvation) is to be joined together into the one Christ (church): "For in Christ Jesus you are all sons of God, through faith. For as many of you as were baptized into Christ have put on Christ. There is nei-

---

[33] Martin Luther, "The Gospel for the Early Christmas Service, Luke 2:[15–20]," in *Luther's Works*, 55 vols., gen. ed. Jaroslav Pelikan (St. Louis: Concordia Publishing House; Philadelphia: Fortress Press, 1955–1975), Vol. 52, 39–40.

[34] John Calvin, *Institutes of the Christian Religion*, ed. John T. McNeill, trans. Ford Lewis Battles, Library of Christian Classics, Vols. 20–21 (Philadelphia: Westminster, 1960), 4.1.1, 4.1.4.

ther Jew nor Greek, there is neither slave nor free, there is no male and female, for you are all one in Christ Jesus" (Gal. 3:26–28; cf. Eph. 3:1–12). In our union with Christ, we are at the same time the church in him. There is, then, no salvation outside of our existence as the church, and there is no complete proclamation of the gospel that is not also the proclamation of the church. Similarly, because the church is constituted by the fact of her intimate, profoundly real, and personal union with the incarnate, crucified, resurrected Christ—our "bodies are members of Christ" (1 Cor. 6:15),[35] we are "one flesh" with Christ (Eph. 5:31–32)—the church is therefore rightly called "the body of Christ." And just as we must insist that there is no salvation outside of this Christ (*extra* Christum *nulla salus*), so there is no salvation outside of the church, which is indeed his body (*extra* ecclesiam *nulla salus*).

Our union with Christ provides a second reason it would be salutary to affirm the *extra ecclesiam*. I suspect that a major reason why contemporary evangelicals hesitate in affirming this dictum stems from a reductionistic view of salvation, in which salvation is essentially synonymous with the justification of the individual. Under this view, it may be difficult to see why the church is necessary to salvation, given that one can presumably trust in Christ for the forgiveness of sins "outside of the church."

I have argued throughout this work, however, that when we consider salvation from the central reality of union with Christ, we see that it includes much more, albeit never less, than forgiveness. For instance, salvation in Christ also necessarily includes our sanctification, which is not only *already ours* in Christ (like justification), but, unlike justification, also includes a progressive aspect: we are presently growing in conformity to Jesus Christ. Our growing conformity to the image of the Holy One is part of what it means that God saves us. If we consider salvation from this more comprehensive point of view, we should be happy to confess that there is no salvation outside

---

[35] It can hardly be stressed enough that Paul's use of "member" language (Greek, *mele*) is very far afield from contemporary notions of membership. Where "membership" for us connotes voluntary association in a social group or club, for Paul it means a vital and organic participation in Christ. As Anthony Thiselton writes, "'Members' of Christ are *constituent elements of the corporeity* of the body of Christ, better understood as 'limbs of Christ' to reinvigorate the metaphor with its Pauline meaning. . . . The church is the corporeity defined as being-in-Christ as one. It is not simply a group of fellow travelers going to the same destination, who enjoy one another's company, companionship and support" (*The Hermeneutics of Doctrine* [Grand Rapids: Eerdmans, 2007], 481).

the church, because it is in and with the body of Christ that we are sanctified. Sanctification, as I showed in chapter 4, is a "bodily" affair in which the church grows up into maturity in Christ (Eph. 4:15–16) through the preached Word, sacraments, and prayer: "And they devoted themselves to the apostles' teaching and the fellowship, to the breaking of bread and the prayers" (Acts 2:42). Our continual salvation (sanctification) takes place primarily in the blessed assembly of the body of Christ, through which Christ is present to bless and save us through the preached and sacramental Word.[36]

It is important to point out that the Protestant Reformers affirmed that there is no salvation outside of the church precisely because there is no salvation outside of *Christ*. They were convinced that the church is the body of Christ, and that Christ is truly present in and through the church in the divinely ordained means of Word and sacrament. For them, a rejection of the *extra ecclesiam* would have meant a rejection of these dearly held, fundamental ecclesiological realities.

A third reason it would be salutary for the evangelical church to affirm that there is no salvation outside the church is the historical significance of this affirmation. Embedded within the historic creeds and confessions of the universal church is the affirmation that we "believe in God the Father Almighty . . . in Jesus Christ His only Son our Lord . . . in the Holy Spirit . . . *in the holy catholic church*."[37] As Torrance has reminded us, the article of the church is essential to evangelical doctrine:

> In the Apostles' Creed the church is given a place within the articles of faith under faith in the Holy Spirit, and is bracketed together with the forgiveness of sins, the resurrection of the body and the life everlasting. The doctrine of the church belongs to the doctrines of saving faith. It does not belong to the periphery of the faith, to some marginal area which is not important and where differences of opinion do not matter very much. On the contrary, it is essentially evangelical

---

[36] The ministry of the preached Word and sacrament, entrusted to the church alone, and through which the church grows into intimacy with the Lord, is the primary sense in which the Reformers and their heirs affirmed the *extra ecclesiam*. For Calvin, God places believers in the church, "not only that they may be nourished by her help and ministry as long as they are infants and children, but also that they may be guided by her motherly care until they mature and at last reach the goal of faith" (*Institutes*, 4.1.1). For growing generations of evangelicals, brought up with individualistic notions of piety, in which personal devotions and "quiet times" form the substance of personal holiness, the notion that holiness is primarily a churchly affair has receded into the background, despite the consistent biblical and historical witness to the contrary.

[37] The Apostles' Creed.

doctrine inseparably bound up with faith in the holy Trinity and with the saving operation of Christ through the Holy Spirit.[38]

To confess that we believe "in the church" is to confess, in agreement with the saints throughout the centuries—and, most importantly, in concert with the scriptural witness—that the church is indeed the body and bride of Christ, the people to whom the promises of Christ belong because we belong to him. Apart from our being his body and bride, there is no salvation: *extra ecclesiam nulla salus.*

Conclusion

By looking at some of the important ways in which Scripture speaks of the church—namely, as the mystery of the gospel and the body of Christ—I have intended to provide some fruitful avenues for a reinvigorated evangelical ecclesiology, one in which the intrinsic connections between salvation and the church are underscored. There are many reasons why evangelical ecclesiology lacks the richness and profundity we witness in the Scriptures and the historic Christian church. Perhaps our ecclesiology can go only as far as our soteriology and Christology will allow. But perhaps the defining reason is that we have failed to take with utter seriousness the words of the One whose body we are:

> I do not ask for these only, but also for those who will believe in me through their word, that they may all be one, just as you, Father, are in me, and I in you, that they also may be in us, so that the world may believe that you have sent me. The glory that you have given me I have given to them, that they may be one even as we are one, I in them and you in me, that they may become perfectly one, so that the world may know that you sent me and loved them even as you loved me. (John 17:20–23)

These words are staggering. Jesus is declaring to us that in our union with him we participate in the most sacred assembly of persons: Father, Son, and Spirit. This means that the church is the most sacred assembly of persons in the entire creation, by reason of our participa-

---

[38] *Atonement*, 358.

tion in the triune persons. We have been joined to the communion, life, and love of Father, Son, and Spirit. This is no "voluntary society of like-minded believers" bound together by common faith interests. It would be far truer to say that the church is a living, organic communion of those who have been united into the life of the crucified, resurrected, living Jesus Christ himself—the body of Christ and the mystery of the gospel. The church derives her identity from her union with the Savior, and thus the church is who she is because salvation is who *he* is for us and in us:

> Through union with Jesus Christ the church shares in his life and in all that he has done for mankind. Through his birth its members have a new birth and are made members of the new humanity. Through his obedient life and death their sins are forgiven and they are clothed with a new righteousness. Through his resurrection and triumph over the powers of darkness they are freed from the dominion of evil and are made one body with him. Through his ascension the kingdom of heaven is opened to all believers and the church waits for his coming again to fulfill in all humanity the new creation which he has already begun in it. Thus the church finds its life and being not in itself but in Jesus Christ alone, for not only is he the head of the church but he includes the church within his own fullness.[39]

Amidst all the uncertainties, perplexities, and vagaries that attend our mortal existence, we can be sure of at least one fantastic truth: Jesus Christ shall never be without his body and bride, the church. Full and complete as the eternal Word of God, the Son nevertheless takes us into existence with himself—he crucifies and buries us into his own death and burial, and raises us with him in his resurrection—and so declares that he shall never be who he is without his church, "the fullness of him who fills all in all." Of this we can be perfectly sure.

---

[39] Ibid., 361.

8

THE WORD AND SACRAMENTS OF CHRIST

Do you not know that all of us who have been baptized
into Christ Jesus were baptized into his death? We were
buried therefore with him by baptism into death, in order
that, just as Christ was raised from the dead by the glory
of the Father, we too might walk in newness of life. For if
we have been united with him in a death like his, we shall
certainly be united with him in a resurrection like his.

ROMANS 6:3–5

The cup of blessing that we bless, is it not a participation
in the blood of Christ? The bread that we break,
is it not a participation in the body of Christ?

1 CORINTHIANS 10:16

Several decades ago, Harry Blamires lamented the deterioration of one
of the essential marks of the Christian mind, what he called its "sacramental cast." He wrote: "The Christian mind thinks sacramentally. The
Christian Faith presents a sacramental view of life."[1] Non-sacramental
thinking, in other words, is non-Christian thinking.

What was true in Blamires's time is no less true for contemporary

---

[1] Harry Blamires, *The Christian Mind* (1963; repr., Vancouver: Regent College Publishing, 2005), 173.

evangelical Protestants, for whom a sacramental mode of thinking has perhaps deteriorated further still. Anecdotally, I have found that my students, who come from a broad range of evangelical Protestant churches, are generally oblivious to sacramental mysteries and consequently have little conceptual space for a robust understanding of baptism and the Lord's Supper. They are surprised to discover that sacramental language and practices, far from being outmoded vestiges of the church from early and medieval times, are, in fact, vital parts of their evangelical heritage. Their curiosity is usually piqued when they learn that Martin Luther and John Calvin, for instance, believed that the sacraments were ordained means of grace, instituted by Jesus Christ, through which the church truly receives him.

Following Augustine, the Reformers believed that a sacrament is a "visible sign of an invisible reality."[2] This meant for them that the visible/physical *signs* of water, bread, and wine refer to, and bring us to participate in, the *reality* to which they point, namely, Jesus Christ. This understanding of the sacraments seems so utterly foreign to my students, much as it did to their professor when he once sat where they do, because evangelical Protestantism has largely abandoned its theological moorings on this point, preferring instead testimonial and memorialistic notions of the sacraments, in which there is a visible sign but no present invisible reality. For most evangelical Protestants, who no longer think in terms of sacramental mysteries, visible sign and invisible reality have become estranged.[3]

Why is this so? As in most matters of theological and historical depth, the answers are complex, and we can by no means address them all. But two important, related points deserve our attention. Robert Letham speaks for those who believe that, at least in sacramental matters, evangelical Protestants have become epistemologically Gnostic or dualistic:

> Underlying opposition to a robust doctrine of the sacraments is a form of Gnosticism that has infected evangelical Protestantism and

---

[2] For historic Protestantism, the sacraments have always been two: baptism and the Lord's Supper.

[3] This is not to say that most evangelicals deny that the signs point to a divine reality, but that they view the signs are *merely* pointers to a past event and not also a divinely ordained means through which Christ is offered and received.

has spread to Reformed churches as well. This takes a subtle form, in which spiritual realities are divorced from the material realm. There needs to be a strong reminder that "in the beginning, God created the heavens *and the earth*."[4]

A failure to think in sacramental terms—particularly of the sacraments themselves, but of much more besides—betrays a dualistic mode of thought that radically separates the visible, created realm from the invisible Creator, from whom the creation derives its very existence. When Christians succumb to this culturally embedded assumption, they inevitably find it difficult to embrace the divinely ordained intersection of the physical and spiritual, which is intrinsic to God's self-revelation in Word and sacrament. Thomas F. Torrance writes:

> God does not reveal himself in abstractions and emptiness, but reveals himself to man within created existence in which he condescends to accommodate himself to the creature through creaturely forms, appointing them as signs and instruments of his Self-disclosure, veiling his truth in lowly forms adapted to creaturely apprehension.[5]

The most stunning demonstration of God's sacramental dealing with his creatures, of course, is the incarnation of the eternal Word of God—in which *God, without ceasing to be God, became that which he created in order to mediate his personal presence*. Christianity has historically embraced sacramental mystery precisely because Christianity is rooted in the mystery of the God-man. If we have become non-sacramental in our thinking, it may be because we have forgotten our confession of the ultimate visible sign of the ultimate invisible reality (Christ himself).

Another reason why evangelical Protestants have ceased to think in robustly sacramental ways may be that the church has ceased thinking of salvation in terms of union with Christ. Perhaps the implicit dualism that characterizes contemporary evangelical opposition to sacramental realism is to be found in the way we think about salvation. Just as surely as our conception of the nature of salvation determines the way

---

[4] Robert Letham, *Union with Christ: In Scripture, History and Theology* (Phillipsburg, NJ: P&R, 2011), 139fn9 (emphasis in original).
[5] Thomas F. Torrance, *The School of Faith: The Catechisms of the Reformed Church* (James Clarke & Co., 1959; repr., Eugene, OR: Wipf & Stock, 1996), lii.

we think about the benefits of salvation and the nature of the church, so it determines the way we think of the sacraments of the church. In other words, if the church ceases to think of salvation as rooted in the mystery of our union with the incarnate, crucified, resurrected, living Christ, she is bound to cease thinking in realistic terms about the sacraments of the church. If the church begins with a soteriology dominated by abstract, impersonal, and extrinsic categories, then the sacraments are bound to follow suit; the church is left with no other hand to play. If, on the other hand, the church begins with a soteriology in which a personal union with the living Christ is central—Christ is truly present to us through faith, in the gospel, by the power of the Spirit—then she is already thinking in sacramental terms.

The purpose of this chapter is to aid in the recovery of a robust evangelical and Reformational understanding of the true presence of Christ in Word and sacrament—the preached Word, baptism, and the Lord's Supper. This sacramental recovery mission depends on the recognition that God employs visible, created, physical means to save us and bless us. And this recognition depends on another, more crucial one. To borrow a phrase from Leonard J. Vander Zee, we must first recognize Christ himself as "the quintessential sacrament." Vander Zee writes:

> In the human Jesus, who completely shares our creaturely existence, God comes to us and unites himself to us. Jesus' death and resurrection seal all God's promises to us. Everything that we experience and know through the sacraments, we experience and know through Christ. Calvin put it this way: "I say that Christ is the matter or (if you prefer) the substance of all the sacraments; for in him they have all their firmness, and they do not promise anything apart from him." Calvin means that the sacraments are one of the ways that God brings us into union with Christ. He is their source, substance and goal. They are the sacraments of Christ.[6]

Christ is the quintessential sacrament because in his full humanity and full deity he is the saving intersection between God and humans.

---

[6] Leonard J. Vander Zee, *Christ, Baptism, and the Lord's Supper: Recovering the Sacraments for Evangelical Worship* (Downers Grove, IL: IVP, 2004), 45. Vander Zee quotes John Calvin from *Institutes of the Christian Religion*, 4.14.16.

He unites in his own person the visible and the invisible, the Creator and the created—his incarnate person is the definitive visible sign of an invisible reality; he is the visible image of the invisible God. God reveals *himself* and mediates *himself* through the Word become flesh. This is the most important reason why Christian thinking is inherently sacramental and why Jesus Christ is the true starting point for reflection on sacramental theology. Just as Christ is the substance of the gospel, so is he the substance of the sacraments. The Christ to whom we are joined in the gospel is the same Christ we continue to receive in Word and sacrament, the audible and visible gospel. What the church receives in Word and sacrament is never more, less, or other than Christ. To deny the true, sacramental presence of Christ in Word and sacrament is to implicitly deny that Christ continually gives himself to the church, his body.

It is right to insist at this point that the preached Word and sacraments do not themselves constitute the presence of Christ to the church, but rather that Christ is the sacramental presence of God *mediated* to us (through faith, by the power of the Holy Spirit) in Word and sacrament. "Christ alone gives himself to us through the Spirit in these creaturely acts; and so, he alone constitutes God's sacramental grace through the Spirit in our midst. Christ mediates himself to his people in the Spirit through Word and Sacrament."[7] Christ alone has been, is, and ever will be our salvation, and so Word and sacrament do not establish or add to our salvation apart from him. Rather, just as Christ gave himself to us in the incarnation and gives himself to us in the gospel, he continues to give himself to the church in Word and sacrament. For Calvin, that is indeed the whole point of the ministry of Word and sacrament:

> The end of the whole gospel ministry is that God, the fountain of all felicity, communicate Christ to us who are disunited by sin and hence ruined, that we may from him enjoy eternal life; that in a word all heavenly treasures be so applied to us that they be no less ours than Christ's himself.[8]

---

[7] Brad Harper and Paul Louis Metzger, *Exploring Ecclesiology: An Evangelical and Ecumenical Introduction* (Grand Rapids: Brazos Press, 2009), 142.

[8] John Calvin, *Calvin: Theological Treatises*, trans. with introduction and notes by J. K. S. Reid, Library of Christian Classics, Vol. 22 (Philadelphia: Westminster, 1954), 171.

Our union with Christ, who is the mystery of our union with God, forms the basis for our understanding of the sacraments. Word and sacrament are what they are precisely because the incarnation, salvation, and the church are what they are. They are not footnotes or appendages to the church service but mysteries that describe, define, and exegete who we are in our existence in Christ. They are the gifts of God for the people of God that allow us continual participation in the one great sacrament: Jesus Christ himself.

Christ Present in the Preached Word

As a necessary prelude to a rich, sacramental understanding of baptism and the Lord's Supper, we must come to an understanding of the sacramental function of the preached Word in relation to them; that is, the real presence of Christ in his Word. The preaching of the gospel is the necessary context for the sacraments, lest the sacraments are left to "hang in the air," devoid of the reality to whom they point. This is why the Reformers rightly rejected an understanding of the sacraments as efficacious in a mechanistic way, by the sacramental action itself (*ex opere operato*),[9] absent the preached gospel or faith. An *ex opere operato* understanding of the sacraments, the Reformers insisted, is a violation of the gospel logic that undergirds the sacraments. The sacraments depend upon the word of promise to be sacraments, and thus they must be accompanied by the hearty and faithful reception of the Word of God. The sacraments are empty signs apart from the preaching of the gospel because it is always in and through the gospel that Christ is communicated to his people—after all, Christ is the substance of the gospel. Therefore, apart from the preaching of the gospel promises, the sacraments have no proper content or referent.

On the other hand, when the gospel is properly preached, the sacraments make clear to us *visibly* what has been offered to us *audibly*; or, to put it another way, the sacraments "exegete" the preached Word just as the preached Word "exegetes" the sacraments—and Christ is

---

[9] This Latin phrase, which could be translated "from the work done," signifies an understanding of the sacraments in which the sacrament is itself an instrument of God, "and that so long as the conditions of its institution are validly fulfilled, irrespective of the qualities or merits of the person administering or receiving it, grace is conferred" (F. L. Cross and E. A. Livingstone, eds., *The Oxford Dictionary of the Christian Church* [Oxford: Oxford University Press, 1997], 588).

offered and received in both. As Calvin put it, "Therefore, let it be regarded as a settled principle that the sacraments have the same office as the Word of God: to offer and set forth Christ to us, and in him the treasures of heavenly grace."[10] The sacraments offer to us visibly and tangibly the One whom the preached Word offers to us audibly. Thus, for Calvin, the preached Word is an instrument ordained by God to unite us with Christ:

> Just as God has set all fullness of life in Jesus, in order to communicate it to us by means of him, so he has ordained his Word as the instrument by which Jesus Christ, with all his benefits, is dispensed to us.[11]

> In the preaching of the Word, the external minister holds forth the vocal word and it is received by the ears. The internal minister the Holy Spirit truly communicates the thing proclaimed through the Word, that is Christ, to the souls of all who will, so that it is not necessary that Christ or for that matter his Word be received through the organs of the body, but the Holy Spirit effects this union by his secret virtue, by creating faith in us by which he makes us living members of Christ, true God and true man.[12]

For the Reformers, the doctrine of the real presence of Christ in the sacraments flowed directly from their belief in the real presence of Christ in the Word. Indeed, both Word and sacrament are ordained, creaturely means by which we are united to Christ and continue to enjoy the benefits of growing intimacy with him. Luther's words poignantly capture this reality:

> Again, I preach the gospel of Christ, and with my bodily voice I bring Christ into your heart, so that you may form him within yourself. If now you truly believe, so that your heart lays hold of the word and holds fast within it that voice, tell me, what have you in your heart? You must answer that you have the true Christ. . . . How that comes about you cannot know, but your heart truly feels his presence, and through the experience of faith you know for a certainty that he is

---

[10] John Calvin, *Institutes of the Christian Religion*, ed. John T. McNeill, trans. Ford Lewis Battles, Library of Christian Classics, Vols. 20–21 (Philadelphia: Westminster, 1960), 4.14.17.
[11] John Calvin, "Short Treatise on the Holy Supper of Our Lord and Only Savior Jesus Christ," in *Calvin: Theological Treatises*, 143.
[12] Ibid., 173.

there . . . [Christ] is distributed whole among all the faithful, so that one heart receives no less, and a thousand hearts no more, than the one Christ. This we must ever confess, and it is a daily miracle. Indeed it is as great a miracle as here in the sacrament. Why then should it not be reasonable that he also distributes himself in the bread?[13]

If robustly sacramental notions of baptism and the Lord's Supper are generally foreign to, or even opposed by, contemporary evangelical Protestants, it may be because the notion of the real presence of Christ in the preached Word is similarly foreign. Why would one affirm the real presence of Christ in the sacraments if one does not already affirm the real presence of Christ in the Word? If our notions of the preached Word are non-sacramental, then surely the notion of the sacramental presence of Christ begins to dissolve elsewhere as well. As T. H. L. Parker has observed, churches that tend to have a memorialistic view of the Lord's Supper—that is, those that view Christ as present merely to the memory of the faithful—also tend toward a non-sacramental view of preaching.[14]

According to this view—which, in my best estimation, is the dominant view among evangelicals—the preaching of the Word is considered primarily informational, educational, and emotive; preaching serves the function of conveying biblically-faithful truths *about* God, but is not thought to serve the function of conveying the very presence *of* God.[15] Preaching is valued more for the exegetical insights provided by the preacher than for its role as a means through which God truly speaks and in which Christ is really present.

---

[13] Martin Luther, *The Sacrament of the Body and Blood—Against the Fanatics*, in *Martin Luther's Basic Theological Writings*, ed. Timothy F. Lull (Minneapolis, MN: Fortress Press, 1989), 319. Luther added: "But [the fanatics] see none of these things, great as it is that Christ dwells thus in the heart and imparts himself completely in every heart and is distributed through the Word. Therefore, whoever can believe this does not find it difficult to believe also that his body and blood are in the sacrament" (ibid.).

[14] *Calvin's Preaching* (Louisville, KY: Westminster John Knox, 1992), 22. I am grateful to J. Mark Beach for this reference, "The Real Presence of Christ in the Preaching of the Gospel: Luther and Calvin on the Nature of Preaching," in *Mid-America Journal of Theology* 10 (1999), 121. I should add that, despite the persistent caricature, Ulrich Zwingli was no mere memorialist. Zwingli's understanding of the Lord's Supper was far richer than that of his present-day namesakes. See Bruce Ware, "The Meaning of the Lord's Supper in the Theology of Ulrich Zwingli (1483–1531)," in *The Lord's Supper: Remembering and Proclaiming Christ Until He Comes* (Nashville: B&H Academic, 2010), 229–247.

[15] I am inclined to wonder whether the dominance of the historical-critical method of interpreting Scripture, for all its benefits, tends to locate the significance of the preached Word "in the past." Dawn DeVries writes: "The sermon does not merely point back to saving events that happened in the life of the Jesus of history, but rather *itself conveys*, or is the medium of, the presence of Christ in the church. Preaching is Christ's 'descent' to us, as Calvin puts it" (*Jesus Christ in the Preaching of Calvin and Schleiermacher*, Columbia Series in Reformed Theology [Louisville, KY: Westminster John Knox, 1996], 95).

While the exegetical labors and attending benefits of the preacher are to be resolutely affirmed, we should be careful not to artificially disassociate the living, present, eternal Word of God from the preached Word of God:

> The Zwinglian-like conception of preaching, at least as it pertains to the real presence of Christ, artificially divides and separates Christ from his Word. If biblical sermons, for example, convey the message of the gospel, how can the sermon not be God's Word to the recipients of that Word? May we legitimately separate the Word *incarnate*, from the Word *inscripturated*, from the Word *preached*?[16]

The problem in separating the presence of Christ from the Word that testifies to him is that the proclamation of the gospel runs the risk of being thought of as a merely cerebral exercise in which the efficacy of God's Word reposes upon the cranial operation of the congregants. When we cease to affirm that Christ is himself the chief benefit conveyed by the preaching of his Word, we are tempted to relegate that benefit elsewhere. Often, this means that the primary benefit we expect to receive from preaching is an increased awareness and cognition of the historical information in the biblical text. We expect (and, indeed, often experience) the blessing of insight into God's sacred Word, from which we hope for spiritual fruit. These expectations are laudable and should be pursued and nurtured in the church. But I wonder whether we can and should expect more than this? Should we expect that in the preaching of God's Word, God himself speaks and is present to us through his Son in the power of the Spirit to bless and nourish us? Should we expect that preaching, while it most certainly includes the imparting of exegetical insight, is ultimately a mysterious, sacramental act in which Christ is really present?

John Koessler has written of preachers: "We declare certainties when we preach, but we also preside over mysteries. Preaching seeks to mediate the presence of Christ."[17] An assertion such as this is certainly in keeping with the theology of our evangelical forebears, who

---

[16] Beach, "The Real Presence of Christ," 121.
[17] John Koessler, *Folly, Grace, and Power: The Mysterious Act of Preaching* (Grand Rapids: Zondervan, 2011), 103.

similarly thought of the faithful preaching of God's Word as a divinely ordained medium through which Jesus Christ is present. "To preach the gospel," Luther wrote, "is nothing else than Christ's coming to us or bringing us to him."[18]

Are there solid biblical and theological grounds for the assertion that Christ is present in the preaching of the Word? After all, even if we think the idea of Christ's presence in the Word is interesting or even exciting, we should be able to articulate the reasons in biblically faithful ways.

I believe the key to substantiating the real presence of Christ in the Word is to address important underlying questions: Do we have good reason to affirm that Christ is *ever* truly present to his people in order to save, bless, and nurture them? This question takes us back to the central thesis of this book—that to be saved means, at its root, to be personally and intimately united to the incarnate, crucified, resurrected Jesus Christ. Recall that this union is not with the "idea" of Christ. The union does not exist merely in our minds or wills, it is not merely a legal or moral union, and neither is it a mere mental assent to the saving work of Christ in the past. It is, rather, a union with the present, living Lord Jesus Christ in the fullness of his saving person, and it occurs through (without being reduced to) faith and by the power of the Holy Spirit. This means, of course, that in order to save us, Christ must have been really, personally present to us. He, in his own person, gathered us into himself so that we might enjoy all the benefits he secured for us.

Recall as well that Jesus insisted that we must partake of him for eternal life, that he would dwell in us and we in him, and that he would join us to the Father through the Spirit (John 6, 14–17). If, as I hope I have shown, these kinds of assertions are not mere "figures of speech" but in fact refer to a reality actualized in our union with Christ, then we might ask a further question: When, where, and how did Jesus assume that he would be personally present to join us to himself? The answer, as John 17 tells us, is that Christ is present in the apostolic proclamation that bears witness to him:

---

[18] Martin Luther, cited in Paul D. L. Avis, *The Church in the Theology of the Reformers* (1981; repr., Eugene, OR: Wipf & Stock, 2002), 89.

I do not ask for these only, but also for those who will believe in me through their word, that they may all be one, just as you, Father, are in me, and I in you, that they may also be in us, so that the world may believe that you have sent me. The glory that you have given me I have given to them, that they may be one even as we are one, I in them and you in me, that they may become perfectly one, so that the world may know that you sent me and loved them even as you loved me. (John 17:20–23)

I referred to the stunning reality of this passage when I discussed the intense intimacy of the union we have with the Father through the Son. Here, I want to highlight the fact that the union we have with Christ is realized in "those who will believe in me through their [the disciples'] word." The reception through faith of the apostolic testimony to Jesus Christ, he prays, will have as its result the unity of believers with the Father through the Son—"just as you, Father, are in me, and I in you, that they may also be in us." The proclamation of Christ is the means through which believers are included in the personal union between the Father and the Son. This proclamation is no mere presentation of information *about* Christ, and neither is believing in Christ the mere reception of information *about* him. Rather, Christ is both presented and received in the preaching of the Word. The reception of the apostolic testimony to Christ is the reception of Christ himself: "Whoever receives you receives me," Jesus told the twelve, "and whoever receives me receives him who sent me" (Matt. 10:40).

To this we may add that the apostle Paul consistently correlated the preaching of the gospel with the real presence of Christ. He affirmed that it is in the faithful preaching and faithful reception of the gospel that the believer is included in Christ: "And you also were included in Christ when you heard the word of truth, the gospel of your salvation" (Eph. 1:13, niv1984). Indeed, Paul makes clear that in his commission to preach, the gospel's content is not only the mystery of "Christ in you" but also the realization of everyone "in Christ":

I have become [the church's] servant by the commission God gave me to present to you the word of God in its fullness—the mystery that has been kept hidden for ages and generations, but is now disclosed to the saints. To them God has chosen to make known among the Gentiles the glorious riches of this mystery, which is Christ in you, the hope of glory. *We proclaim him, admonishing and teaching everyone with all wisdom, so that we may present everyone perfect in Christ. To this end I labor, struggling with all his energy, which he so powerfully works in me.*" (Col. 1:25–29, NIV1984)

Notice that the goal of Paul's proclamation is the same as the content of that proclamation—"Christ in you" and "everyone perfect in Christ." To that he adds that it is actually Christ himself who "powerfully works in me." Christ is the content, source, and personal goal (what Calvin called the "substance") of the proclamation of the gospel. It is no wonder, then, that Paul called the gospel the "power of God for salvation to everyone who believes" (Rom. 1:16), for there is no salvation apart from the Savior. And it is no wonder that we find Paul exclaiming in Romans 10:14: "How then will they call on him in whom they have not believed? And how are they to believe in him of whom they have never heard? And how are they to hear without someone preaching?"[19] Evidently, for Paul, the preaching of Christ is no mere preaching *about* Christ. It is the preaching *of* Christ—Christ speaking through the human proclamation of the Word and being received in faith.

So, the preaching of the gospel is the "arena" in which Christ is present to join himself to us through faith. And the presence of Christ in the proclamation of the gospel is no mere punctiliar event. Christ is always the One on offer in the gospel—then, now, and whenever he is preached and received in faith. "So then, just as you received Christ Jesus as Lord, continue to live in him, rooted and built up in him, strengthened in the faith as you were taught" (Col. 2:6–7, NIV1984; cf. Eph. 3:16–17; 4:15).

There are certainly biblical and historical grounds for the claim that Christ is really present in the proclamation of his Word, but the

---

[19] There is a host of scholars who feel that Romans 10:14b is often mistranslated. The phrase, they think, should be translated, "And how are they to believe in him *whom* they have never heard?" indicating that Christ himself speaks through the gospel preached. See J. D. G. Dunn, *Romans 9–16*, Word Biblical Commentary, Vol. 38b (Dallas, TX: Word Books, 1988), 620; C. E. B Cranfield, *A Critical and Exegetical Commentary on the Epistle to the Romans*, International Critical Commentary, 2 volumes (Edinburgh: T&T Clark, 1979), 534; John R. W. Stott, *The Message of Romans* (Downers Grove, IL: IVP, 1994), 286; Beach, "The Real Presence of Christ," 126.

acceptance of such a claim, I suspect, ultimately rests on the way we conceive of the nature of salvation. If our salvation depends on an intimate and profoundly real union with the incarnate, crucified, risen, living person of Jesus Christ, then it is necessary that Christ be present to us in his Word. Similarly, if our ongoing salvation depends on the continual and growing communion we have with the Lord, then it is also necessary that Christ be ever-present in that same Word, the Word preached and received by the church in faith.

After all, what are the alternatives to Christ's real presence in the preaching of the gospel? Is it possible that the apostolic testimony to Christ, then and now, is merely historical information *about* Christ that the hearer can only mentally appropriate? If so, how is anyone joined to the living Christ? If Christ is not present in his Word to be received in faith, then how is anyone ever saved? Further, if Christ is not present in the preached Word, what is the significance of the sermon exactly? Is the church's ministry of the Word merely the words of fallible human preachers? "If Christ is not present in the proclamation of the gospel, isn't preaching for that reason an exercise in futility, an inevitable corruption or diminishment of the Word, a wholly human and fallible enterprise?"[20]

Finally, if the Christ who is preached is merely the Christ of history—a Savior who is present only to our redemptive memories—could we not just as readily recall him apart from the church? If we do not encounter Christ in the preaching of his Word, what takes place in the sermon that could not be duplicated in private study?[21] Perhaps Dietrich Bonhoeffer was right to insist that the vitality of the church depends on Christ's presence in his Word—Christ present not just as the collective spirit or faith of the church, not just as the mere subject of the written text, but as the Word in his personal presence:

> Christ is not only present *in* the Word of the Church, but also *as* the Word of the Church, . . . the spoken Word of preaching. *In* the Word

---

[20] Beach, "The Real Presence of Christ," 128. Speaking anecdotally, I cannot help but wonder whether non-sacramental views of the preached Word have led to an increasing malaise among evangelicals, even among students preparing for ministry, about the significance of the church.

[21] "Although many believers are more than prepared to affirm the exalted nature of Scripture as the inspired Word of God, and rightly so, they fail to reckon with Scripture's own testimony regarding the necessity of preaching. Scripture, as divine revelation, emphatically ranks the public proclamation of the gospel above private Bible reading" (ibid., 133).

could be too little because it could separate Christ from his Word. Christ's presence is his existence as proclamation. The whole Christ is present in preaching, humiliated and exalted. His presence is not the power of the congregation or its objective spirit, out of which the preaching is made, but his existence as preaching. If this were not so, preaching could not have had that prominent place which the Reformation insisted upon. . . . It is the form of the present Christ to which we are bound and to which we must hold. If the complete Christ is not in the preaching, then the Church is broken.[22]

The Visible Words of God

I began this chapter on Word and sacrament in the church with the claim that the preaching of the Word is "sacramental" in the sense that the proclaimed Word is the ordained and inspired sign of which Christ himself is the invisible reality. However, while the preaching of the Word is certainly sacramental, it is not properly called a "sacrament." The sacraments of the church, as historic Protestantism has defined them, are baptism and the Lord's Supper.

As we have seen, the Reformers drew an inseparable connection between the sacraments and the Word of God (especially preached), insisting that the sacraments are merely "empty signs" apart from the promises of God contained in that Word. The whole purpose of the sacraments, after all, is to clarify and confirm the promises of God in Christ. "We might call them mirrors," Calvin wrote, "in which we may contemplate the riches of God's grace."[23] The sacraments "mirror" the riches of the gospel because they explain, in living pictures, what the gospel is all about. In order to achieve this end, the sacraments must be sustained and explained by the Word.

Thus, to best understand the sacraments, we can begin by stating that they are the "visible words of God" that impress on our hearts the promise of the gospel, Jesus Christ. The Christ who is offered and received in the "audible" gospel is also offered and received in the "visible" gospel—always and only through faith and by the power of the Holy Spirit. God's Word, whether audible or visible, whether inscripturated or incarnate, is never devoid of his real presence.

---

22 Dietrich Bonhoeffer, *Christ the Center* (New York: Harper and Row, 197), 51–52.
23 Calvin, *Institutes*, 4.14.6.

BAPTISM

Let me then begin with the sacrament we call baptism and offer a definition:

> Baptism is God's pledge to us, in the visible sign and seal of water, of our incorporation into the death and resurrection of Christ, the cleansing of our sins, and our inclusion into Christ's body, the church, by the power of the Holy Spirit and through faith.

Baptism is a visible word of God that "exegetes" the gospel, showing us in a tangible and experientially powerful way what salvation is about. It is a gift of God that brings to clear expression the promises of the gospel, showing forth our new existence and identity in Christ. How does baptism do this?

(1) *As a "visible word of God," baptism is God's pledge to us that we have been so included in Jesus Christ that we are joined with him in his death, burial, and resurrection.* As Paul writes:

> Do you not know that all of us who have been baptized into Christ Jesus were baptized into his death? We were buried therefore with him by baptism into death, in order that, just as Christ was raised from the dead by the glory of the Father, we too might walk in newness of life. For if we have been united with him in a death like his, we shall certainly be united with him in a resurrection like his. (Rom. 6:3–5)

The waters of baptism press upon us the truth of our union with the crucified, buried, resurrected Christ. In the incarnation, Christ took upon himself our humanity, crucifying and resurrecting that humanity so that through the baptism of the Spirit and through faith we have a new crucified and resurrected existence in him. Baptism shows us that we have been put to death in Christ and have been raised to new life in him.[24] Those united to Christ, in other words, are both mortified and vivified. Mortification means that our sinful nature has been put to death in Christ's crucifixion and we are no longer enslaved

---

[24] The question as to the *mode* of baptism ought to be thought through in relation to the *meaning* of baptism. If baptism is meant to be a living picture of our crucifixion, burial, and resurrection with Christ, then it follows that the mode of baptism should attempt to best approximate that reality. Immersion seems preferable to sprinkling on this logic.

to sin (Rom. 6:6). In Vander Zee's words, "The baptismal font becomes our coffin."[25] Vivification means that we have new resurrection life in Christ with the freedom to offer ourselves to God "as instruments for righteousness" (Rom. 6:13). Baptism is the sacrament of our new crucified and resurrected identity in Jesus Christ, who took upon himself our alienated, broken, and enslaved existence and crucified it, so that we may have a reconciled, healed, and free existence through his resurrection life. Torrance writes:

> The central truth of baptism, therefore, is lodged in Jesus Christ himself and all that he has done for us within the humanity he took from us and made his own, sharing to the full what we are that we may share to the full what he is. *Baptism is the sacrament of that reconciling and atoning exchange in the incarnate Saviour.*[26]

As we think through our baptism in Christ, we must not allow the reality of our crucifixion and resurrection in him to dissolve into mere sentiment. Because our union with Christ is profoundly real, we must insist, with Paul, that our new mortified and vivified existence is similarly real. Paul is no idealist. He assumes the reality of our new existence and indeed grounds his exhortations to holiness in that reality (Col. 2:20; 3:1). In other words, Paul calls us to newness of life not on the basis of the "notion" that we have died and are resurrected with Christ, but on the basis that the power of Christ's death and resurrection is an *operative reality* in our lives. Those baptized into Christ, Calvin wrote, "truly feel the effective working of Christ's death in the mortification of their flesh, together with the working of his resurrection in the vivification of the Spirit."[27]

(2) As a *"visible word of God," baptism is God's tangible and experiential pledge to us that we have been wholly cleansed of our sins.* On the day of Pentecost, Peter cried out, "Repent and be baptized every one of you in the name of Jesus Christ for the forgiveness of your sins" (Acts 2:38). Just

---

[25] *Christ, Baptism, and the Lord's Supper*, 108.

[26] Thomas F. Torrance, *The Trinitarian Faith: The Evangelical Theology of the Ancient Catholic Church* (Edinburgh: T&T Clark, 1988), 294 (emphasis added).

[27] *Institutes*, 4.15.5. "But as it is not enough to know Christ as crucified and raised up from the dead unless you experience, also, the fruit of this, [Paul] speaks expressly of efficacy. Christ therefore is rightly known, when we feel how powerful his death and resurrection are, and how efficacious they are in us" (John Calvin, *Calvin's Commentaries* [Edinburgh: Calvin Translation Society, 1844–56; reprinted in 22 vols., Grand Rapids: Baker, 2003], Phil. 3:10).

as the water of baptism is a tangible symbol of our incorporation into Christ, so it is a symbol of our purification. The two are inseparably related: there is no forgiveness of sins apart from our incorporation into Christ's crucifixion, and having been crucified in Christ, we are no longer under the condemnation of sin. Baptism is a vivid picture of the costly love of Christ for his bride, the church. He so loves his church that he "gave himself up for her, that he might sanctify her, having cleansed her by the washing of water with the word, so that he might present the church to himself in splendor, without spot or wrinkle or any such thing, that she might be holy and without blemish" (Eph. 5:25–27).

Baptism is a sacrament of the gospel because it so poignantly and powerfully captures the benefits we receive in Christ. It is God's promise to us that we have been justified in Christ—our sins washed away so that we are now without condemnation, "blameless" in him. Baptism is also God's promise to us that we have been sanctified in Christ—set apart to holiness by our purification in him. Further, baptism is God's pledge to us that we have been adopted in Christ—"for in Christ Jesus you are all sons of God, through faith. For as many of you as were baptized into Christ have put on Christ" (Gal. 3:26–27). The cleansing water of baptism is our assurance from God that we are indeed the sanctified and justified children of God in Christ.

(3) *As a "visible word of God," baptism is God's promise to us that we have been included in the body of Christ—Christ himself and therefore his church.* Paul writes: "For just as the body is one and has many members, and all the members of the body, though many, are one body, *so it is with Christ.* For in one Spirit we were all baptized into one body—Jews or Greeks, slaves or free—and all were made to drink of one Spirit" (1 Cor. 12:12–13). Baptism into Christ cannot be separated from baptism into his body, the church. This is precisely why baptism has been understood as a sacrament of *initiation* in the church.[28] It is a very clear and comprehensive picture of the new reality into which the believer

---

[28] Given the centrality of the doctrine of justification in evangelical soteriology, we would do well to remember that new converts are to be taken to the waters of baptism—a powerful demonstration of their union with Christ—not to the halls of a courtroom. Baptism, to be sure, includes within it the promise of justification, but it is not primarily a forensic reality that is pictured there; rather, it is a profoundly personal and participatory reality that defines the new identity of the people of God.

has been included. Baptized into Christ, believers are assured of their participation in his death and resurrection, the cleansing of their sin, and their incorporation into a people who are together united to the one Christ.

Baptism constitutes a decisive judgment against individualistic notions of salvation, reminding us that salvation is a communal reality—communion with the Father through the Son in the Spirit, and communion with all the others defined by that same reality. Thus, baptism tells us that salvation and the church are not to be thought of as separable realities, but as two realities inextricably joined by their common source, Jesus Christ. Believers are at one and the same time the saved *and* the one body of Christ in their union with the Savior. The mystery of the gospel, we should recall, is the mystery of "Christ in you." That gospel mystery is, therefore, the mystery of salvation and the mystery of the church, and baptism is a sacrament of this mystery.

I must conclude this section on baptism with a brief note on the sacramental function of baptism. I suspect that most evangelicals are wary of referring to baptism as a sacrament because they are wary of the Roman Catholic connotations, especially the idea that the sacramental rite confers saving benefits to the recipient simply by the performance of the rite (a "quasi-magical" conception of the sacraments). This is a good evangelical instinct, for, as we have seen, the Reformers rejected this notion wholesale, primarily because it violated the principle that grace is received only through faith in the promises of the gospel. The sacraments have meaning or efficacy only in tandem with the gospel promises that they attest, and only insofar as they are received in faith.[29] However—and this is an important however—the Reformers did not cease to affirm that baptism is a sacrament. Sacraments, by their very nature as visible gospel promises, bring us to participate in the benefits of the gospel (Jesus Christ). God's promises are never empty. Baptism, as a visible word of God's promise, is a means by which he brings us into real communion with Christ, though always through faith, always by the Spirit, and always accompanied by the Word.

---

[29] "But what is a sacrament received apart from faith but the most certain ruin of the church?" (Calvin, *Institutes*, 4.14.14).

While it is perfectly evangelical and Protestant to reject a "quasi-magical" conception of the sacrament of baptism, this is no reason to so minimize the significance of baptism that it becomes nothing more than a testimony to one's faith experience, or perhaps a sometimes-optional step of obedience. The apostolic authors refer to baptism in far more urgent and robust terms than these, so closely associating baptism with salvation that we often feel the need to qualify their words to account for our doctrine (cf. Acts 2:38). If we feel a certain kind of unease with the way in which Jesus and the apostles referred to baptism, perhaps that is because we have forgotten—or have ceased affirming—that God does indeed use instrumental means to effect what he promises. The written Word of God, the preached Word of God, the humans who preach that Word, and faith are all creaturely means ordained by God to bring us to salvation in Christ. These creaturely *means* have as their *end* Jesus Christ. This is another way of saying that God gives himself to us in Christ through the gospel, and he does so through means he has specifically ordained for that purpose. If baptism is in fact a visible proclamation of the gospel, can we not expect that God gives us, or seals in us through faith, what he promises there? The physical act of baptism can no more save us than the Bible, the preaching of the gospel, or faith can save us. We are only and ever saved in and through Christ. But where do we come to know and experience God in Christ? To this we must answer that Christ is offered and received by way of his self-revelation in the gospel.

As Christ is the substance of the gospel, to be received in faith, so he is the substance of the visible gospel of baptism, to be received in faith. That is why the context for baptism is the promises of God in Christ. Baptism is always to be accompanied by the Word. Baptism is not something *other* than the gospel, it is the gospel in three-dimensional form, the experience and assurance of which we live in for the rest of our lives. It is in baptism that we experience, in a way especially suited to our physical existence, God's promise that we are *Christ*-ians.[30] We are the ones who have been joined to the crucified and resurrected Christ. We are the ones who are justified, sanctified,

---

[30] "Baptism is sometimes called 'christening.' That, it seems to me, is exactly what happens in baptism—we are christened, we are made Christ-ians, we are identified with Christ" (Vander Zee, *Christ, Baptism and the Lord's Supper*, 109).

and adopted in this Christ. We are the ones who are members of his living body. Baptism is the sacramental mystery of our identity—we are his and he is ours.

THE LORD'S SUPPER

Like baptism, the Lord's Supper is a sacrament of the gospel that "exegetes" salvation. It interprets for us what it means that we are *Christians*. It, too, is a visible, tangible—and, in this case, edible—sign of the invisible reality of our union with Jesus Christ. What we believe about the Supper, John Williamson Nevin said, is a confession about what we believe about salvation, allowing us to experience tangibly and visibly the promise that we have been joined to the Savior. Nevin writes:

> Any theory of the Eucharist will be found to accord closely with the view that is taken at the same time of the nature of the union generally between Christ and his people. Whatever the life of the believer may be as a whole in this relation, it must determine the form of his communion with the Saviour in the sacrament of the Supper, as the central representation of its significance and power.[31]

Nevin wrote these words as part of a lament about the quickly fading sense of the significance of the Lord's Supper in American Protestantism in the mid-nineteenth century. The diminution of the sacrament of the Supper, Nevin thought, was occurring in large part because Protestantism had lost sight of the Reformational understanding of how the nature and significance of the church's saving union with Christ are inextricably bound up with the nature and significance of the Supper. His basic contention—rooted in Calvin's theology and in the confessions and catechisms of the Reformed tradition—was that our thinking on the Lord's Supper inevitably mirrors our thinking on the nature of salvation more generally. He saw that evangelicals were failing to follow the Reformers on the nature and significance of our saving union with Christ, and therefore they also were failing to follow them on the nature and significance of the Supper, losing their grip

---

[31]John Williamson Nevin, *The Mystical Presence: A Vindication of the Reformed or Calvinistic Doctrine of the Holy Eucharist*, in American Religious Thought of the 18th and 19th Centuries, Vol. 20 (New York: Garland, 1987), 54.

on a crucial aspect of the evangelical tradition. In other words, our soteriology determines our ecclesiology and sacramentology, whether consciously or not.

Although Nevin's lament went largely unheard, he proved remarkably prescient.[32] The vast majority of evangelical Protestants, having largely abandoned or minimized the central significance of union with Christ soteriologically, have similarly abandoned or minimized the significance of the sacrament of the Lord's Supper. If we no longer view salvation in terms of a personal and profoundly real union with Jesus Christ, it is no surprise that we no longer see the intrinsic connection between the Lord's Supper and the gospel:

> According to the old Reformed doctrine the invisible grace of the sacrament, includes a real participation in his *person*. That which is made present to the believer, is the very life of Christ himself in its true power and substance. *The doctrine proceeds on the assumption, that the Christian salvation stands in an actual union between Christ and his people,* mystical but in the highest sense real, in virtue of which they are as closely joined to him, as the limbs are to the head in the natural body. They are in him, and he is in them, not figuratively but truly.[33]

Nevin's fears have been especially realized among contemporary evangelicals, for whom the eucharistic views of the Reformers have become quite foreign. Because the vast majority of evangelicals are accustomed to think of the presence of Christ in the Supper in "memorialist" terms,[34] we are shocked to find out (if ever we are told) that our evangelical forebears held resolutely to the *real presence* of

---

[32] We could say, as in the case of the eminent Princeton theologian Charles Hodge, that Nevin was heard and rejected. In a scathing 1848 review of Nevin's book, Hodge offered a rebuttal in which, most importantly, he dismissed Calvin's eucharistic views as an "uncongenial foreign element" in Reformed doctrine. Hodge went on to accuse Nevin of abandoning Reformed soteriology and of jeopardizing the doctrine of justification with his understanding of union with Christ. Apparently, Hodge was unaware that in rejecting Calvin's view of the eucharistic presence of Christ, he was at the same time rejecting Calvin's view of union with Christ more generally. It did not occur to Hodge that this put him at odds with Calvin's *soteriology*, in which justification is a consequence of union with Christ, the nature of which union Calvin sets forth in his understanding of the Lord's Supper. For a helpful overview of the debate between Nevin and Hodge, see Keith Mathison, *Given for You: Reclaiming Calvin's Doctrine of the Lord's Supper* (Phillipsburg, NJ: P&R, 2002), 136–56.
[33] Nevin, *The Mystical Presence*, 122 (emphasis added).
[34] This is the view of the Lord's Supper in which the bread and wine serve the exclusive function of recalling to believers' hearts and minds the sacrificial death of Christ on their behalf. While all Protestants agree that the Supper includes the idea of the remembrance of Christ's death, the doctrine of the "real presence" of Christ in the Supper goes on to affirm that the church truly participates in the Christ who is offered to believers in the bread and wine.

Christ in the sacrament of the Supper—the view that in the Lord's
Supper we truly participate (through faith and by the power of the
Holy Spirit) in the life-giving flesh and blood of the incarnate, crucified, resurrected Christ. Though Luther and Calvin rejected the idea
of "transubstantiation,"[35] they by no means rejected the notion that we
really and truly receive what is offered in the supper: Christ himself.
The Lord's Supper was, for them, a sacrament of the church, a visible
word of the gospel ordained by Christ through which we are nourished by his living presence. Thus, it is thoroughly evangelical and
Protestant to affirm the real presence of Christ in the Supper.[36]

If, as this book has attempted to demonstrate, our salvation consists in a vital, personal, and profoundly real union with the incarnate Christ, then we have good reason to revisit the question of the
sacrament of the Lord's Supper. In so doing, we may find an internal
theological coherence that binds together the mystery of the gospel of
Jesus Christ and the visible sign of that gospel, the sacramental mystery of bread and wine.

In my view, the best way to proceed on this course is to return
to the theology of Calvin, one of the fountainheads of the evangelical
theological tradition, to find out why he accorded such significance to
the Lord's Supper—why he was willing to affirm what so few modern
evangelicals would: that Christ is truly present to bless and nourish us
with his life-giving flesh and blood in the visible word of the Supper.
This brief exercise may help us to see the intrinsic connection between
how we think of salvation and how we think of the Lord's Supper. Four
key elements to Calvin's eucharistic thought are particularly relevant
for our purposes:

(1) *For Calvin, the Lord's Supper is not something* other *than the gospel*.
He believed the Supper is an ordained means by which God testifies
to us of our salvation in Christ. Why? Because at the center of his understanding of salvation was the conviction that believers are joined

---

[35] This is the theory of the Eucharist that asserts that the whole substance of the bread and wine is
converted, or "transubstantiated," into the whole substance of the body and blood of Jesus Christ. The
seemingly unchanged appearance of the bread and wine after this conversion is, thus, accidental to
their true substance. See *The Oxford Dictionary of the Christian Church*, 1637.
[36] Luther and Calvin never questioned the affirmation that in the Supper we truly participate in the
flesh and blood of Jesus Christ, by which they meant the fullness of the incarnate Christ in his saving person and work. What they rejected was the *manner* of that reception as defended by the Roman
Catholic Church, namely, transubstantiation.

to the living Christ; Christ himself is the offer of the gospel, and in our union with him we enjoy all of his benefits. Here it is important to recall the passage I cited in the introduction:

> First, we must understand that as long as Christ remains outside of us, and we are separated from him, all that he has suffered and done for the salvation of the human race remains useless and of no value to us. Therefore, to share in what he has received from the Father, he had to become ours and to dwell within us . . . for, as I have said, all that he possesses is nothing to us until we grow into one body with him.[37]

The Lord's Supper is thus a "picture painted from life" that testifies to God's promise that we receive from him our greatest need, the indwelling Christ. The bread and wine are a confirmation and a seal of our participation in the Christ who accomplished our salvation. This means that the Supper has the same function and the same substance as the written Word of God, "to offer and set forth Christ to us, and in him the treasures of heavenly grace. But they avail and profit nothing unless received in faith."[38]

The Supper, then, is God's gracious condescension by which he presents to us the gospel of Jesus Christ in visible, tangible, edible form. Because the nature of our saving union with Christ remains a mystery to us, God shows it to us in ways accommodated to our creaturely existence: "For this reason, the Lord instituted for us his Supper, in order to sign and seal in our consciences *the promises contained in the gospel concerning our being made partakers of his body and blood*."[39] Indeed, in the signs of bread and wine, God "makes it as certain to us as if we had seen it with our own eyes."[40] Because the gospel is the offer of Christ, the Lord's Supper is a sacrament of the gospel.

(2) *With the other Reformers, and in concert with the consensus of the historic Christian church, Calvin affirmed that in the Supper believers are re-*

---

[37] Calvin, *Institutes*, 3.1.1.
[38] Ibid., 4.14.17.
[39] Calvin, "Short Treatise on the Holy Supper," 144 (emphasis added). Thomas Davis explains, "Since union with Christ, union with not just his spirit but also his body, constituted the essence of the Christian life for Calvin, then it is the Sacrament of the Eucharist that most assures the believer that such a union takes place" (*This Is My Body: The Presence of Christ in Reformation Thought* [Grand Rapids: Baker, 2008], 88).
[40] Calvin, *Institutes*, 4.17.1.

ally and truly nourished by the flesh and blood of Christ that was offered for our salvation. By this, Calvin did not mean that the bread and wine are "transubstantiated" into Christ's physical body. He rejected this idea. But he nevertheless insisted that the church receives Christ himself in the promissory signs of bread and wine: "For the analogy of the sign applies only if souls find their nourishment in Christ—which cannot happen unless Christ truly grows into one with us, and refreshes us by the eating of his flesh and the drinking of his blood."[41]

Why did he assert such a thing? He did so because his understanding of salvation demanded it: "[A]s long as Christ remains outside of us . . . all that he has suffered and done for the salvation of the human race remains useless and of no value to us." Thus, the Supper is not a special, unique occurrence of the presence of Christ to us; it is our ongoing participation in the very Christ in union with whom is our salvation. The Supper is the continuing benefit of what has already happened to us through the gospel—our union with the incarnate, crucified, resurrected, living Christ.[42] Calvin's perception of the real presence of Christ in the Supper is best understood, therefore, not as a "theory of the Eucharist," but as a natural extension of his view of the nature of salvation. Because Christ's very body is the instrument through which God has accomplished our salvation, it is his body that constitutes the gift of salvation and the Supper.

But what of the objection that physical acts, such as the Lord's Supper, are unable to convey saving grace? Is Calvin saying that the physical act of participating in the Supper conveys the grace of Christ to us? To answer this question, we must recall that God always ordains physical means to bring us to salvation. The most important and indeed foundational physical means is the incarnate Christ himself—the "quintessential sacrament," to use Vander Zee's term. To reject physical means as divinely ordained instruments of salvation implies a rejection of the logic of the incarnation. Suspicion about divinely ordained

---

[41] Ibid., 4.17.10.

[42] This point underscores the significance of the relation between Word and sacrament. The sacrament is not a word above or beyond the word of the gospel, as if God's Word were insufficient. The sacrament is rather an aid to our insufficient belief: "The addition of the sacrament is not a critique of the mode of God's spoken revelation, but a critique of man's insensitive, unreceptive, resisting and contradicting heart. The significance of the sacrament lies in the divine act in which God directs our attention again to the trustworthiness of his Word, upon which man can depend without fear and with great boldness" (G. C. Berkouwer, *Studies in Dogmatics: The Sacraments* [Grand Rapids: Eerdmans, 1969], 53).

physical means that convey salvation would also have to extend to the other physical means through which God brings us into Christ, such as the Bible, the preached Word, and faith, all of which involve physical processes and elements. There is no more reason to fear idolatrous excesses in the Supper than there is to fear such excesses in our understanding of the Bible, preaching, or faith.[43] The danger is not in affirming that God employs physical processes in our salvation, but in substituting means for ends. Whether we are speaking of the Bible, the gospel, preaching, the sacraments, or faith, we must insist that these are divinely given *means* that bring us to the divine *end*: Jesus Christ. The question is not whether God *does* use such means, the question is *what* means he uses. This is why Calvin affirmed the Supper as a means of grace: it is a visible word of God.

(3) *For Calvin, there is no question that we are truly joined to the living Christ in the gospel, and therefore the Supper; there is only the question of how we are so joined*. The answer—whether we are speaking of the Supper or outside of the Supper—is always the same: in the proclamation of the gospel, through faith, and by the power of the Holy Spirit. This is the particular genius of Calvin's understanding of the real presence of Christ in the Supper. He did not need to devise a special "theory of the eucharistic presence" to explain our participation in Christ. All that he had already affirmed of the presence of Christ in the gospel could equally be said of the Supper. In Calvin's mind, theories of the Supper that insisted on the *local, physical* presence of Christ (whether Roman Catholic or Lutheran) insisted on too much. Christ's presence—the real presence of the incarnate humanity of Christ—is always mediated to the church through faith and by the power of the Holy Spirit. There is no reason, therefore, to "drag Christ down from heaven" in order for us to be nourished by his flesh and blood:

> And there is no need of this for us to enjoy a participation in [Christ's body], since the Lord bestows this benefit upon us through his Spirit so that we may be made one in body, spirit, and soul with him. The bond of this connection is therefore the Spirit of Christ, with whom

---

[43] "In short, to attack the eucharist as a physical act is to leave the Christian nothing but mental prayer and wordless contemplation. The parishioner who hangs on the words of the preacher stands in the same peril of idolatry as the communicant who relies on the visible elements of bread and wine" (David Steinmetz, *Luther in Context*, second edition [Grand Rapids: Baker, 2002], 83).

we are joined in unity, and is like a channel through which all that Christ himself is and has is conveyed to us.[44]

By insisting that we partake of "Christ himself" by the Holy Spirit, Calvin does not mean that we merely partake of Christ's Spirit, as if Christ's body were not the substance of the Supper, or that the manner of eating is merely "spiritual" (lower-case "s," as in the sense of religious sentimentality). He means that by the *power* of the Holy Spirit we partake of the body and blood of Christ.[45] "Moreover," Calvin writes, "I am not satisfied with those persons who, recognizing that we have some communion with Christ, when they would show what it is, make us partakers of the Spirit only, omitting mention of flesh and blood."[46]

A similar caution needs to be exercised when we note Calvin's assertion that we partake of Christ through faith. When Calvin says that we receive Christ as he is promised in the gospel *through faith*, he does not mean that our participation in Christ *is* faith; to *believe* in Christ is different from being *united* to Christ. In order to avoid any notion that union with Christ can be equated with our faith expression or experience, Calvin states in no uncertain terms that faith is the instrument through which we enjoy communion with the flesh and blood of Christ:

> For there are some who define the eating of Christ's flesh and the drinking of his blood as, in one word, nothing but to believe in Christ. But it seems to me that Christ meant to teach something more definite and more elevated in that noble discourse in which he commends to us the eating of his flesh [John 6:26ff]. It is that we are quickened by the true partaking of him; and he has therefore designated this partaking by the words "eating" and "drinking," in order that no one should think that the life we receive from him is received by mere knowledge.[47]

The gift of the gospel, in short, is the real presence of Christ. He cannot be replaced by the Spirit (though he is present *by* the Spirit) or

---

[44] Calvin, *Institutes*, 4.17.12.
[45] Letham writes, "No amount of stress on the spiritual aspect of the Supper, which is of course a correct stress, can ever diminish the real and true feeding that takes place [in the Supper]" (*Union with Christ*, 125).
[46] Calvin, *Institutes*, 4.17.7. In the words of Canlis: "Here Calvin is not allowing the Spirit to be the scapegoat for a thoroughly unsatisfactory doctrine of presence. The Spirit is not a spiritualized mode of Christ; rather, the Spirit is the person in whom we now have access to the embodied Jesus" (*Calvin's Ladder*, 117).
[47] Calvin, *Institutes* 4.17.5.

by our faith (though he is present *through* faith). Christ gives *himself* to us in the gospel and continues to give himself to us in the visible gospel of the Supper. The Supper functions to set forth Christ to us in the visible elements, and through our Spirit-wrought faith in the promise of his flesh and blood we truly receive what is offered.

(4) *Finally, Calvin was not concerned to empirically validate or rationalize the real presence of Christ in the Supper.* Just as the union of God and man in the incarnate Christ is an incomprehensible mystery, and just as our union with the incarnate Christ is an incomprehensible mystery, so too is our union with Christ in the Supper. We are not under the obligation to explain the mysteries of the gospel; we are under the blessed obligation to *confess and adore them.* Calvin was no rationalist. He was content to submit his reason to the wonder and mystery of the Lord's Supper:

> For, whenever this matter is discussed, when I have tried to say all, I feel that I have as yet said little in proportion to its worth. And although my mind can think beyond what my tongue can utter, yet even my mind is conquered and overwhelmed by the greatness of the thing. Therefore, nothing remains but to break forth in wonder at this mystery, which plainly neither the mind is able to conceive nor the tongue to express.[48]

The mystery of our union with Christ lies at the heart of Calvin's understanding of the mystery of the real presence of Christ in the Supper. Indeed, they are the same mystery. Whatever Calvin was willing to say about the nature of our union with Christ soteriologically, he was willing to say sacramentally. This soteriological coherence should commend him to the contemporary evangelical church once again. Once we embrace the profoundly real and personal nature of our saving union with the incarnate Christ, the Lord's Supper will find its place in the center of the church's life and worship.

Conclusion

We do well, as we partake of bread and wine, to "do this in remembrance" of Christ (1 Cor. 11:24–26; Luke 22:19), but let us go on to re-

---

[48] Ibid., 4.17.7.

member that what is being offered is his body and blood: "The cup of blessing that we bless, is it not a participation in the blood of Christ? The bread that we break, is it not a participation in the body of Christ?" (1 Cor. 10:16). Our memories of Christ are no substitute for his living presence. Our recollections of Christ's death, as meaningful and enriching as they are, cannot replace our very participation in the One who was crucified. Vander Zee writes:

> Ask most any Protestant about the meaning of the Supper, and you will hear the word *remembrance*.[49] The problem is that a too-simplistic understanding of the Lord's command has limited the meaning of the sacrament in the minds of many to the recollection of a long-ago historical event. It tends to place the weight of the sacramental meaning in the minds, heart and faith of the participant, as he or she struggles to remember, with faith and gratitude, what the Lord did for them on the Cross. Rather than coming as a gift, it comes as a mental exercise, an act of pious, prayerful reflection. In that sense, the Supper offers the believer, not a gift of grace, but a mere reminder of grace; not an assuring seal of God's forgiveness, but a distant memory of its basis; not a union with the risen and living Christ, but a memory of him. This represents a fundamental diminution of the sacrament's meaning and intent.[50]

Our mental remembrance of the significance of Christ's death is not able, and is not meant, to sustain us in our fragile and compromised states, full of the perplexities, doubts, tragedies, griefs, and despair that inevitably accompany us. Only Christ is able, and is meant, to do that. The Lord's Supper is God's assurance to us that we really belong to Christ in the fullness of his saving person; that we really do share in the One who, in flesh and blood, is our justification, sanctification, and redemption. All that he is *for us* he is *in us* as well. Christ is the incarnate, crucified, resurrected, living Savior who gives *himself* to us in the gospel, and continues to nourish us with himself in the Supper of that gospel, until that great day when we shall experience, "face to face," full and eternal satiation in communion with the glorified Lord.

---

[49] We may additionally note that the meaning of the word *remember*, biblically speaking, is not merely to recall a past event but to render an event in the past the operative truth and reality in one's present life. See, for instance, Gal. 2:10: "Only, they asked us to *remember* the poor, the very thing I was eager to do."
[50] Vander Zee, *Christ, Baptism, and the Lord's Supper*, 210.

BIBLIOGRAPHY

Ames, William. *The Marrow of Theology*. Translated by John D. Eusden. Grand Rapids: Baker, 1997.

Athanasius. *On the Incarnation*. Crestwood, NY: St. Vladimir's Seminary Press, 1977.

Augustine. *Confessions*. Translated by Henry Chadwick. Oxford: Oxford University Press, 2009.

Avis, Paul D. L. *The Church in the Theology of the Reformers*. London: Marshall, Morgan and Scott, 1981. Reprint, Eugene, OR: Wipf & Stock, 2002.

Badcock, Gary D. "The Church as 'Sacrament." *The Community of the Word: Toward An Evangelical Ecclesiology*. Edited by Mark Husbands and Daniel J. Treier. Downers Grove, IL: IVP, 2005, 188–200.

———. *The House Where God Lives: The Doctrine of the Church*. Grand Rapids: Eerdmans, 2009.

Barth, Karl. *Church Dogmatics*. Translated by G. W. Bromiley. Edited by Thomas F. Torrance and G. W. Bromiley. Edinburgh: T&T Clark, 1975.

Bavinck, Herman. *Reformed Dogmatics*, Vol. 2. Grand Rapids: Baker, 2004.

Beach, J. Mark. "The Real Presence of Christ in the Preaching of the Gospel: Luther and Calvin on the Nature of Preaching." *Mid-America Journal of Theology* 10 (1999): 77–134.

Berkhof, Louis. *Systematic Theology*. 1938. Reprint, Grand Rapids: Eerdmans, 1996.

Berkouwer, G. C. *Studies in Dogmatics: The Church*. Grand Rapids: Eerdmans, 1976.

———. *Studies in Dogmatics: Divine Election*. Grand Rapids: Eerdmans, 1960.

———. *Studies in Dogmatics: The Sacraments*. Grand Rapids Eerdmans, 1969.

———. *Studies in Dogmatics: Sin*. Grand Rapids: Eerdmans, 1971.

Billings, Todd. *Union with Christ: Reframing Theology and Ministry for the Church*. Grand Rapids: Baker, 2011.

Bird, Michael F. "Incorporated Righteousness: A Response to Recent Evangelical Discussion Concerning the Imputation of Christ's Righteousness in Justification." *Journal of the Evangelical Theological Society* 47, no. 2 (June 2004): 253–75.

Blamires, Harry. *The Christian Mind*. 1963. Reprint, Vancouver, BC: Regent College Publishing, 2005.

Blocher, Henri. *Original Sin: Illuminating the Riddle*. Downers Grove, IL: IVP, 1997.

Boersma, Hans. *Heavenly Participation: The Weaving of a Sacramental Tapestry*. Grand Rapids: Eerdmans, 2011.

Bonhoeffer, Dietrich. *Christ the Center*. New York: Harper and Row, 1978.

———. *The Cost of Discipleship*. New York: Touchstone, 1995.

Boston, Thomas. *Human Nature in its Fourfold State*. Carlisle, PA: Banner of Truth Trust, 1964. Reprint, 1989.

Brown, Raymond E. *The Gospel According to John I–XII*. Garden City, NY: Doubleday, 1966.

Burke, Trevor. *Adopted into God's Family: Exploring a Pauline Metaphor*. Downers Grove, IL: IVP, 2006.

Caldwell, Robert W. *Communion in the Spirit: The Holy Spirit as the Bond of Union in the Theology of Jonathan Edwards*. Studies in Evangelical History and Thought. Eugene, OR: Wipf & Stock, 2007.

Calvin, John. *Calvin: Theological Treatises*. Translated with introduction and notes by J. K. S. Reid. Library of Christian Classics, Vol. 22. Philadelphia: Westminster Press, 1954.

———. *Calvin's Commentaries*. Edinburgh: Calvin Translation Society, 1844–56. Reprinted in 22 volumes. Grand Rapids: Baker, 2003.

———. *Institutes of the Christian Religion*. Edited by John T. McNeill. Translated by Ford Lewis Battles. Library of Christian Classics, Vols. 20–21. Philadelphia: Westminster Press, 1960.

Campbell, Constantine. *Paul and Union with Christ: An Exegetical and Theological Study*. Grand Rapids: Zondervan, 2012.

Canlis, Julie. *Calvin's Ladder: A Spiritual Theology of Ascent and Ascension*. Grand Rapids: Eerdmans, 2010.

Carson, D. A. *The Gospel According to John*. Pillar New Testament Commentary. Grand Rapids: Eerdmans, 1991.

———. "The Vindication of Imputation: On Fields of Discourse and Semantic Fields." *Justification: What's at Stake in the Current Debates*. Edited by Mark Husbands and Daniel J. Treier. Downers Grove, IL: IVP, 2004, 46–78.

Cranfield, C. E. B. *A Critical and Exegetical Commentary on the Epistle to the Romans.* International Critical Commentary. 2 volumes. Edinburgh: T&T Clark, 1979.

Crisp, Oliver. "Federalism vs. Realism." *International Journal of Systematic Theology* 8, no. 1 (January 2006): 55–71.

———. "The Theological Pedigree of Jonathan Edwards's Doctrine of Imputation." *Scottish Journal of Theology* 56, no. 3 (2003): 308–327.

Cross, F. L., and E. A. Livingstone. *The Oxford Dictionary of the Christian Church.* Oxford: Oxford University Press, 1997.

Davis, Thomas J. *This Is My Body: The Presence of Christ in Reformation Thought.* Grand Rapids: Baker, 2008.

Demarest, Bruce. *The Cross and Salvation.* Wheaton, IL: Crossway, 1997.

Dennison Jr., James T. *Reformed Confessions of the 16th and 17th Centuries in English Translation: Vol. 2, 1552–1566.* Grand Rapids: Reformation Heritage Books, 2010.

DeVries, Dawn. *Jesus Christ in the Preaching of Calvin and Schleiermacher.* Columbia Series in Reformed Theology. Louisville, KY: Westminster John Knox Press, 1996.

Dunn, J. D. G. *Romans 9–16.* Word Biblical Commentary, Vol. 38b. Dallas: Word Books, 1988.

———. *The Theology of Paul the Apostle.* Grand Rapids: Eerdmans, 2006.

Edwards, Jonathan. *The Works of Jonathan Edwards.* 26 volumes. Edited by Ava Chamberlain. New Haven, CT: Yale University Press, 1957–2009.

Edwards, Mark J., ed. *Ancient Christian Commentary on Scripture, New Testament VIII, Galatians, Ephesians, Philippians.* Downers Grove, IL: IVP Academic, 1999.

Elowsky, Joel C., ed. *Ancient Christian Commentary on Scripture, New Testament IVb, John 11–21.* Downers Grove, IL: IVP Academic, 2007.

Elwell, Walter A., ed. *Evangelical Dictionary of Theology.* Grand Rapids: Baker, 2001.

Erickson, Millard J. *Christian Theology.* Grand Rapids: Baker, 1998.

Evans, William B.. *Imputation and Impartation: Union with Christ in American Reformed Theology.* Studies in Christian History and Thought. Eugene, OR: Wipf & Stock, 2009.

Fairbairn, Donald. *Life in the Trinity: An Introduction to Theology with the Help of the Church Fathers.* Downers Grove, IL: IVP, 2009.

———. "Patristic Soteriology: Three Trajectories." *Journal of the Evangelical Theological Society* 50, no. 2 (June 2007): 289–310.

Ferguson, Sinclair. *The Holy Spirit.* Downers Grove, IL: IVP, 1996.

———. "Ordo Salutis." In *New Dictionary of Theology*. Edited by S. B. Ferguson and D. F. Wright. Downers Grove, IL: IVP, 1988.

Fesko, J. V. *Justification: Understanding the Classic Reformed Doctrine*. Phillipsburg, NJ: P&R, 2008.

Fung, R. Y. K. "Body of Christ." In *Dictionary of Paul and His Letters*. Edited by Gerald F. Hawthorne, Ralph P. Martin, and Daniel G. Reid. Downers Grove, IL: IVP Academic, 1993.

Gaffin Jr., Richard B. "Justification and Union with Christ." In *A Theological Guide to Calvin's Institutes: Essays and Analysis*. Edited by David Hall. Phillipsburg, N.J: P&R, 2008, 248–69.

———. *Resurrection and Redemption: A Study in Paul's Soteriology*. Philipsburg: P&R, 1987.

———. "Union with Christ: Some Biblical and Theological Reflections." In *Always Reforming: Explorations in Systematic Theology*. Edited by A. T. B. McGowan. Downers Grove, IL: IVP, 2006, 271–88.

Garland, David. *1 Corinthians*. Baker Exegetical Commentary on the New Testament. Grand Rapids: Baker, 2003.

Greenslade, S. L., ed. *Early Latin Theology*. Library of Christian Classics, Vol. 5. Philadelphia: Westminster, 1956.

Gregory of Nazianzus. "Against Apollinarius" (Epistle 101). *Nicene and Post-Nicene Fathers*, Second Series, Vol. 7. Edited by Philip Schaff and Henry Wace. Grand Rapids: Eerdmans, n.d.

Griffiths, Paul J. "Christians and the Church." In *Oxford Handbook of Theological Ethics*. Edited by Gilbert Meilaender and William Werpehowski. Oxford: Oxford University Press, 2005.

Grounds, Vernon. "The Postulate of Paradox." *Bulletin of the Evangelical Theological Society*, 7, no. 1 (Winter 1964): 3–21.

Grudem, Wayne. *Systematic Theology: An Introduction to Bible Doctrine*. Grand Rapids: Zondervan, 1994.

Gundry, Robert. "The Nonimputation of Christ's Righteousness." In *Justification: What's at Stake in the Current Debates*. Edited by Mark Husbands and Daniel J. Treier. Downers Grove, IL: IVP, 2004, 17–45.

Habets, Myk. *Theosis in the Theology of Thomas Torrance*. Burlington, VT: Ashgate, 2009.

———. "Theosis, Yes; Deification, No." In *The Spirit of Truth: Reading Scripture and Constructing Theology with the Holy Spirit*. Edited by Myk Habets. Eugene, OR: Pickwick, 2010.

Harper, Brad and Paul Louis Metzger. *Exploring Ecclesiology: An Evangelical and Ecumenical Introduction*. Grand Rapids: Brazos Press, 2009.

Hart, D. G. "The Church in Evangelical Theologies, Past and Future." In *The Community of the Word: Toward an Evangelical Ecclesiology*. Edited by Mark Husbands and Daniel J. Treier. Downers Grove, IL: IVP, 2005, 23–40.

Hilary of Poitiers. *De Trinitate*. In *Nicene and Post-Nicene Fathers*, Second Series, Vol. 9. Edited by Philip Schaff and Henry Wace. Grand Rapids: Eerdmans, n.d.

Hindmarsh, Bruce. "Is Evangelical Ecclesiology an Oxymoron? A Historical Perspective." In *Evangelical Ecclesiology: Reality or Illusion?* Edited by John G. Stackhouse Jr. Grand Rapids: Baker Academic, 2003.

Hoehner, Harold. *Ephesians: An Exegetical Commentary*. Grand Rapids: Baker Academic, 2002.

Hoekema, Anthony. *Created in God's Image*. Grand Rapids: Eerdmans, 1986.

———. *Saved by Grace*. Grand Rapids: Eerdmans, 1989.

Hooker, Richard. *Laws of Ecclesiastical Polity*. In *The Works of That Learned and Judicious Divine Mr. Richard Hooker*, Vol. 50. Oxford: Clarendon Press, 1865.

Horton, Michael. *The Christian Faith: A Systematic Theology for Pilgrims on the Way*. Grand Rapids: Zondervan, 2011.

———. *Covenant and Salvation: Union with Christ*. Louisville, KY: Westminster John Knox, 2007.

Husbands, Mark, and Daniel J. Treier, eds. *The Community of the Word: Toward an Evangelical Ecclesiology*. Downers Grove, IL: IVP, 2005.

Irenaeus. *Against Heresies*. In *Ante-Nicene Fathers*, Vol. 1. Edited by Alexander Roberts and James Donaldson. 1865. Reprint, Peabody, MA: Hendrickson, 1994.

Jeffrey, Steve, Michael Ovey, and Andrew Sach. *Pierced for Our Transgressions: Rediscovering the Glory of Penal Substitution*. Wheaton, IL: Crossway, 2007.

Jenson, Robert. "The Church and the Sacraments." In *The Cambridge Companion to Christian Doctrine*. Edited by Colin Gunton. New York: Cambridge University Press, 1997.

Johnson, Marcus. "'The Highest Degree of Importance': Union with Christ and Soteriology in Evangelical Calvinism." In *Evangelical Calvinism: Essays Resourcing the Continuing Reformation of the Church*. Princeton Theological Monograph Series. Edited by Myk Habets and Robert Grow. Eugene, OR: Pickwick, 2012.

———. "Luther and Calvin on Union with Christ." *Fides et Historia* 39, no. 2 (Summer 2007): 59–77.

————. "A Way Forward on the Question of the Transmission of Original Sin." In *Evangelical Calvinism: Essays Resourcing the Continuing Reformation of the Church*. Princeton Theological Monograph Series. Edited by Myk Habets and Robert Grow. Eugene, OR: Pickwick, 2012.

Johnson, S. Lewis. "Romans 5:12—An Exercise in Exegesis and Theology." In *New Dimensions in New Testament Study*. Edited by Richard N. Longenecker and Merrill C. Tenney. Grand Rapids: Zondervan, 1974.

Keener, Craig S. *The Gospel of John: A Commentary*, Vol. 2. Peabody, MA: Hendrickson, 2003.

Kittel, Gerhard, and Gerhard Friedrich, eds. *Theological Dictionary of the New Testament*. 10 volumes. Grand Rapids: Eerdmans, 1965–1977.

Koessler, John. *Folly, Grace, and Power: The Mysterious Act of Preaching*. Grand Rapids: Zondervan, 2011.

Leith, John H. *Creeds of the Churches: A Reader in Christian Doctrine from the Bible to the Present*. Third edition. Louisville, KY: Westminster John Knox, 1982.

Letham, Robert. *The Holy Trinity: In Scripture, History, Theology, and Worship*. Phillipsburg, NJ: P&R, 2004.

————. *Union with Christ: In Scripture, History and Theology*. Phillipsburg, NJ: P&R, 2011.

Lewis, C. S. *Mere Christianity*. San Francisco: Harper, 2001.

Lillback, Peter. "Calvin's Development of the Doctrine of Forensic Justification: Calvin and the Early Lutherans on the Relationship of Justification and Renewal." In *Justified in Christ: God's Plan for us in Justification*. Edited by K. Scott Oliphint. Ross-shire, Scotland: Mentor, 2007, 51–80.

Lohse, Bernhard. *Martin Luther's Theology: Its Historical and Systematic Development*. Minneapolis: Fortress Press, 1999.

Luther, Martin. *Luther's Works*. 55 volumes. Edited by Jaroslav Pelikan. St. Louis: Concordia Publishing House; Philadelphia: Fortress Press, 1955–1975.

————. *Martin Luther's Basic Theological Writings*. Edited by Timothy F. Lull. Minneapolis: Fortress Press, 1989.

Mathison, Keith. *Given for You: Reclaiming Calvin's Doctrine of the Lord's Supper*. Phillipsburg, NJ: P&R, 2002.

McGrath, Alister. *Iustitia Dei: A History of the Christian Doctrine of Justification*. Second edition. Cambridge: Cambridge University Press, 2002.

McKnight, Scot. *A Community Called Atonement: Living Theology*. Nashville: Abingdon Press, 2007.

Metzger, Paul Louis. "Mystical Union with Christ: An Alternative to Blood Transfusions and Legal Fictions." *Westminster Theological Journal* 65 (2003): 201–13.

Moo, Douglas J. *The Epistle to the Romans.* New International Commentary on the New Testament. Grand Rapids: Eerdmans, 1996.

Murray, John. "The Imputation of Adam's Sin." *Westminster Theological Journal* 19, no. 1 (1956): 25–44.

———. *Redemption Accomplished and Applied.* Grand Rapids: Eerdmans, 1955.

Nevin, John Williamson. *The Mystical Presence: A Vindication of the Reformed or Calvinistic Doctrine of the Holy Eucharist.* American Religious Thought of the 18th and 19th Centuries, Vol. 20. New York: Garland, 1987.

O'Brien. Peter T. *The Epistle to the Philippians.* New International Greek Testament Commentary. Grand Rapids: Eerdmans, 1991.

———. *The Letter to the Ephesians.* Pillar New Testament Commentary. Grand Rapids: Eerdmans, 1999.

———. "Mystery." In *Dictionary of Paul and His Letters.* Edited by Gerald F. Hawthorne, Ralph P. Martin, and Daniel G. Reid. Downers Grove, IL: IVP Academic, 1993.

Oden, Thomas, ed. *Ancient Christian Commentary on Scripture.* 28 volumes. Downers Grove, IL: IVP, 2001.

Oliphint, K. Scott. *God with Us: Divine Condescension and the Attributes of God.* Wheaton, IL: Crossway, 2012.

Packer, J. I. "Justification." In *Evangelical Dictionary of Theology.* Edited by Walter A. Elwell. Grand Rapids: Baker, 2001.

———. *Keep in Step with the Spirit.* Grand Rapids: Fleming H. Revell, 1984.

———. *Knowing God.* Downers Grove, IL: IVP, 1973.

Partee, Charles. *The Theology of John Calvin.* Louisville: Westminster John Knox Press, 2008.

Perriman, Andrew. "'His body, which is the church . . .' Coming to Terms with Metaphor." *Evangelical Quarterly* 62, no. 2 (1990): 123–42.

Peterson, Robert. *Adopted by God: From Wayward Sinners to Cherished Children.* Phillipsburg, NJ: P&R, 2001.

Piper, John. *Brothers, We Are Not Professionals.* Nashville: B&H, 2002.

———. *The Future of Justification: A Response to N. T. Wright.* Wheaton, IL: Crossway, 2007.

Plantinga, Cornelius. *Not the Way It's Supposed to Be: A Breviary of Sin.* Grand Rapids: Eerdmans, 1995.

Purves, Andrew, and Charles Partee. *Encountering God*. Louisville, KY: Westminster John Knox, 2000.

Ramm, Bernard. *Them He Glorified: A Systematic Study of the Doctrine of Glorification*. Grand Rapids: Eerdmans, 1963.

Reid, J. K. S. *Our Life in Christ*. Philadelphia: Westminster Press, 1963.

Reymond, Robert. *A New Systematic Theology of the Christian Faith*. Nashville: Thomas Nelson, 1998.

Ridderbos, Herman. *Paul: An Outline of His Theology*. Grand Rapids: Eerdmans, 1975.

Ryrie, Charles. *So Great Salvation*. Wheaton, IL: Victor Books, 1989.

Sanders, Fred. *The Deep Things of God: How the Trinity Changes Everything*. Wheaton, IL: Crossway, 2011.

Schaff, Philip, ed. *The Creeds of Christendom, Vol. III: Evangelical Creeds*. Grand Rapids: Baker, 1966.

Scott, J. M. "Adoption, Sonship." In *Dictionary of Paul and His Letters*. Edited by Gerald F. Hawthorne, Ralph P. Martin, and Daniel G. Reid. Downers Grove, IL: IVP, 1993.

Shedd, W. G. T. *Dogmatic Theology*. Nashville: Thomas Nelson, 1980.

Smedes, Lewis. *Union with Christ: A Biblical View of the New Life in Jesus Christ*. Grand Rapids: Eerdmans, 1983.

Spurgeon, Charles Haddon. "Perseverance in Holiness." In *Metropolitan Tabernacle Pulpit*, Vol. 35. Pasadena, TX: Pilgrim, 1975.

Steinmetz, David. *Luther in Context*. Second edition. Grand Rapids: Baker, 2002.

Stewart, James S. *Man in Christ*. 1935. Reprint, Vancouver, BC: Regent College Press, 2002.

Stott, John R.W. *The Message of Ephesians*. Downers Grove, IL: IVP, 1979.

———. *The Message of Romans*. Downers Grove, IL: IVP, 1994.

Strong, Augustus. *Systematic Theology*. 1907. Reprint, Valley Forge, PA: Judson Press, 1976.

Sweeney, Douglas. *The American Evangelical Story: A History of the Movement*. Grand Rapids: Baker, 2005.

Thielman, Frank. *Ephesians*. Baker Exegetical Commentary on the New Testament. Grand Rapids: Baker, 2010.

Thiselton, Anthony C. *The First Epistle to the Corinthians*. New International Greek Testament Commentary. Grand Rapids: Eerdmans, 2000.

———. *The Hermeneutics of Doctrine*. Grand Rapids: Eerdmans, 2007.

Tipton, Lane. "Union with Christ and Justification." In *Justified in Christ: God's Plan for Us in Justification*. Edited by K. Scott Oliphint. Ross-shire, Scotland: Mentor, 2007, 23–49.

Torrance, Thomas F. *Atonement: The Person and Work of Christ*. Edited by Robert T. Walker. Downers Grove, IL: IVP Academic, 2009.

———. *Conflict and Agreement in the Church*. London: Lutterworth Press, 1959.

———. *Incarnation: The Person and Life of Christ*. Downers Grove, IL: IVP Academic, 2008.

———. "Justification: Its Radical Nature and Place in Reformed Doctrine and Life." In *Theology in Reconstruction*. London: SCM Press, 1965.

———. *The Mediation of Christ*. Colorado Springs, CO: Helmer & Howard, 1992.

———. *The School of Faith: The Catechisms of the Reformed Church*. James Clarke & Co., 1959. Reprint, Eugene, OR: Wipf & Stock, 1996.

———. *The Trinitarian Faith: The Evangelical Theology of the Ancient Catholic Church*. Edinburgh: T&T Clark, 1988.

Trumper, Tim. "The Metaphorical Import of Adoption: A Plea for Realisation. I: The Adoption Metaphor in Biblical Usage." *Scottish Bulletin of Evangelical Theology* 14, no. 2 (1996): 129–45.

———. "The Metaphorical Import of Adoption: A Plea for Realisation. II: The Adoption Metaphor in Theological Usage." *Scottish Bulletin of Evangelical Theology* 15, no. 2 (1997): 98–115.

Vander Zee, Leonard J. *Christ, Baptism, and the Lord's Supper: Recovering the Sacraments for Evangelical Worship*. Downers Grove, IL: IVP, 2004.

Vickers, Brian. *Jesus' Blood and Righteousness: Paul's Theology of Imputation*. Wheaton, IL: Crossway, 2006.

Ware, Bruce. "The Meaning of the Lord's Supper in the Theology of Ulrich Zwingli (1483–1531)." In *The Lord's Supper: Remembering and Proclaiming Christ Until He Comes*. Edited by James M. Hamilton and Thomas R. Schreiner. Nashville: B&H Academic, 2010, 229–247.

Webster, John. *Holy Scripture: A Dogmatic Sketch*. Cambridge: Cambridge University Press, 2003.

Wright, N. T. *Justification: God's Plan & Paul's Vision*. Downers Grove, IL: IVP Academic, 2009.

———. "Paul in Different Perspectives: Lecture 1: Starting Points and Opening Reflections." www.ntwrightpage.com.

———. *What Saint Paul Really Said: Was Saul of Tarsus the Real Founder of Christianity?* Grand Rapids: Eerdmans, 2005.

GENERAL INDEX

1 John, book of, adoption in, 179

adoption, 145–47; definition of, 147; distortions and misunderstandings of, 147–51; the English word *adoption*, 162n35; in first-century Roman culture, 157, 157–58n27; and glorification in Christ, 185–86; in the Johannine corpus, 150, 152–55, 156; and justification, 121–22, 161–62; in the Pauline corpus, 150, 156–62; and preservation in Christ, 179; and sanctification, 121–22; as sharing in the Son's relationship to the Father, 151–56
aliena iustitia (Latin: "alien righteousness"), 72, 110
Ames, William, 94, 94n12
Apostles' Creed, 209–10
Athanasius of Alexandria, 21, 37, 78
Augustine of Hippo, 21, 42; on adoption, 160; on the sacraments, 214

Badcock, Gary D., 191, 198
baptism, 28, 141, 227–32; definition of, 227; as God's pledge to us that we have been cleansed of our sins, 228–29; as God's pledge to us that we have been so included in Jesus Christ that we are joined with him in his death, burial, and resurrection, 227–28; as God's promise to us that we have been included in the body of Christ, 229–30; mode of, 227n24; as a sacrament of initiation, 229, 229n28; the sacramental function of, 230–31
Barth, Karl, 128n13
Bavinck, Herman, 134n24
Beach, J. Mark, 221, 224n19, 225, 225n21
Belgic Confession, 100
Berkhof, Louis, 61n5, 62n6–7, 63n10, 67n23, 74n41, 76n49, 77, 98n20, 113n47; on adoption, 147–48; on justification (two unions with Christ), 74, 96–98, 97n17; on the *ordo salutis*, 162, 164–65, 164n38, 165n41; on union with Christ, 69n30
Berkouwer, G. C., 36n4, 64n13, 66n21, 69n28, 236n42
Beza, Theodore, 24, 94; on sanctification, 125n10
Billings, Todd, 26n20; on adoption, 149n12, 151
Bird, Michael, 108n38
Blamires, Harry, 213
Blocher, Henri, 63n10, 67n25
Boersma, Hans, 27, 27n22
Bonhoeffer, Dietrich, 202, 225–26
Boston, Thomas, 24, 111n44; on adoption, 161; on the mysteries of the gospel, 49
Brown, Raymond E., 51
Bucer, Martin, 24

Burke, Trevor, 146n4; on adoption, 147n6, 149, 149n13, 157n26

Calvin, John, 15–16, 42, 47n27, 53, 181, 206n30; on adoption, 146, 160; on baptism, 228, 228n27; on the body of Christ, 204n25, 205; on the church, 207, 209n36; on election, 36; on faith, 99, 140; on the Holy Spirit, 45; on imputation, 109; on the incarnation, 38, 38n9; on justification, 88, 89, 93, 93n8, 104; on justification and sanctification, 122; on the Lord's Supper, 234, 234n36, 234–39; on the ministry of Word and sacrament, 217; on the mystery of union with Christ, 49; objection to Zwingli's views, 52, 52n37, 53–54n41; on the sacraments, 142, 214, 219, 226, 230n29; on sanctification, 125n10, 131n20, 132n21; on "this is my body," 204n26; on union with Christ, 22–23
Campbell, Constantine, 26n20
Canlis, Julie, 148n10, 238n46
Carson, D. A., 47, 71, 108n38, 114, 174
Chalcedonian Creed, 81, 82, 155n21
children of God. *See* adoption
Christification, 51n32
christological realism, 62, 69–71; as a chastened, evangelical Reformed version of classical realism, 69; how the pollution of Adam's nature becomes ours, 73–75; how we become guilty of Adam's sin, 71–73; the relationship between the declaration of our guilt and the corruption of our nature, 75–77; union with Christ as vital, organic, and personal, 69, 74, 75
christology, 190; "applied christology," 85
Chrysostom, John, 159–60
church, the: as the body of Christ, 28, 141, 192, 196–206; ministry of Word and sacrament in, 180, 180n10, 209n36, 217; as the mystery of the gospel, 192, 192–96; unity of, 154n15; as the wife or bride of Christ, 46, 46nn25–26. *See also extra ecclesiam nulla salus* (Latin: "outside the church there is no salvation")
"Come, Thou Fount of Every Blessing" (Robinson), 179–80
condemnation, 73
consummation. *See* glorification in Christ; resurrection
corruption, 76
Cotton, John, 24
Cranfield, C. E. B., 224n19
creation, restoration of, 186
Crisp, Oliver, 64, 65n16, 65n19
cross, the, 18n4, 193
Cyprian, 206

SCRIPTURE INDEX